Knowledge and Data Management in GRIDs

Knowledge and Data Management in GRIDs

edited by

Domenico Talia
University of Calabria
Italy

Angelos Bilas
ICS-FORTH
Greece

Marios D. Dikaiakos
University of Cyprus
Cyprus

Domenico Talia
Università Calabria
Dipto. Elettronica Informatica
Sistemistica (DEIS)
via P. Bucci,41 c
87036 RENDE
ITALY

Angelos Bilas
ICS-FORTH
P O BOX 1385
711 10 HERAKLION
GREECE

Marios D. Dikaiakos
75 Kallipoleos Str.
University of Cyprus
Dept. Computer Science
P.O.Box 20537
1678 NICOSIA
CYPRUS

Knowledge and Data Management in GRIDs
edited by Domenico Talia, Angelos Bilas and Marios D. Dikaiakos

ISBN-13: 978-1-4419-4252-4

e-ISBN-13: 978-0-387-37831-2
e-ISBN-10: 0-387- 37831-6

Printed on acid-free paper.

Printed in the United States of America.

9 8 7 6 5 4 3 2 1

springer.com

Contents

Foreword

While Grids have initially emerged from the need to get access to more computing power by combining several high-performance computers, it has been quickly evident that there is a similar need to get access to data, such as databases, file systems, and digital libraries which are widely spread in the Internet. By accessing these distributed data and processing them using Grid computing resources to produce knowledge, we can expect to extend the scope of Grid Technologies to new applications. In fact, research activities in this area are being pursued by several research teams and, at the same time, big companies are very active in the area.

The huge amount of dispersed data and information repositories have arisen new challenges in the field of Grid computing. Grids are evolving towards flexible and knowledge-based infrastructures, in which services will be dynamically composed, allowing applications to access heterogeneous resources to be exploited in complex distributed applications. The field of Grid computing can take advantage of related paradigms, such as Workflows, Services, and Ontologies in order to provide an infrastructure with mentioned features. This new approach can be referred as the Knowledge and Data Management in Grids, and it must address issues related to data services composition, knowledge discovery, data and knowledge integration to provide the ability for extracting useful knowledge from unmanageable volume of data, by exploiting storage management, database and data mining techniques in a Grid context.

The strategic importance of Data and Knowledge Management in the context of Grid Technologies, have led CoreGRID, the only one Network of Excellence in Grid and P2P technologies funded by EU 6th Framework Programme, to have a dedicated institute to investigate research issues in this area. This book is the result of the efforts carried out by researchers involved in this CoreGRID Institute during the first year. While the CoreGRID ambition is to foster integration and collaboration, the first year was mainly to let CoreGRID researchers to know one each other. Several meetings and workshops were organized to give the opportunity to researchers to exchanged and confront their ideas. This was the goal of the first Workshop on Knowledge and Data Management in Grids that has been held in Poznan (Poland) on September 13-14, 2005. I would like to take this opportunity to express my gratitude to the organizers of this workshop as well as to all contributors.

Thierry Priol, CoreGRID Scientific Co-ordinator

Preface

Data and knowledge play a key role in current and future Grid applications and services. The issues concerning representation, querying, discovery, and integration of data and knowledge in dynamic distributed environments can be addressed by exploiting features offered by Grid Technologies. Current research activities are leveraging the Grid for the provision of generic- and domain-specific solutions and services for data management and knowledge discovery. The goal is to promote a wide diffusion and use of knowledge-based Grid services for the Semantic Grid and the Knowledge Grid. To this end, researchers are focusing on problems related to (i) providing commodity-based distributed frameworks for storing, accessing, and handling data, (ii) developing semantic-based techniques and tools for supporting data intensive applications, and (iii) designing distributed data analysis techniques and services for information and knowledge extraction on Grids.

The CoreGRID Network of Excellence aims at strengthening and advancing scientific and technological excellence in the area of Grid and Peer-to-Peer technologies. To achieve its objectives, CoreGRID brings together a critical mass of well-established researchers from more than forty European institutions active in the fields of distributed systems and middleware, models, algorithms, tools and environments.

In the CoreGRID NoE, the Institute on Knowledge and Data Management (KDM) has the objective to improve integration of research activities in the fields of data management, knowledge discovery and Grid computing for providing knowledge-based Grid services for the Semantic Grid through a tight coordination of European researchers active in those areas. The research tasks undertaken in the context of the KDM Institute compose a unified scenario of the data and knowledge management in GRIDs through a layered approach that starts from efficient data storage techniques up to information management and knowledge representation and discovery. At the same time, joint research activities pursued by the Institute partners are providing single solutions for data and knowledge management that will bring benefits to research and industry in GRID technology. Within its activities. the KDM Institute organized the first Workshop on Knowledge and Data Management in Grids that has been held in

Poznan (Poland) on September 13-14, 2005. The purpose of the workshop was bringing together CoreGRID researchers and invited external scientists doing research in Knowledge and Data Management in Grid and Peer-to-Peer Systems. The workshop provided a forum for the presentation and exchange of views on the latest Grid Technology research in the area of knowledge and data management.

This book is the third volume of the CoreGRID series and, as a result of that workshop and some additional invited papers, it brings together scientific contributions by researchers and scientists working on storage, data, and knowledge management in Grid and Peer-to-Peer systems. The book chapters present the latest Grid solutions and research results in key areas of knowledge and data management such as distributed storage management, Grid databases, Semantic Grid and Grid-aware data mining. All the addressed topics are discussed in the context of recent research projects.

The book includes four parts: Grid Data Management, Grid Data Storage, Semantic Grid, and Distributed Data Mining. All those sections are concerned with key topics in the area of knowledge and data management on Grids. They provide a general view of the main challenges in implementing data- and knowledge-intensive applications in a Grid computing scenario.

The first part includes four chapters. The first one presents an overview of the OGSA-DAI (Open Grid Service Architecture - Data Access and Integration) software, which provides a uniform and extensible framework for accessing structured and semi-structured data and provide some examples of its use in significant Grid projects. The second chapter discusses data integration and query reformulation in service-based Grids. The XMAP data integration algorithm is presented and service-based architecture for data integration-enabled query processing on the Grid is discussed. In the third chapter are evaluated the benefits of using OGSA-DAI in bioinformatics GRIDs by establishing communication between OGSA-DAI and GRID project developers as well as through practical case studies involving current projects. The last chapter of this part discusses fault-tolerance in Grid-based distributed query processing. A new scheme for adding fault-tolerance to distributed query processing through a rollback-recovery mechanism is evaluated in the context of the OGSA-DQP system.

The Grid Data Storage part includes a chapter on Conductor, a rule-based production system providing the ability to configure storage systems to meet resource constraints and application requirements. Conductor is able to evaluate alternatives and minimize system costs based on certain criteria. Then an autonomous distributed system built on top of the Violin framework is presented that is able to configure and reconfigure the storage hierarchy by detecting service breaches and take actions to eliminate them. The third chapter of this part presents the Clusterix Data Management System (CDMS), a solution for data management on Grids. Taking into account Grid specific networking conditions - different bandwidth, current load and network technologies between geographically distant sites, CDMS tries to optimize data throughput via replication and replica selection techniques.

The third part includes five chapters discussing key topics in the Semantic Grid area. The first chapter describes the dynamic aspects of the Semantic Grid reference architecture, S-OGSA, by presenting the typical patterns of interaction among these services. The next chapter describes a science metadata model developed at CCLRC providing interoperability of scientific information systems in the organization and form a specification of the type and categories of metadata that studies should capture about their investigations. Then the Semantic Grid part includes a chapter that argues that providing the appropriate means for accessing and using ontologies effectively is a key factor in enriching current Grid with semantic technologies and supporting progress towards the next generation Grid. That work was performed in the OntoGrid project. The fourth chapter in this part proposes an ontology-based metascheduler as a Grid service for co-allocating resources on multiple grid nodes based on semantic information. Finally, the part finishes with a chapter that presents the implementation of Atlas, a P2P system for the distributed storage and querying of RDF(S) metadata describing OntoGrid resources and services.

The last part of the book includes contributions on Distributed Data mining in Grids. The first chapter describes the composition of distributed knowledge discovery services according to the WSRF model by using the Knowledge Grid environment. The chapter focuses in particular on the application modeling. Applications are designed using a UML model, which is translated into a BPEL representation, in turn processed by the Knowledge Grid services for its execution. The second chapter addresses the problem of mining frequent closed itemsets in a highly distributed setting like a Grid. Authors show how frequent closed itemsets, mined independently at each site, can be merged in order to derive globally frequent closed itemsets. The last chapter reports progress made by using data mining techniques in the TELEMAC project concerned with enhancing the efficacy of anaerobic digestion in potentially unstable digesters. After placing the specific TELEMAC situation in a generic Grids context, authors present a classification approach to attributes for metadata and indicate some examples of model resource discovery.

From recent developments we can see the Grid moving from a computation platform to a data and knowledge management infrastructure. This trend needs new models, tools and solutions for enabling Grid computing to support advanced Grid applications. This book discusses some of the key technologies needed to support this trend and presents solutions recently designed to implement scalable applications.

We would like to thank all the participants for their contributions to making the KDM workshop a success. The workshop program committee for reviewing the submissions; the PSNC colleagues in Poznan for their support, and all the authors that contributed chapter for publication in this volume. A special thank to the Springer staff, Vladimir Getov and Paolo Trunfio for their assistance in editing the book.

Our thanks also go to the European Commission for sponsoring under grant number 004265 this volume of the CoreGRID project series of publications.

Domenico Talia, Angelos Bilas, Marios D. Dikaiakos

Contributing Authors

Pinar Alper School of Computer Science, The University of Manchester, United Kingdom (penpecip@cs.man.ac.uk)

Mario Antonioletti EPCC, The University of Edinburgh, JCMB, The King's Buildings, Mayfield Road, Edinburgh, EH9 3JZ, United Kingdom (mario@epcc.ed.ac.uk)

Malcolm Atkinson National e-Science Centre, 15 South College Street, Edinburgh, EH8 9AA, United Kingdom (mpa@nesc.ac.uk)

Sean Bechhofer School of Computer Science, The University of Manchester, United Kingdom (seanb@cs.man.ac.uk)

Angelos Bilas Institute of Computer Science (ICS), Foundation for Research and Technology - Hellas, P.O.Box 1385, Heraklion, GR 71110, Greece (bilas@ics.forth.gr)

Neil P. Chue Hong EPCC, The University of Edinburgh, JCMB, The King's Buildings, Mayfield Road, Edinburgh, EH9 3JZ, United Kingdom (N.ChueHong@epcc.ed.ac.uk)

Carmela Comito DEIS, University of Calabria, Via P. Bucci 41C, 87036 Rende (CS), Italy (ccomito@deis.unical.it)

Antonio Congiusta DEIS, University of Calabria, Via P. Bucci 41C, 87036 Rende (CS), Italy (acongiusta@deis.unical.it)

Oscar Corcho School of Computer Science, The University of Manchester, United Kingdom (ocorcho@cs.man.ac.uk)

Shirley Crompton CCLRC, Daresbury Laboratory, Warrington WA4 4AD, United Kingdom (s.y.crompton@dl.ac.uk)

Maurice Dixon Computing, Communications Technology and Mathematics, London Metropolitan University, 31 Jewry Street, London, EC3N 2EY, UK (M.Dixon@Londonmet.ac.uk)

Michail D. Flouris Department of Computer Science, University of Toronto, Toronto, Ontario M5S 3G4, Canada (flouris@cs.toronto.edu)

Julian R. Gallop e-Science, CCLRC Rutherford Appleton Laboratory, Chilton, Didcot, Oxon, OX11 0QX, UK (J.R.Gallop@rl.ac.uk)

Carole Goble School of Computer Science, The University of Manchester, United Kingdom (carole@cs.man.ac.uk)

Asunción Gómez-Pérez Ontology Engineering Group, Universidad Politécnica de Madrid, Campus de Montegancedo s/n, 28660, Boadilla del Monte, Madrid, Spain (asun@fi.upm.es)

Anastasios Gounaris School of Computer Science, University of Manchester, UK (gounaris@cs.man.ac.uk)

Alex Gray Cardiff School of Computer Science, Cardiff University, Cardiff CF24 3AA, United Kingdom (w.a.gray@cs.cardiff.ac.uk)

Miguel Esteban Gutiérrez Ontology Engineering Group, Universidad Politécnica de Madrid, Campus de Montegancedo s/n, 28660, Boadilla del Monte, Madrid, Spain (mesteban@fi.upm.es)

Stratos Idreos CWI, Amsterdam, The Netherlands (S.Idreos@cwi.nl)

Andrew Jones Cardiff School of Computer Science, Cardiff University, Cardiff CF24 3AA, United Kingdom (Andrew.C.Jones@cs.cardiff.ac.uk)

Zoi Kaoudi Dept. of Informatics and Telecommunications, National and Kapodistrian University of Athens, Athens, Greece (zoi@di.uoa.gr)

Konstantinos A. Karasavvas National e-Science Centre, 15 South College Street, Edinburgh, EH8 9AA, United Kingdom (kostas@nesc.ac.uk)

Konrad Karczewski Institute of Computer and Information Sciences, Czestochowa University of Technology (xeno@icis.pcz.pl)

Ioannis Kotsiopoulos School of Computer Science, The University of Manchester, United Kingdom (ioannis@cs.man.ac.uk)

Manolis Koubarakis Dept. of Informatics and Telecommunications, National and Kapodistrian University of Athens, Athens, Greece (koubarak@di.uoa.gr)

Lukasz Kuczynski Institute of Computer and Information Sciences, Czestochowa University of Technology (lkucz@icis.pcz.pl)

Renaud Lachaize Institute of Computer Science (ICS), Foundation for Research and Technology - Hellas, P.O.Box 1385, Heraklion, GR 71110, Greece (rlachaiz@ics.forth.gr)

Simon C. Lambert e-Science, CCLRC Rutherford Appleton Laboratory, Chilton, Didcot, Oxon, OX11 0QX, UK (S.C.Lambert@rl.ac.uk)

Erietta Liarou Dept. of Electronic and Computer Engineering, Technical University of Crete, Greece (erietta@intelligence.tuc.gr)

Claudio Lucchese Dept. of Computer Science, Ca' Foscari University of Venice, Via Torino 155, 30172 Venezia, Italy (clucches@dsi.unive.it)

Matoula Magiridou Dept. of Informatics and Telecommunications, National and Kapodistrian University of Athens, Athens, Greece (matoula@di.uoa.gr)

Brian Matthews CCLRC, Rutherford-Appleton Laboratory, Didcot, Oxfordshire OX11 0AX, United Kingdom (b.m.matthews@rl.ac.uk)

Iris Miliaraki Dept. of Informatics and Telecommunications, National and Kapodistrian University of Athens, Athens, Greece (iris@di.uoa.gr)

Paolo Missier School of Computer Science, The University of Manchester, United Kingdom (pmissier@cs.man.ac.uk)

Zsolt Németh MTA SZTAKI Computer and Automation Research Institute, P.O. Box 63, Budapest, H-1518, Hungary (zsnemeth@sztaki.hu)

Raffaele Perego HPC Laboratory, ISTI-CNR of Pisa, via G. Moruzzi 1, 56124 Pisa, Italy (perego@isti.cnr.it)

Salvatore Orlando Dept. of Computer Science, Ca' Foscari University of Venice, Via Torino 155, 30172 Venezia, Italy (orlando@dsi.unive.it)

Rizos Sakellariou School of Computer Science, University of Manchester, UK (rizos@cs.man.ac.uk)

Claudio Silvestri Dept. of Computer Science, Ca' Foscari University of Venice, Via Torino 155, 30172 Venezia, Italy (silvestri@dsi.unive.it)

Jim Smith Newcastle University, Newcastle upon Tyne, UK (Jim.Smith@ncl.ac.uk)

Shoaib Sufi CCLRC, Daresbury Laboratory, Warrington WA4 4AD, United Kingdom (s.a.sufi@dl.ac.uk)

Domenico Talia DEIS, University of Calabria, Via P. Bucci 41C, 87036 Rende (CS), Italy (talia@deis.unical.it)

Paolo Trunfio DEIS, University of Calabria, Via P. Bucci 41C, 87036 Rende (CS), Italy (trunfio@deis.unical.it)

Paul Watson Newcastle University, Newcastle upon Tyne, UK (Paul.Watson@ncl.ac.uk)

Richard White Cardiff School of Computer Science, Cardiff University, Cardiff CF24 3AA, United Kingdom (r.j.white@cs.cardiff.ac.uk)

Philipp Wieder Grid Computing and Distributed Systems Group, Research Centre Jülich, 52425 Jülich, Germany (ph.wieder@fz-juelich.de)

Wolfgang Ziegler Fraunhofer Institute SCAI, Department of Bioinformatics, 53754 Sankt Augustin, Germany (wolfgang.ziegler@scai.fraunhofer.de)

I

GRID DATA MANAGEMENT

ACCESSING DATA IN GRIDS USING OGSA-DAI

Neil P. Chue Hong and Mario Antonioletti
EPCC, The University of Edinburgh
JCMB, The King's Buildings, Mayfield Road,
Edinburgh, EH9 3JZ,
United Kingdom
N.ChueHong@epcc.ed.ac.uk
mario@epcc.ed.ac.uk

Konstantinos A. Karasavvas and Malcolm Atkinson
National e-Science Centre
15 South College Street,
Edinburgh, EH8 9AA,
United Kingdom
kostas@nesc.ac.uk
mpa@nesc.ac.uk

Abstract

The grid provides a vision in which resources, including storage and data, can be shared across organisational boundaries. The original emphasis of grid computing lay in the sharing of computational resources but technological and scientific advances have led to an ongoing data explosion in many fields. However, data is stored in many different storage systems and data formats, with different schema, access rights, metadata attributes, and ontologies all of which are obstacles to the access, integration and management of this information.

In this chapter we examine some of the ways in which these differences can be addressed by grid technology to enable the meaningful sharing of data. In particular, we present an overview of the OGSA-DAI (Open Grid Service Architecture - Data Access and Integration) software, which provides a uniform, extensible framework for accessing structured and semi-structured data and provide some examples of its use in other projects. The open-source OGSA-DAI software is freely available from http://www.ogsadai.org.uk.

Keywords: OGSA-DAI, databases, data access, data management.

1. Introduction

The grid provides a vision [1, 7] in which resources, such as high performance computers, people and, for the purposes of this chapter, storage and data, can be shared across organisational boundaries. Each individual organisation contributes resources to this *Virtual Organisation* (VO) [2], a dynamic collection of individuals and institutions sharing resources in a flexible, secure and coordinated manner, while still maintaining ownership and control of its own resources. There are clear benefits to a VO's members in allowing resources to be shared, as well as many technological and political obstacles to overcome. To facilitate the process a number of organisations are developing *middleware*: software that allows the VO federation to be realised through the use of grids. Notable amongst these are: Globus, UNICORE and the UK OMII, as well as others [4]. By itself, the base middleware provided is usually insufficient to construct a fully functional VO – it requires configuration and customisation to achieve full operational status. We, as grid technology providers, are still some way from being able to produce an *out of the box grid* but nevertheless grid toolkits amortise the development costs and ensure a level of inter-operability between distinct grids, allowing dynamic and hierarchical VOs to be composed.

The original emphasis in grids lay in the sharing of computational resources. Technological and scientific advances have led to an ongoing data explosion in many fields [5–7] and there are clear benefits to being able to share and combine data from different sources [8–9]. With the decreasing cost of storage, more data is being maintained online and thus readily available. However, data is stored in many different storage systems and data formats, with different schema, access rights, metadata attributes, and ontologies. The volumes of data concerned could vary from small to very large, stored in one system or across many. All these differences can produce significant obstacles in a grid. Not all are immediately tractable and trying to solve the general problem is hard; nevertheless some of these obstacles may be overcome or reduced by middleware specifically targeted at addressing data management issues. These products (of which OGSA-DAI is an example) provide an infrastructure which, in particular contexts, allows the meaningful sharing of data to take place.

The *Open Grid Services Architecture - Data Access and Integration* (OGSA-DAI) software is intended to make the process of combining data from multiple, distributed, heterogenous and autonomously managed data sources easier to establish, maintain and operate by providing middleware that delivers many commonly required functions in a form that is easily used. It focuses on cases where the assembly of all the data into a single data warehouse is inappropriate. Instead, it enables application developers to build virtual data resources that draw on up-to-date data from an identified set of other data resources. Users can then explore these combined virtual data resources by requesting the enactment of compositions of OGSA-DAI activities, often via application-specific higher-level tools.

The remainder of this chapter discusses how data access can be managed in grids, focusing in particular on the perspective taken by the current version of OGSA-DAI. The next section discusses why web services are being used by some of the middleware products to build grids, section 3 examines some of the data middleware architectural requirements arising from grids, and sections 4 and 5 provide an overview of OGSA-DAI. Section 6 briefly reviews how OGSA-DAI is being used in a selection of projects and section 6 considers other currently available middleware products that cater for data in grids. Finally, before concluding, section 8 examines how OGSA-DAI considers standards as a means of ensuring interoperability between different grid middlewares.

2. Web Services and Grids

A large number of different types of resources could be contributed by a member organisation to a VO. Grid middleware needs to be able to accommodate these and abstract away some of the inherent differences to facilitate shared access and use. *Web Services* (WS) [10], originating in the business-to-business world, offered a number of transparencies: *platform independence*, *programming language neutrality*, *clearly defined interfaces* and *transport neutrality* that could be used to construct grids.

However, a number of important perceived grid requirements such as: the provision of *service state* with a standard access interface, *lifecycle management* to ensure services are cleaned up, *service groups* to facilitate the aggregation and discovery of services and *inheritance* to facilitate the development of complex grid services [7] were not provided by web services. The *Open Grid Services Infrastructure* (OGSI) [8] specification attempted to add this missing functionality, but its implemention threatened a schism in the base technology used by grid and web services. This undesirable outcome was avoided by deprecating the OGSI specification and developing a new set of specifications, the *Web Services Resource Framework* (WSRF) [12–16], motivated by OGSI and providing the same functionality in a manner consistent with web services. The consequence of this forced and rapid change between OGSI, on which a lot of the grid infrastructure being developed was based, and WSRF led to a reticence by some in the grid community to adopt emerging standards until they had wide acceptance and adoption within the community [17]. For this reason, some products, like OGSA-DAI, have had to support more than one infrastructure, to allow information to be shared across grid implementations. At present OGSA-DAI provides support for the Globus Toolkit 4 (www.globus.org), OMII 2 (www.omii.ac.uk) and Axis 1.2 (xml.apache.org/axis); versions have also been adapted to run on the GRIA (www.gria.org) and UNICORE (www.unicore.org) platforms[1].

Currently, web services are regarded as a suitable means to construct grids and, importantly, the abstractions offered are useful to satisfy the requirements for data sharing [18–19], in particular lowering the barriers created by the heterogeneity of different data sources. OGSA-DAI has subscribed to the use of web services for grids and provides its functionality through web services. However, web services do not offer a perfect solution: for instance SOAP is not a a good mechanism for transporting large amounts of data and there are associated overheads with the processing of XML. We must assume that many of the current web service limitations will be overcome in the future.

3. Architectural Requirements for Data Middleware

The previous section examined the suitability of web services to build grid infrastructure. In this section we examine some of the architectural requirements that arise from the provision of middleware for grids in general and in particular to address data requirements of grids.

The fundamental requirement is to provide a middleware layer, between data resources and their clients, that provides some level of uniformity in terms of virtualisation, access, federation and data integration. This can be expressed through a number of goals for these *data services*:

- it must be easy for users to combine data from multiple sources in ways that suit their particular analysis by assisting:
  - application developers building services for a target community of users
  - data integration users through provision of higher-level tools that compose sets of data services
- it must provide a uniform access layer that allows data services to be composed including:
  - a common set of access mechanisms covering all the types of data source and their metadata
  - a set of operations providing all of the elemental data selections, transformations, combinations and partitions
  - a set of data movement capabilities suitable for all destinations and data sizes

[1]Further porting work will be carried out as part of the EU FP6 OMII-Europe project.

  - an abstraction to allow different security models to be bridged

- it must minimise data transfer and copying by allowing:
  - composition and enactment of multiple operations on a service
  - transfer of computation closer to the data source
  - efficient, streaming, data transfer both internally and between services

The OGSA-DAI software has aimed to meet these goals by providing:

- *An extensible framework* – which allows new operations, data resources and security models to be exposed.
- *Perform Documents* – which allow multiple operations to take place in a single web service interaction.
- *Activity Framework* – which provides a powerful mechanism to combine activities within sessions, allowing one to specify control and data flows while creating pipelines to process data in streams.
- *Interoperability with other grid infrastructure* – by working closely with other grid middleware providers, to ensure that OGSA-DAI services will interoperate with their software.
- *Application development support* – OGSA-DAI has provided a client toolkit that makes it easier to develop OGSA-DAI applications and hides the differences in the message infrastructures supported by OGSA-DAI.

Most of the grid middleware development that is taking place is not aimed directly at end-users but rather at other developers. This second tier of developers can customise the middleware functionality for the needs of their own particular communities, hence the importance of a flexible and extensible framework.

4. An Overview of OGSA-DAI

OGSA-DAI has adopted a *service oriented architecture* (SOA) solution for integrating data and grids through the use of WS. This section presents an overview of OGSA-DAI features as present in the 2.1 WSRF and WSI releases of OGSA-DAI. A high-level view of the basic OGSA-DAI components and their interactions is shown in Figure 1.

The base unit of functionality within OGSA-DAI is the *activity*. Activities expose one or more capabilities of an underlying data resource, for instance the ability to execute an SQL query on a relational database, or they add functionality at the service layer: transforming data as it comes out of the data resource

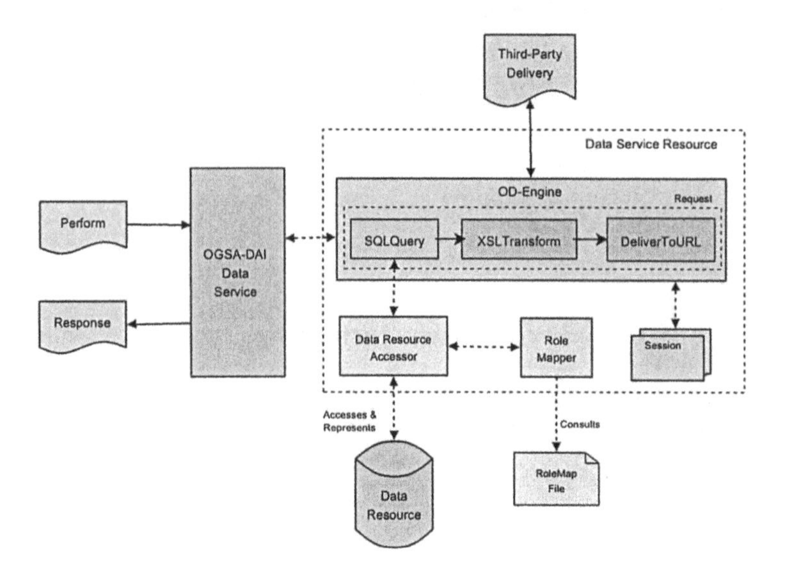

Figure 1. An overview of OGSA-DAI components

while still at the service or delivering data to a third party using a non-SOAP based protocol. A *perform document* collects a number of these activities, represented as XML fragments in an XML document, chained together using a set of named inputs and outputs that describes the data flow through the activities. The data is operated on by each activity as the data flows through it. The details of perform documents and activities are discussed in more detail in section 5.

An OGSA-DAI interaction thus begins with a client sending a perform document to an OGSA-DAI *Data Service* (DS). The DS can expose zero or more *Data Service Resources* (DSR). A DSR presents a high-level abstraction of a *Data Resource* (DR), a WS-Resource in WSRF terms, and contains the OGSA-DAI infrastructure necessary to interact with the DR. For instance, the DSR knows about the activities it can execute. In the case where no data resources are bound to the service only translation and delivery capabilities are supported. In the case where more than one DSR is associated with a DS then more capabilities are supported but the client must be able to specify which DSR a perform document is targeting. As OGSA-DAI supports more than one messaging framework the way that this is done varies: for the WSRF case the *end point reference* of the DSR targeted is specified in the SOAP header using mechanisms specified in WS-Addressing [20]; for the non-WSRF case, referred to as the WSI flavour of OGSA-DAI, the DSR *name*, which is determined when a DSR is instantiated, is appended to the service URL. Once the message has passed through the DS and the perform document has been extracted the behaviour of OGSA-DAI is identical regardless of the messaging framework used.

The bulk of the processing in OGSA-DAI takes place at the *Data Service Resource* (DSR). The DSR accepts a perform document from the DS and passes it to its *OGSA-DAI Engine* (ODE). The ODE is responsible for processing perform documents and generating response documents. It checks the syntax of the perform document, instantiates and starts the activities required and coordinates the data flow between them. If an activity needs to access a resource it does so through the *Data Resource Accessor* (DRA). This provides an activity with the appropriate connection type to communicate with the underlying data resource. The DRA consists of an interface that, when implemented, provides the functionality required for any activity to be able to interact with the particular type of data resource it is trying to access, e.g. for an XML database it might return an XMLDB connection. This abstraction facilitates the inclusion of new types of data resource to operate within the existing OGSA-DAI framework. Currently, OGSA-DAI supports DRAs for: DB2, Oracle DB, SQLServer, MySQL, PostgreSQL, HSQLDB, eXist, file systems and indexed files.

The security mechanism provided is also extensible. In order for the DRA to provide access to the underlying data resource, the grid credentials used to access the service need be mapped to a suitable username/password with which to access the data resource. This is done by the *Role Mapper* which maps the *distinguished name* obtained from the grid credentials to suitable credentials to access the underlying data resource. This functionality has been separated from the DRA in order to allow third parties to replace the role mapper functionality with their own version [21–22]. For this reason, the role mapper provided in the OGSA-DAI distribution is intentionally basic and not intended to be used in a production environment. The current authorisation granularity employed by OGSA-DAI relies on that provided by the existing underlying security infrastructure and associated policies. Support for a finer level of authorisation at the activity level will be provided within future versions of OGSA-DAI. These interfaces would provide another extensibility point that could use external authorisation services such as PERMIS [23].

Assuming that all activities successfully run to completion, the results from the activities are aggregated into a *response document* by the ODE which is then sent back to the original client. This will contain any data produced, unless a delivery activity has been explicitly used in which case the data will be transferred separately (note that data may also be pulled into the service using a delivery activity, rather than just extracted from a DR). The original requester will still get a response document with the completion status of all the activities present in their perform document. In the case where not all the activities complete successfully, the client will be informed about the completion status of each activity including those that failed. Currently no transactional capabilities are supported by OGSA-DAI so such an outcome would mean that some modifications will have been done and others will not. However, the final status should be clear from the response document. Transactional capabilities will be supported in future OGSA-DAI releases, including roll back mechanisms and distributed transactional capabilities. Early prototyping work has shown the viability of wrapping the transactional capabilities of an underlying resource and running a set of activities atomically and identified the appropriate interfaces that could be implemented for resources that not provide their own transactional functionality.

This completes the description of a simple interaction with an OGSA-DAI service. In addition, a perform request can create a *session* in order for its activities to store state within a named context. A follow-on perform document can then re-join a session to access any previously stored state. This avoids having to pass a context through in the request-response messages and allows intermediate state to be stored at the service. Sessions facilitate the external decision-making process to take place. For example, storing intermediate results in a session allows a client to decide how the process should continue in a follow-on request: results could be delivered or collected at a later time depending on their size. In addition, sessions will help in the provision of transactional behaviour, and provide a naming scheme for status monitoring, logging and diagnostics.

Finally, in order to help support the development of OGSA-DAI applications a *Client Toolkit* (CTk) has been developed that provides an *Application Programmer's Interface* (API) that facilitates the programmatic construction of perform documents and interaction with OGSA-DAI services. The CTk also abstracts away the differences between the WSRF/WSI messaging frameworks supported by OGSA-DAI – the same API can be used for flavours of OGSA-DAI running on different underlying platforms.

5. Activities and Perform Documents

Activities constitute the logical unit of work within OGSA-DAI. They are defined by an XML Schema fragment that dictates the syntax of its XML representation in perform documents, a service side Java implementation that implements the functionality at the service and a CTk representation that allows the activity to be used by the client toolkit. Activities can provide any kind of functionality, but typically they fall into one of the three broad categories: *statement activities* interact with a data resource; *transformation activities* transform the data while it is still at the service; and *delivery activities* deliver, or collect, data to/from third parties (which could include the original client). A comprehensive set of activities are provided with each OGSA-DAI distribution covering general functionality including SQL and XPath queries, XSLT transformations and delivery via GridFTP, FTP and SOAP, as well of examples of some statistical (projections) and data integration (SQLBag) operations – consult the documentation for more details. However, it is unlikely that all the required functionality for a particular application will be there. Thus, OGSA-DAI has been designed to allow new activities to be easily added, or existing functionality customised, to operate within the same OGSA-DAI framework.

As we have seen a perform document collects together activities so that these can be sent to a DS in a single request, reducing the number of interactions required between client and DS to achieve a desired outcome. Figure 2 schematically shows two perform documents being executed at the service.

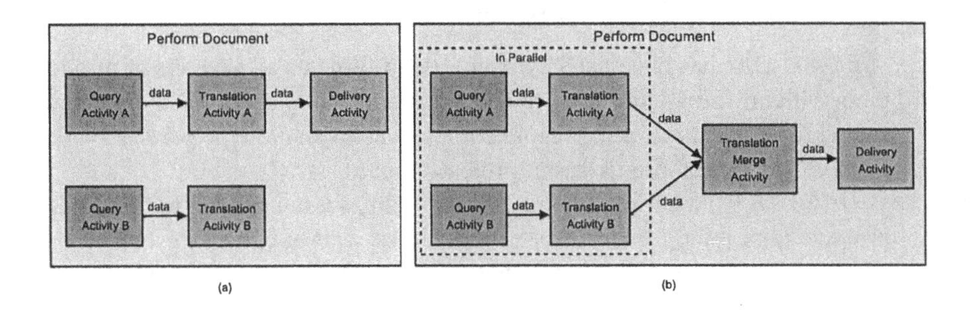

Figure 2. An example of two perform documents; (a) a perform document containing two requests, and (b) a perform document that contains parallel execution and multiple inputs/outputs to activities

In case (a) the perform document contains two independent sets of requests (*activity pipelines*) which, by default, will be executed in parallel. For each activity its name, parameters, inputs and outputs are defined. The data flow between activities can be set up by chaining them together; the output of the first becomes the input of the second and so on. This creates a pipeline between activities where data is streamed between them.

It is possible express the control flow that takes place between activities in a perform document more explicitly. In the previous case the control flow was implicitly sequential as the inputs of activities down the pipeline depend on the output of earlier activities (though the order of the execution of the pipelines cannot be determined). However, if activities are not explicitly linked it is possible to guarantee sequential processing. In some instances, you may also want to declare that a set of activities should be run in parallel. For example, in case (b) in Figure 2 we can see that two queries and the subsequent transformations are executed in parallel up to the synchronised point at the

Transformation-Merge activity. The example also demonstrates that activities can have multiple inputs and outputs.

A taxonomy for activities will be published by the OGSA-DAI team in the near future which will help with the composition and semantics of activities. The perform document represents a powerful and efficient way for managing data access and integration within grids. We aim to extend perform documents to be able to target multiple data resources within the same document, along with new generic data integration and transform activities. Finally support for distributed transactions will enable multi-resource perform documents to run atomically. This should facilitate several types of simple data integration use cases and provide users with a powerful set of tools for data integration.

6. How OGSA-DAI is being Used

OGSA-DAI has been used by a number of projects as a means of providing them with uniform data access to data resources. Only a very brief overview of some projects is given here, a more complete list with more projects is available from www.ogsadai.org.uk/about/projects.php.

OGSA-DQP (www.ogsadai.org.uk/dqp) [24] a sister project to OGSA-DAI, provides distributed query processing across read-only data resources using OGSA-DAI to provide access to these. OGSA-DQP provides an additional set of services over and above the OGSA-DAI ones: a *coordinator* that coordinates the various services involved in a distributed query and a set of *evaluators* that accept query partitions and evaluate them. OGSA-DQP provide data integration capabilities using OGSA-DAI.

The *e-Diamond* project (www.ediamond.ox.ac.uk) [25] was a pilot project within the UK to pool and distribute information on breast cancer treatement allowing specialists to review mammographs produced at different institutions. OGSA-DAI was used to provide access to the databases where the images were stored, and was extended to include a wrapper for IBM Content Manager.

The *STORM* project (storm.bmi.ohio-state.edu) [26] provides a framework designed to support processing of large datasets in a distributed environment. STORM allows SQL-type queries on file-based datasets by providing data model abstractions, e.g. object-relational. To leverage the existing framework in grids, STORM uses OGSA-DAI. The latter regards STORM as a data resource and provides the standard grid interfaces to it. Moreover, OGSA-DQP can now be used on top to provide distributed query processing over the large datasets (virtualised via STORM).

The *ConvertGrid* project (pascal.mvc.mcc.ac.uk:9080/convert/) produced a demonstrator which showed how grid technologies could automate complex social science workflows and facilitate the integrated use of multiple georeferenced datasets. It used OGSA-DAI to access a subset of UK census and neighbourhood statistics data and allows relationships between data to be graphically represented based on postcode.

The *LEAD* project (lead.ou.edu) [27] is a large US initiative to improve the forecasting of medium scale weather phenomena such as tornados. OGSA-DAI was used in the LEAD project to provide a metadata catalogue, myLEAD, which aims to provide a personal workspace for users faced with enormous amount of information. In this case, LEAD extended OGSA-DAI to allow the use of streaming data.

7. Related Work

Data access and integration is a large domain which features a variety of software and techniques which address at least some of the issues raised in earlier sections. However, there are relatively few products which aim to provide general solutions, in particular for grids. Here we restrict our discussion to middleware that provides some form of abstracted access to data.

Storage Resource Broker (SRB): (http://www.sdsc.edu/srb/) is produced by San Diego Supercomputer Center (SDSC). An SRB server provides a way of accessing *collections*, a logical name given to a set of data objects, based on their attributes and/or logical names rather than their physical names and/or locations. SRB supported data objects are file and archival systems, BLOBs in DBMSs, database objects that can be queried using SQL and tape library systems. In addition SRB servers may be combined to form a federation using *zoneSRB*.

SRB is mainly file orientated and uses its own protocols. By default it is not WS enabled. OGSA-DAI is mainly database orientated and can only be accessed through WS mechanisms. In both cases there is some cross over where SRB can support databases and OGSA-DAI has some support for files. Indeed the two architectures do not prevent OGSA-DAI being used to access SRB servers or for OGSA-DAI resources to be exposed through SRB.

WebSphere Information Integrator (WSII): (www.ibm.com/software/data/integration/) from IBM provides a number of desirable capabilities to deal with data in a VO. These include: search operation across the organisational domains, data federation, data replication, data transformation and data event publishing. The data federation can allow multiple data sources to be queried and accessed through a single access point. For a comparison between earlier versions of this product and OGSA-DAI see [28].

The abstraction capabilities provided by OGSA-DAI have been exploited through the provision of a *grid wrapper* that uses OGSA-DAI to wrap data resources that WebSphere Information Integrator can then access [29–30] allowing more data resources to be associated with this product.

Virtual Data System (VDS): (vds.uchicago.edu) developed within the GriPhyN project and work with the *Virtual Data Toolkit* (vdt.cs.wisc.ed). This allows a *Directed Acyclic Graph* (DAG) to express a workflow, similar to the OGSA-DAI perform document but wider in scope, that allows a data recipe to be specified to generate *derived data* from a number sources with a number of transformations acting on the source data. The workflow is then stored as the provenance for the data that has been generated.

Mobius: (projectmobius.osu.edu) aims to create a set of tools and services to provide data as well as metadata sharing and management in a grid and/or a distributed computing environment. To expose a resource in Mobius it must be described in an XML schema which will be shared via the Global Model Exchange (GME) and then later accessed by querying that schema using for example XPath. OGSA-DAI does not require an XML schema to be created for a resource, rather it directly exposes that information (data and metadata/schema) to be queried by the resource's querying mechanisms.

There are a number of other products that attempt to provide access to data in the context of grids, including ELDAS (www.edikt.org/eldas/) and Spitfire (edg-wp2.web.cern.ch/edg-wp2/spitfire/) but it is not clear whether these are currently being actively developed at the moment.

8. Importance of Standards

In order to provide some cohesion to the disparate efforts that are going on to produce components to construct grids at the moment it is important to ensure that these inter-operate at some level. For this reason standards are important. Bodies such as the *Global Grid Forum* (www.ggf.org), OASIS (www.oasis-open.org), W3C (www.w3c.org) and the IETF (www.ietf.org) are providing the basic blue prints for grid components. Of course, a standard by itself is not sufficient condition as it also requires adoption and consensus. One problem is that the ecosystem is rather too rich in standards and it is difficult to understand what will be successful and what will not, e.g. OGSI. At some level this richness is good in that the space will be sufficiently explored and the best candidate standards will be adopted. Of course, in order for grids to become successful there has to be some stability in the standards space, and their implementations, so that end-users gain sufficient confidence to migrate to the new technology.

Within the context of OGSA-DAI the intent was to have a twin track approach: OGSA-DAI would be the implementation and through the GGF DAIS Working Group (forge.gridforum.org/projects/dais-wg) the implementation would both be standardised and at the same time inform the standardisation process – a symbiotic process. In reality, the implementation and DAIS specifications diverged, with the implementation having to support existing users and the specification having to agree details with all parties. Nevertheless, the resulting *Web Services – Database Access and Integration* (WS-DAI) [32, 31] family of specifications attempt to promote databases to be first class citizens within the grid world. Currently, relational and XML databases are catered for but the model is extensible to allow other types of data models such as files, object databases and RDF data sources[2]. The intent is for OGSA-DAI to track and implement these where possible.

Standards help to enable interoperability between implementations, something which we have pursued through DIALOGUE (www.datagrids.org). In particular, OGSA-DAI has been keen to see the emergence of a standard for bulk data transfer between web services (for which we currently provide the proprietary *Grid Data Transport* porttype).

Thus despite the proliferation of standards, they still serve to provide the vision, such as OGSA [34], and the basic nuts and bolts to allow the construction of interoperable grids.

9. Conclusions

This chapter has reviewed the benefits of being able to construct grids that address the data requirements of a VO and how web services offer one possible abstraction that facilitates this process. OGSA-DAI has taken the web service approach to sharing data – particularly structured data like databases – within grids. OGSA-DAI has been constructed with extensibility in mind allowing additional functionality to be added through *activities*, new *data resources* through *data resource accessors* and the security mechanisms to be extended through the *authorization callouts*. A number of design principles have been employed which attempt to maximise the benefits in using OGSA-DAI: minimising data movement, encapsulating multiple web service interactions in a single document – the *perform document* – and to moving computation close to the data. As such, OGSA-DAI occupies a unique position with regard to related products that also facilitate access to data on grids. Development of OGSA-DAI is driven by user requirements and scenarios and future extensions include extensions to the perform document, support for transactions, security at the activity level and general data integration activities.

The grid world is progressing rapidly and we hope OGSA-DAI will continue to evolve and satisfy the needs of those building grids. The OGSA-DAI project continues to address the differences that prevent data sharing and enable the acheivement of additional data scenarios. Up-to-date information on the project is available from our website (www.ogsadai.org.uk).

[2]A prototype implementation of RDF as an OGSA-DAI resource already exists, see www.gtrc.aist.go.jp/dbgrid/sc05/.

Acknowledgments

We would like to thank the following people: Bartosz Dobrzelecki, Ally Hume, Mike Jackson, Amy Krause, Steven Lynden, Arijit Mukherjee, Mark Parsons, Norman Paton, Jen Schopf, Tom Sugden, Elias Theocharopoulos, Paul Watson, as well as others not mentioned above but that have been involved in the OGSA-DAI project in the past.

This work has been supported by the UK eScience Core Programme, EPSRC and the DTI.

References

[1] I. Foster and C. Kesselman (editors). The Grid 2: Blueprint for a New Computing Infrastructure. Morgan Kaufmann Pub. December 2003.

[2] I. Foster, C. Kesselman, S. Tuecke. The Anatomy of the Grid: Enabling Scalable Virtual Organizations. *International J. Supercomputer Applications*, 15(3), 2001.

[3] I. Foster, C. Kesselman, J. Nick, S. Tuecke. The Physiology of the Grid: An Open Grid Services Architecture for Distributed Systems Integration. Open Grid Service Infrastructure WG, Global Grid Forum, June 22, 2002.

[4] K. Krauter, R. Buyya, M. Maheswaran. A taxonomy and survey of grid resource management systems for distributed computing. Software: Practice and Experience Vol 32, p135-164, 2002.

[5] T. Hey and A. Trefethen. The data deluge: An e-Science perspective. Chapter 36, In Grid Computing, Editors: F. Berman, G. Fox, T. Hey. John Wiley & Sons, Ltd, 2003.

[6] J. Thornton. The future of bioinformatics. Trend in Ecology and Evolution. VOL 13; NUMBER 11; SUPP 1, pages 30-31, 1998.

[7] L. Reiser, L.A. Mueller, S.Y. Rhee. Surviving in a sea of data: a survey of plant genome data resources and issues in building data management systems. Plant Molecular Biology, Volume 48, Issue 1-2, Jan 2002, Pages 59-74.

[8] Virtual observatory finds black holes in previous data. News in brief. Nature 429, 494-495, June 2004.

[9] Astronomers Detect New Category of Elusive 'Brown Dwarf'. The New York Times, Tuesday, June 1 1999.

[10] D. Booth, H. Haas, F. McCabe, M. Champion, C. Ferris, D. Orchard. Web Services Architecture. W3C Working Group Note, February 2004.

[11] S. Tuecke, K. Czajkowski, I. Foster, J. Frey, S. Graham, C. Kesselman, T. Maguire, T. Sandholm, P. Vanderbilt and D. Snelling. Open Grid Services Infrastructure (OGSI) Version 1.0. Global Grid Forum Draft Recommendation GFD.15, June 2003.

[12] S. Graham, J. Tredwell. Web Services Resource Properties 1.2 (WS-ResourceProperties). OASIS, January 2006

[13] S. Graham, A. Karmarkar, J. Mischkinsky, I. Robinson, I. Sedukhin. Web Services Resource 1.2 (WS-Resource). OASIS, January 2006.

[14] L. Srinivasan, T. Banks Web Services Resource Lifetime 1.2 (WS-ResourceLifetime)/ OASIS, January 2006.

[15] T. Maguire, D. Snelling, T. Banks. Web Services Service Group 1.2 (WS-ServiceGroup). OASIS, January 2006.

[16] L. Liu, S. Meder. Web Services Base Faults 1.2 (WS-BaseFaults). OASIS, January 2006.

[17] M. Atkinson, D. DeRoure, A. Dunlop, G. Fox, P. Henderson, T. Hey, N. Paton, S. Newhouse, S. Parastratidis, A. Trefethen, P. Watson, J. Webber Web Service Grids: an evolutionary approach. Concurrency and Computation: Practice and Experience, 2005. 17(2): p. 377-390.

[18] M.P. Atkinson, V. Dialani, L. Guy, I. Narang, N.W. Paton, D. Pearson, T. Storey, and P. Watson. Grid Database Access and Integration: Requirements and Functionalities. DAIS-WG, Global Grid Forum Informational Document (GFD.13), March 2003.

[19] V. Raman, C. Crone, L. Haas, S. Malaika, T. Mukai, D. Wolfson and C. Baru. Services for Data Access and Data Processing on Grids. DAIS-WG, Global Grid Forum Informational Document (GFD.14), February 2003.

[20] M. Gudgin, M. Hadley, T. Rogers. Web Services Addressing 1.0 - Core (WS-Addressing). W3C Proposed Recommendation, 21 March 2006.

[21] D. Power, M. Slaymaker, E. Politou and A. Simpson. A Secure Wrapper for OGSA-DAI. Lecture Notes in Computer Science, Volume 3470, Pages 485-494, June 2005.

[22] A.L. Pereira, V. Muppavarapu and S.M. Chung. Role-Based Access Control for Grid Database Services. First DIALOGUE Workshop: Applications-Driven Issues in Data Grids, Columbus, Ohio, 2005.

[23] D. W. Chadwick and A. Otenko The PERMIS X.509 role based privilege management infrastructure. Future Generation Computer Systems, 19(2):277-289, 2003.

[24] N. Alpdemir, A. Mukherjee, A. Gounaris, N.W. Paton, P. Watson, and A.A.A. Fernandes. OGSA-DQP: A grid service for distributed querying on the grid. LNCS Volume 2992, p 858-861, 2004.

[25] J.M. Brady, D.J. Gavaghan, A.C. Simpson, M. Mulet-Parada, R.P. Highnam. eDiaMoND: A grid-enabled federated database of annotated mammograms. In Berman, F., Fox, G.C., Hey, A.J.G., eds.: Grid Computing: Making the Global Infrastructure a Reality. Wiley Series (2003) 923-943.

[26] S. Narayanan, T. M. Kurc, U. V. Catalyurek, J. H. Saltz. Servicing Seismic and Oil Reservoir Simulation Data through Grid Data Services. In Very Large Databases (VLDB) Workshop on Data Management in Grids Trondheim, Norway, 2005.

[27] B. Plale, Using Global Snapshots to Access Data Streams on the Grid, Lecture Notes in Computer Science, Volume 3165, Jan 2004, Pages 191 - 201.

[28] R.O. Sinnott, D. Houghton. Comparison of Data Access and Integration Technologies in the Life Science Domain. Proceedings of the UK e-Science All Hands Meeting 2005, September 2005.

[29] IBM Alphaworks. Grid Wrapper for WebSphere Information Integrator. http://www.alphaworks.ibm.com/tech/gridwrapper

[30] A. Lee, J. Magowan, P. Dantressangle, F. Bannwart. Bridging the integration gap, Part 1: Federating grid data. IBM Developer Works. August 2005.

[31] M. Antonioletti, A. Krause, S. Hastings, S. Langella, S. Laws, S.Malaika and N.W. Paton. Web services data access and integration - the XML realization (WS-DAIX), Version 1.0. GGF, 2005

[32] M. Antonioletti, M. Atkinson, A. Krause, S. Laws, S. Malaika, N.W. Paton, D. Pearson, G. Riccardi. Web services data access and integration Ž013 the core (WS-DAI) Specification, Version 1.0. GGF, 2005.

[33] M. Antonioletti, B. Collins, A. Krause, S. Laws, S. Malaika, J. Magowan and N.W. Paton. Web services data access and integration - the relational realization (WS-DAIR), Version 1.0. GGF, 2005.

[34] I. Foster, H. Kishimoto, A. Savva, D. Berry, A. Djaoui, A. Grimshaw, B. Horn, F. Maciel, F. Siebenlist, R. Subramaniam, J. Treadwell, J. Von Reich The Open Grid Services Architecture, Version 1.0. GGF Document (GFD30), January 2005.

SERVICE CHOREOGRAPHY FOR DATA INTEGRATION ON THE GRID

Anastasios Gounaris and Rizos Sakellariou
School of Computer Science, University of Manchester, UK
gounaris@cs.man.ac.uk
rizos@cs.man.ac.uk

Carmela Comito and Domenico Talia
DEIS, University of Calabria, Italy
ccomito@deis.unical.it
talia@deis.unical.it

Abstract To date there have been several efforts with a view to developing services that support and enable data integration on the Grid; however there is a lack of a comprehensive solution to this issue. This paper summarises the work thus far on the XMAP data integration framework and query reformulation algorithm and on middleware with regard to Grid query processing services, namely OGSA-DQP. Furthermore, it presents an architecture for data integration-enabled query processing on the Grid, which combines the two aforementioned pieces of work and provides an extended set of e-Services. These services allow users to submit queries over a single database and receive the results from multiple databases that are semantically correlated with the former one. The paper focuses on the service choreography involved by elaborating on the interactions between the services, and discusses the extensions to OGSA-DQP that are required in order to make the services interoperable.

Keywords: service choreography, data integration, XMAP, OGSA-DQP.

1. Introduction

The Grid, as an emerging infrastructure for the discovery, access and use of distributed computational resources [15], offers new opportunities and raises new challenges in data management. Many aspects differentiate the Grid from a traditional distributed environment; such aspects include the large scale, dynamic, autonomous, and distributed nature of data sources. A Grid can include related data resources maintained in different syntaxes, managed by different software systems, and accessible through different protocols and interfaces. Due to this diversity in data resources, one of the most demanding issue in managing data on Grids is reconciliation of data heterogeneity [8]. Therefore, in order to provide facilities for addressing requests over multiple heterogeneous data sources, it is necessary to provide data integration models and mechanisms.

Data integration is one of the most persistent problems that the database and information management community has to deal with. Although significant progress has been made in several aspects of data integration, the increase in availability of web-based data sources has led to new challenges. More specifically, efficient techniques have been developed and approaches have been devised to schema mediation languages, query answering algorithms, optimisation strategies, query execution policies, industrial development, and so on [17]. However, effective techniques for the generation and handling of semantic mappings are still in their infancy. The need for semantic correlation of data sources is particularly felt in Grid settings. Moreoever, in a Grid, a centralized structure for coordinating all the nodes may not be practical because it can become a bottleneck and, more importantly, it cannot accommodate the dynamic and distributed nature of Grid resources.

Data access and integration services have been attracting significant interest from the Grid community. Data Grids that rely on the coordinated sharing of and interaction across multiple autonomous database management systems play a key role in many industrial and scientific initiatives. To this end, middleware services have been developed. Two notable examples are the *OGSA Data Access and Integration* (OGSA-DAI) [6] and the *OGSA Distributed Query Processor* (OGSA-DQP)[1] [5, 4] projects. These projects have moved toward a servide-oriented architecture quite early in their lifecycle. OGSA-DAI exposes database management systems (including Oracle, MySQL, SQLServer, DB2, and so on) in a uniform way, whereas OGSA-DQP provides distributed query processing functionalities on top of OGSA-DAI. As such, OGSA-DQP can combine and integrate data from multiple data sources. To enhance performance, it employs parallel query execution techniques; nevertheless it relies

[1]OGSA-DQP is publicly available in open source form from www.ogsadai.org.uk/dqp.

on the user for the semantic interpretation of the data and does not address any schema integration requirements.

To date, only few projects (e.g., [11, 9]) actually meet the schema-integration requirements that are necessary for establishing semantic connections among heterogeneous data sources. To address this limitation, the use of the *XMAP* framework for integrating heterogeneous data sources distributed over a Grid has been proposed [12] . The aim of this framework is to develop a decentralized network of semantically related schemas, so that the formulation of distributed queries over heterogeneous data sources is enabled. XMAP employs a decentralized point-to-point mediation approach to connect different data sources based on schema mappings in order to combine remote XML documents. The XMAP framework is also exposed as an additional e-Service, called *Grid Data Integration Service* (GDIS). The contribution of the paper is the presentation of a unifying infrastructure for distributed query processing and query reformulation driven by semantic connections. The infrastructure proposed exploits the middleware provided by OGSA-DQP and OGSA-DAI, to provide schema-integration services. The integration and coordination of different services is the topic of service choreography. In this paper, we examine in detail how OGSA-DAI/DQP and GDIS are combined.

The remainder of the paper is organized as follows. Section 2 presents a short analysis of data integration systems focusing on the issues that are more relevant to Grids. The integrative architecture that combines the query reformulation and the query processing services, along with their interaction, is the subject of Section 3. Section 4 presents the XMAP integration framework, and describes the underlying integration model and the XMAP query reformulation algorithm. Section 5 discusses a simple example of applying the XMAP algorithm to OGSA-DQP supported relational databases, elaborating on how the service integration is achieved in practice and how the architecture proposed can be further extended. Finally, Section 6 concludes the paper.

2. Background

Both areas of data integration and Grid computing benefit from their combination:

- data integration is a key issue for exploiting the availability of large, heterogeneous, distributed and highly dynamic data volumes on Grids;

- integration formalisms can benefit from an OGSA-based Grid infrastructure, since such an infrastructure facilitates dynamic discovery, allocation, access, and use of both data and computational resources, which are required to support computationally demanding database operations such as query reformulation, compilation and evaluation.

Data integration on Grids has to deal with unpredictable, highly dynamic data volumes provided by unpredictable membership of nodes that happen to be participating at any given time. So, traditional approaches to data integration, such as federation database management systems (FDBMS) [22] and the use of mediator/wrapper middleware [21], are not suitable in Grid settings.

The federation approach is a rather rigid configuration where resource allocation is static and optimization cannot take advantage of evolving circumstances in the execution environment. The design of mediator/wrapper integration systems must be done globally, and the coordination of mediators is performed by a central administrator, which is an obstacle to the exploitation of evolving characteristics of dynamic environments. As a consequence, these approaches are insufficient when data sources change often and to a significant extent, since such changes may violate the mappings to the mediated schema.

Recently, several works on data management in peer-to-peer (P2P) systems are moving towards decentralized, wide-scale sharing of semantically-related data [7, 10, 16, 18, 19]. All these systems focus on an integration approach, which is not based on a global schema: each peer represents an autonomous information system, and data integration is achieved by establishing mappings between the various peers.

To the best of our knowledge, there are only few works designed to provide schema-integration in Grids. The most notable ones are *Hyper* [11] and *GDMS* [9]. Both systems are based on an approach similar to ours, i.e., to build data integration services by extending the reference implementation of OGSA-DAI. The *Grid Data Mediation Service* (GDMS) is part of the GridMiner project [16] and uses a wrapper/mediator approach based on a global schema. GDMS presents heterogeneous, distributed data sources as one logical virtual data source in the form of an OGSA-DAI service. The main difference from our work is that it relies on the existence of a global schema, which is not that realistic in Grids. *Hyper* is a framework that integrates relational data in P2P systems built on Grid infrastructures. As in other P2P integration systems, the integration is achieved without using any hierarchical structure for establishing mappings among the autonomous peers. In that framework, the authors use a simple relational language for expressing both the schemas and the mappings. Our integration model follows an approach not based on a hierarchical structure as well, however it focuses on XML data sources and is based on schema-mappings that associate paths in different schemas. Finally, semantic mapping across relational databases coupled with a global-as-view approach is investigated in the context of the SASF project [3].

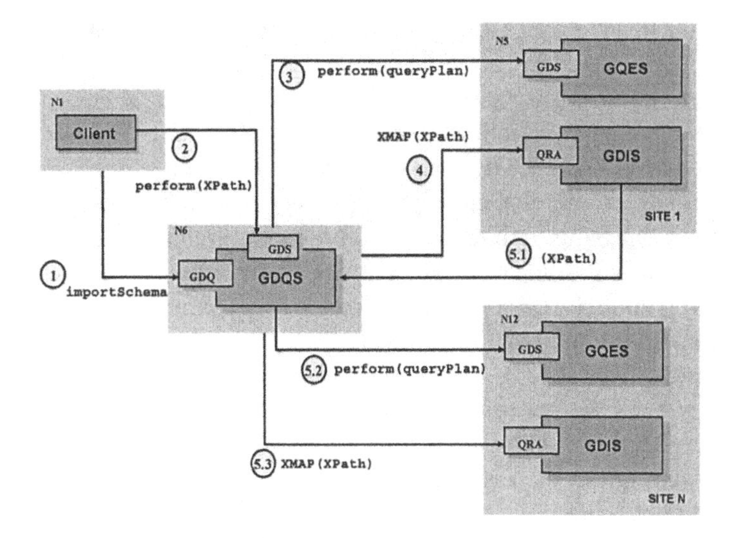

Figure 1. Data integration-enabled query processing on the Grid: service interactions.

3. Architecture and Service Interactions

The XMAP query reformulation algorithm, presented in more detail in the following section, is deployed as a stand-alone service, called *Grid Data Integration Service (GDIS)*. Given an XPath query over a local database, it returns the equivalent XPath queries that retrieve semantically similar data from remote databases. Figure 1 provides an overview of the service interactions involved in the incorporation of data integration functionality in distributed query processing on the Grid. It focuses on the interactions that concern the *GDIS*, and thus it hides all the complexities that relate to (distributed) query submission and execution. As such, it complements the service interactions between the OGSA-DAI and DQP services.

OGSA-DQP is an open source service-based Distributed Query Processor; as such, it supports the evaluation of queries over collections of potentially remote data access and analysis services. OGSA-DQP uses Grid Data Services provided by OGSA-DAI to hide data source heterogeneities and ensure consistent access to data and metadata from any database resource. The current version of OGSA-DQP, OGSA-DQP 3.0 is Globus Toolkit 4 compliant [9]. Thus OGSA-DQP builds upon the WSRF infrastructure.

OGSA-DQP provides two additional types of services, *Grid Distributed Query Services (GDQSs)* and *Grid Query Evaluation Services (GQESs)* or simply *Query Evaluation Services (QESs)*. The former are visible to end users, accept queries from them, construct and optimise the corresponding query plans and coordinate the query execution. GQESs implement the query engine, interact with other services (such as OGSA-DAI services, ordinary Web Services and other instances of GQESs), and are responsible for the execution of the query plans created by a GDQS. The interactions and functionality of OGSA-DQP services are described in detail in [4]. In the latest OGSA-DQP version, GQESs have been refactored as ordinary Web Services, augmenting the applicability of OGSA-DQP, as its deployment has been simplified significantly, whereas several interdependencies have been removed.

For the unifying architecture, the following architectural assumptions are made. A *GDIS* is deployed at each site participating in a dynamic database federation and has a mechanism to load local mapping information. It implements an additional *portType*, namely *Query Reformulation Algorithm (QRA)* portType, which accepts XPath expressions, applies the XMAP algorithm to them, and returns the results. A database can join the system as in OGSA-DQP: registering itself in a registry and informing the *GDQS*. The only difference is that, given the assumptions above, it should be associated with both a *GQES* and a *GDIS*.

Also, there is one *GQES* per site to evaluate (sub)queries, and at least one *GDQS*. As in classical OGSA-DQP scenarios, the *GDQS* contains a view of the schemas of the participating data resources, and a list of the computational resources that are available. The users interact only with a GDQS service through a client application that need not be exposed as a service.

A comprehensive data integration architecture needs to combine both the query reformulation and the query processing services. The interactions of the services, which form the choreography for data integration, are as follows (see also Figure 1):

1 The client contacts the *GDQS* and requests a view of the schema for each database he/she is interested in. At this point, there is no assumption that the user has an a-priori knowledge of the semantics of this and the semantically-related databases.

2 Based on the retrieved schema, he/she composes an XPath query, which is sent to the *GDQS*, and not directly to the corresponding database service, following the OGSA-DQP approach.

3 The *GDQS* transforms, parses, optimises, schedules and compiles a query execution plan [23]. This process entails the identification of the relevant sites, and consequently their local *GQES* and *GDIS*. The resulting query execution plan is sent to the corresponding *GQES*, which returns the results asynchronously, after contacting the local database via an OGSA-DAI service.

4 The initial XPath expression is sent to the *GDIS* that is co-located with the *GQES* of the previous step to perform the XMAP algorithm. *GDIS*

retrieves the locally stored mapping schema, which contains the mapping information that links the paths in the submitted query with paths referring to other databases.

5 As long as the call to the *GDIS* returns at least one XPath expression that has not been considered yet in the same session, the following steps are executed in an iterative manner.

   (a) The results of the call to the *GDIS*, which contain a set of XPath expressions, are collected by the *GDQS*. Subsequently, the *GDQS* filters out the ones that have already been processed in the current session.

   (b) Each remaining XPath expression is processed as in Step 3 to collect results from databases other than the one initially considered.

   (c) The same XPath expressions are processed as in Step 4 to find additional correlated queries. I.e. there is a loop which continuously generates XPath queries until all the relevant data has been retrieved.

4. The XMAP Integration Framework

The primary design goal of the XMAP framework is to develop a decentralized network of semantically related schemas that enables the formulation of queries over heterogeneous, distributed data sources. The environment is modelled as a system composed of a number of Grid nodes, where each node can hold one or more XML databases. These nodes are connected to each other through declarative mappings rules.

The XMAP integration [12] model is based on schema mappings to translate queries between different schemas. The goal of a schema mapping is to capture structural as well as terminological correspondences between schemas. Thus, in [12], we propose a decentralized approach inspired from [18] where the mapping rules are established directly among source schemas without relying on a central mediator or a hierarchy of mediators. The specification of mappings is thus flexible and scalable: each source schema is directly connected to only a small number of other schemas. However, it remains reachable from all other schemas that belong to its transitive closure. In other words, the system supports two different kinds of mapping to connect schemas semantically: point-to-point mappings and transitive mappings. In transitive mappings, data sources are related through one or more *"mediator schemas"*.

We address structural heterogeneity among XML data sources by associating paths in different schemas. Mappings are specified as path expressions that relate a specific element or attribute (together with its path) in the source schema to related elements or attributes in the destination schema. The mapping rules are specified in XML documents called XMAP documents. Each source schema in the framework is associated to an XMAP document containing all the mapping rules related to it.

The key issue of the XMAP framework is the XPath reformulation algorithm. When a query is posed over the schema of a node, the system utilizes data from any node that is transitively connected by semantic mappings, and reformulates the given query expanding and translating it into appropriate, equivalent queries over semantically related nodes. Every time the reformulation reaches a node that stores no redundant data, the appropriate query is posed on that node, and additional answers may be found. As a first step, we consider only a subset of the full XPath language.

Figure 2 shows the service interface of the *Grid Data Integration Service*, which defines *Query Reformulation Algorithm (QRA)* portType. Such a service is interoperable with any other common Web and Grid Services.

5. Combining query processing and reformulation services

The XMAP algorithm can be used for data integration-enabled query processing in OGSA-DQP. The example discussed in this section aims to show how the XMAP algorithm can be applied on top of the OGSA-DAI and OGSA-DQP services. In the example, we will assume that the underlying databases, of which the XML representation of the schema is processed by the XMAP algorithm, are, in fact, relational databases, like those supported by the current version of OGSA-DQP.

We assume that there are two sites, each holding a separate, autonomous database that contains information about artists and their works. Figure 3 presents two self-explanatory views: one hierarchical (for native XML databases), and one tabular (for object-relational DBMSs).

In OGSA-DQP, the table schemas are retrieved and exposed in the form of XML documents, as shown in Figure 4.

The XMAP mappings need to capture the semantic relationships between the data fields in different databases, including the primary and foreign keys. This can be done in two ways, which are illustrated in Figures 5 and 6, respectively. Both the ways seem to be feasible. However, the second one is slightly more comprehensible, and thus more desirable.

The actual query reformulation occurs exactly as described in [12]. Initially, the users submit XPath queries that refer to a single physical database. E.g., `/S1/Artist[style="Cubism"]/name` extracts the names of the artists whose style is Cubism and their data is stored in the *S1* database. Similarly, `/S1/Artefact/title` returns the titles of the artifacts in the same database. When the XMAP algorithm is applied for the second query, two

```
<?xml version="1.0"?> <!-- root element wsdl:definitions defines
set of related services-->

<wsdl:definitions name="QueryReformulation"
  xmlns:qr="http://.../QueryReformulation.wsdl"
  xmlns:qrxsd="http://.../QueryReformulation.xsd"
  xmlns:soap="http://schemas.xmlsoap.org/wsdl/soap/"
  xmlns:wsdl="http://schemas.xmlsoap.org/wsdl/">
<wsdl:types>
 <xsd:schema targetNamespace="..."
      xmlns:xsd="http://www.w3.org/1999/XMLSchema">
   <xsd:element name="ArrayOfString">
    <xsd:complexType >
     <xsd:sequence>
      <xsd:element name="XPathQuery"
         type="xsd:string" minOccurs="0" maxOccurs="unbounded"/>
    </xsd:sequence>
   </xsd:complexType>
  </xsd:element>
 </xsd:schema>
</wsdl:types> <wsdl:message name="queryToReformulate" >
 <wsdl:part name="inputQuery" element="xsd:string"/>
</wsdl:message> <wsdl:message name="reformulatedQueries" >
 <wsdl:part name="reformulatedQuery" element="qrxsd:ArrayOfString"/>
</wsdl:message> <wsdl:portType name="QRAPortType">
  <wsdl:operation name="reformulation">
     <wsdl: input message="qr:queryToReformuate/>
     <wsdl: input message="qr:reformulatedQueries/>
 <wsdl:operation/>
<wsdl:portType/> <wsdl:binding
name="QueryReformulationSoapBinding" type="qr:QRAPortType">
 <soap:binding style="document"
              transport="http://schemas.xmlsoap.org/soap/http"/>
    <wsdl:operation name="reformulation">
      <soap:operation soapAction="..."/>
       <wsdl:input>
        <soap:body use="literal"  namespace="..."/>
      </wsdl:input>
      <wsdl:output>
        <soap:body use="literal" namespace="..."/>
      </wsdl:output>
      <wsdl:fault>
        <soap:body use="literal"  namespace="..."/>
      </wsdl:fault>
    </wsdl:operation>
  </wsdl:binding>
  <wsdl:service name="QueryReformulationService">
    <wsdl:documentation>...</wsdl:documentation>
    <wsdl:port name="QRAPortType"
              binding="qr:QueryReformulationSoapBinding">
      <soap:address location="..."/>
    </wsdl:port>
  </wsdl:service>
 </wsdl:definitions>
```

Figure 2. The interface of the Grid Data Integration Service.

more XPath expressions will be created that refer to the *S2* database: `/S2/Painting/Title` and `/S2/Sculptor/Artefact`. At the back-end, the following queries will be submitted to the underlying databases (in SQL-like format):

```
select title from Artefact;,
```

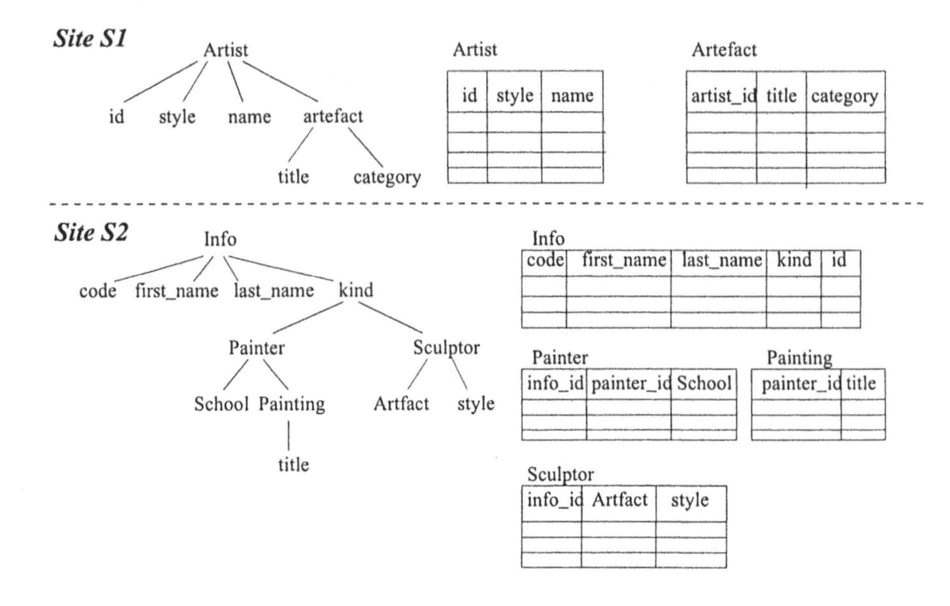

Figure 3. The example schemas.

`select title from Painting;`, and
`select Artefact from Sculptor;`

Note that the mapping of simple XPath expressions to SQL/OQL is feasible [20]. However, solving the mismatch between OQL and XPath, is not the only problem. The grid querying services provided from OGSA-DQP cannot support the proposal of this paper as they are. The modifications required are presented in more detail in the following subsection.

5.1 A Summary of the Extensions Envisaged to the Current Querying Services

The afore-mentioned architecture, apart from the development of the new *GDIS* service, implies some extensions to the current services and clients that are available from OGSA-DAI and OGSA-DQP. These extensions are, in our view, reasonable and feasible, and thus make the overall proposal of practical interest. They are summarised below:

- Currently, *GDQS* does not reveal any information on the database to which a table belongs, as the purpose of OGSA-DQP is to present a unified view of all the database schemas to the user hiding the locality details. However, in the proposed architecture, the user requirements change and the queries are submitted to a single physical database. As such, the client should expose the schemas per database rather than as a

```
<databaseSchema dbname="S1">
    <table name="Artist">
        <column name="id" />
        <column name="style" />
        <column name="name" />
        <primaryKey>
            <columnName>id</columnName>
        </primaryKey>
    </table>
    <table name="Artefact">
        <column name="artist_id" />
        <column name="title" />
        <column name="category" />
    </table>
</databaseSchema>

<databaseSchema dbname="S2">
    <table name="Info">
        <column name="id" />
        <column name="code" />
        <column name="first_name" />
        <column name="last_name" />
        <column name="kind" />
        <primaryKey>
            <columnName>id</columnName>
        </primaryKey>
    </table>
    <table name="Painter">
        <column name="painter_id" />
        <column name="info_id" />
        <column name="school" />
        <primaryKey>
            <columnName>painter_id</columnName>
        </primaryKey>
    </table>
    <table name="Painting">
        <column name="painter_id" />
        <column name="title" />
        <primaryKey>
            <columnName>title</columnName>
        </primaryKey>
    </table>
    <table name="Sculptor">
        <column name="info_id" />
        <column name="artefact" />
        <column name="style" />
    </table>
</databaseSchema>
```

Figure 4. The XML representation of the schemas of the example databases.

```
i)   databaseSchema[@dbname=S1]/table[@name=Artist]/column[@name=style] ->
     databaseSchema[@dbname=S2]/table[@name=Painter]/column[@name=school],
     databaseSchema[@dbname=S2]/table[@name=Sculptor]/column[@name=style]
ii)  databaseSchema[@dbname=S1]/table[@name=Artefact]/column[@name=title] ->
     databaseSchema[@dbname=S2]/table[@name=Painting]/column[@name=title],
     databaseSchema[@dbname=S2]/table[@name=Sculptor]/column[@name=artefact]

iii) databaseSchema[@dbname=S1]/table[@name=Artist/column[@name=id ->
     databaseSchema[@dbname=S2]/table[@name=Info/column[@name=id]

iv)  databaseSchema[@dbname=S1]/table[@name=Artefact]/column[@name=artist_id]
     -> databaseSchema[@dbname=S2]/table[@name=Painter]/column[@name=info_id],
     databaseSchema[@dbname=S2]/table[@name=Sculptor]/column[@name=info_id]
```

Figure 5. The XMAP mappings.

```
i) S1/Artist/style -> S2/Painter/school, S2/Sculptor/style
ii)S1/Artefact/title -> S2/Painting/title, S2/Sculptor/artefact
iii) S1/Artist/id -> S2/Info/id
iv) S1/Artefact/artist_id->S2/Painter/info_id,S2/Sculptor/info_id
```

Figure 6. A simpler form of the XMAP mappings.

unified view, so that it becomes evident what exactly data each database holds.

- *GDQS* should be capable of accepting XPath queries, and of transforming these XPath queries to OQL before parsing, compiling, optimizing and scheduling them. Such a transformation falls in an active research area (e.g., [14, 8]), and, in our architecture, is realised as an additional component within the query compiler.
- *GDQS* should implement an additional XMAP-related activity that, given an XPath expression, finds the corresponding *GDIS*, and calls the XMAP on it. The activity returns a set of corresponding XPaths.
- The client should be capable of aggregating results stemming from multiple queries.
- *GDQS* should be capable of accepting requests that contain more than one (XPath) statement.
- Also, *GDIS* should be capable of processing requests that clean, update and install mapping documents.

5.2 Looking Ahead

The proposed architecture provides added value to the existing querying services, and increases the scope of the applications that may use them. It creates a middleware infrastructure that can be enhanced with more functionality. With a view to incorporating more features, the following stages of extensions have been identified:

Stage A: XPath is a simple language, and, as such, it cannot cover many of the common user requests. It is expected that more extensive use of the knowledge about key/foreign-key relationships will be required in order to reformulate more expressive queries (such as XQuery, SQL and OQL correctly) or to support a more complete set of XPath. When the paths in a XPath query refer to different branches of the tree of the corresponding XML document, the relevant OQL/SQL query typically contains a join, as it is more convenient to map such branches to distinct relational tables. However, the join condition is implied and cannot be directly derived from the XPath expression. Consequently, the knowledge of the key/foreign-key between tables is essential for the correct reformulation of a wider range of XPath queries in our proposal.

Stage B: OGSA-DQP naturally provides the capability to submit queries over distributed sources in a manner that is transparent to the user. The XMAP reformulation algorithm, as presented in [12], returns a new query only if that query can be evaluated across a single database as well; this is one of the validity criteria. In order to use the capability of OGSA-DQP to evaluate distributed queries across multiple databases in the future, some (non-extensive) changes in the validity criteria of reformulated queries in the XMAP algorithm will be required.

Stage C: A more challenging problem is to allow distributed query reformulation. This raises a new set of issues, which include the selection of the site that should hold the mappings, the identification of any further meta-data at the GDQS-level that is required, and ensuring that non-duplicate results are produced. More specifically, in the proposed architecture, the decision on which *GDI* Service should perform the query reformulation is straightforward; it is the one that is co-located with the database that holds the data retrieved by the relevant query, and this service contains the full set of the mapping information required. However, when multiple databases are accessed in the same query, this policy has to be revised.

Stage D: Finally, we plan to explore alternative architectures, and especially architectures in which the *GDISs* may not be co-located with *GQESs*, and can be shared between multiple sites. A simple approach could be to have a single *GDI* Service that contains the full mapping information concerning all the semantically similar databases. However, such an approach is not scalable. If there are multiple *GDISs*, which are not co-located with *GQESs*, then a co-ordination issue arises as to how (i.e., according to which protocol) the services interact and exchange knowledge. To this end, adopting techniques from peer-to-peer models is a promising strategy.

6. Conclusions

The contribution of this work is the proposal of a unifying architecture and of an approach that integrates a data integration methodology with existing e-Services for querying distributed databases with a view to providing an enhanced, data integration-enabled service middleware. The resulting architecture remains service-oriented, and, as such, the service choreography issues are important. The paper explains in detail how the distinct services can interact in order to accomplish the non-trivial task of evaluating remote queries submitted by the user, while, at the same generating automatically new queries that return semantically similar results from different data sources. The data integration is based upon the XMAP framework that takes into account the semantic and syntactic heterogeneity between different data resources, and provides a recursive query reformulation algorithm. The Grid services used as a basis are the outcome of the OGSA-DAI/DQP projects, which have paved the way towards uniform access and combination of distributed databases.

In summary, in this paper (i) we propose an integrated service-oriented architecture; (ii) we explain how we can achieve interaction between the various services; (iii) we show how these services can be used together through an example; (iv) we discuss in detail the implementation issues involved; and (v) finally, we provide insights into how the architecture can be further extended.

Acknowledgments

The collaboration between the Universities of Manchester and Calabria is supported through the CoreGrid European Research Network on Foundations, Software Infrastructures and Applications for large scale distributed, GRID and Peer-to-Peer Technologies project. We are pleased to acknowledge their support.

References

[1] The Globus toolkit, http://www.globus.org.

[2] GridMiner, http://www.gridminer.org/.

[3] SASF: service-based approach to schema federation, http://sasf.grid.leena34.com/.

[4] M. N. Alpdemir, A. Mukherjee, N. W. Paton, P. Watson, A. A. Fernandes, A. Gounaris and J. Smith. Service-based distributed querying on the grid. In Maria E. Orlowska, Sanjiva Weerawarana, Mike P. Papazoglou, and Jian Yang, editors, *Service-Oriented Computing - ICSOC 2003, First Int. Conference, Trento, Italy, December 15-18, 2003, Proceedings*, pages 467–482. Springer, 2003.

[5] M. N. Alpdemir, A. Mukherjee, A. Gounaris, N. W. Paton, P. Watson, A. A. Fernandes and D. J. Fitzgerald. OGSA-DQP: A service for distributed querying on the grid. In *Advances in Database Technology - EDBT 2004, 9th Int. Conference on Extending Database Technology*, pages 858–861, March 2004.

[6] M. Antonioletti et al. OGSA-DAI: Two years on. In *Global Grid Forum 10 — Data Area Workshop*, March 2004.

[7] Ph. A. Bernstein, F. Giunchiglia, A. Kementsietsidis, J. Mylopoulos, L. Serafini and I. Zaihrayeu. Data management for peer-to-peer computing : A vision. In *Proc. of the 5th Int. Workshop on the Web and Databases (WebDB 2002)*, pages 89–94, June 2002.

[8] K. S. Beyer, R. Cochrane, V. Josifovski, J. Kleewein, G. Lapis, G. M. Lohman, B. Lyle, F. Ozcan, H. Pirahesh, N. Seemann, T. C. Truong, B. Van der Linden, B. Vickery and

C. Zhang. System rx: One part relational, one part xml. In *SIGMOD Conference 2005*, pages 347–358, 2005.

[9] P. Brezany, A. Woehrer and A. M. Tjoa. Novel mediator architectures for grid information systems. *Future Generation Computer Systems*, 21(1):107–114, 2005.

[10] D. Calvanese, E. Damaggio, G. De Giacomo, M. Lenzerini and R. Rosati. Semantic data integration in P2P systems. In *Proc. of the First Int. Workshop on Databases, Information Systems, and Peer-to-Peer Computing (DBISP2P)*, pages 77–90, September 2003.

[11] D. Calvanese, G. De Giacomo, M. Lenzerini, R. Rosati and G. Vetere. Hyper: A framework for peer-to-peer data integration on grids. In *Proc. of the Int. Conference on Semantics of a Networked World: Semantics for Grid Databases (ICSNW 2004)*, volume 3226 of *Lecture Notes in Computer Science*, pages 144–157, 2004.

[12] C. Comito and D. Talia. Xml data integration in ogsa grids. In *1st Int. Workshop on Data Management in Grids (DMG)*, pages 4–15, 2005.

[13] K. Czajkowski et al. The WS-resource framework version 1.0. The Globus Alliance, Draft, March 2004. `http://www.globus.org/wsrf/specs/ws-wsrf.pdf`.

[14] W. Fan, J. Xu Yu, H. Lu and J. Lu. Query translation from xpath to sql in the presence of recursive dtds. In *VLDB Conference 2005*, 2005.

[15] I. Foster, C. Kesselman and S. Tuecke. The Anatomy of the Grid: Enabling Scalable Virtual Organizations. *Int. J. Supercomputer Applications*, 15(3), 2001.

[16] E. Franconi, G. M. Kuper, A. Lopatenko and L. Serafini. A robust logical and computational characterisation of peer-to-peer database systems. In *Proc. of the First Int. Workshop on Databases, Information Systems, and Peer-to-Peer Computing (DBISP2P)*, pages 64–76, September 2003.

[17] A. Y. Halevy. Data integration: A status report. In *BTW*, pages 24–29, 2003.

[18] A. Y. Halevy, D. Suciu, I. Tatarinov and Z. G. Ives. Schema mediation in peer data management systems. In *Proc. of the 19th Int. Conference on Data Engineering*, pages 505–516, March 2003.

[19] A. Kementsietsidis, M. Arenas and R. J. Miller. Mapping data in peer-to-peer systems: Semantics and algorithmic issues. In *Proc. of the 2003 ACM SIGMOD Int. Conference on Management of Data*, pages 325–336, June 2003.

[20] G. Lapis. Xml and relational storage - are they mutually exclusive? available at http://www.idealliance.org/proceedings/xtech05/papers/02-05-01/ (accessed in july 2005).

[21] A. Y. Levy, A. Rajaraman and J. J. Ordille. Querying heterogeneous information sources using source descriptions. In *Proc. of 22th Int. Conference on Very Large Data Bases (VLDB'96)*, pages 251–262, September 1996.

[22] A. P. Sheth and J. A. Larson. Federated database systems for managing distributed, heterogeneous, and autonomous databases. *ACM Computing Surveys*, 22(3):183–236, 1990.

[23] J. Smith, A. Gounaris, P. Watson, N. W. Paton, A. A. Fernandes and R. Sakellariou. Distributed query processing on the grid. In Manish Parashar, editor, *Grid Computing - GRID 2002, Third Int. Workshop, Baltimore, MD, USA, November 18, 2002, Proceedings*, pages 279–290. Springer, 2002.

ACCESSING WEB DATABASES USING OGSA-DAI IN BDWORLD*

Shirley Crompton
CCLRC, Daresbury Laboratory, Warrington WA4 4AD, United Kingdom
s.y.crompton@dl.ac.uk

Brian Matthews
CCLRC, Rutherford-Appleton Laboratory, Didcot, Oxfordshire OX11 0AX, United Kingdom
b.m.matthews@rl.ac.uk

Alex Gray, Andrew Jones, Richard White
Cardiff School of Computer Science, Cardiff University, Cardiff CF24 3AA, United Kingdom
w.a.gray@cs.cardiff.ac.uk
Andrew.C.Jones@cs.cardiff.ac.uk
r.j.white@cs.cardiff.ac.uk

Abstract The BioDA project is investigating how Bioinformatics Grids, a data and compute intensive domain, could benefit from using a standard framework, such as OGSA-DAI, to manage access and integration of distributed heterogeneous data resources. In this paper, we outline the common data access and integration requirements from the bioinformatics community. We then highlight some specific issues encountered while designing an OGSA-DAI exemplar application for BiodiversityWorld, a Biodiversity Grid that specialises in extracting knowledge from correlating a plethora of distributed heterogeneous data sources accesible via the Web in the study of biodiversity patterns.

Keywords: bioinformatics, biodiversity, biodiversity informatics, data access, data integration, OGSA-DAI.

*Work supported by Biotechnology and Biological Sciences Research Council grant BB/C510840/1

1. Introduction

Within the diverse field of bioinformatics, there are many types of data analysis, both inter- and intra-disciplinary, which generate as many types of data and databases. The increased computational capacity of the Grid makes it possible for scientists to correlate and combine large numbers of datasets to identify patterns and formulate hypotheses, which can be tested using further datasets and transformed into useful knowledge [1]. The output from such research activities, in turn, generate yet more datasets that will need to be integrated into further analyses.

The bioinformatics projects supported within the UK eScience programme have recognised the need for accessing and integrating data from both new and legacy data sources. As a consequence, solutions to the data management problems have been implemented individually by each project according to their needs.

For example, the Biodiversity World (BDWorld [2–4]) Project is creating a problem-solving environment (PSE) targeted at providing support for biodiversity researchers to use common software tools in a Grid environment, and to use them to analyse data held in a variety of databases and data stores. BDWorlds middleware for data access and communications has been developed so that it can cope with changes caused by the evolving Grid middleware. BDWorld is being interfaced to software previously developed by project partners in the SPICE project [5] to co-ordinate access to some of the databases and analytic tools that have been made available to BDWorld. In SPICE a CAS (Common Access System) hub was created to allow heterogeneous databases (often managed by legacy database systems) to be wrapped, accessed and linked to form a Catalogue of Life for the international Species 2000 project [6]. In the BDWorld project this prototype Catalogue of Life is used to provide taxonomic data about species which is then linked with data from biotic and abiotic datastores. These are wrapped in a somewhat different way from the SPICE databases, since a fixed common data model is not appropriate for the more diverse range of data used in BDWorld (see Section 3). This data includes geographical data about the distribution of species, climate data, genetic structure and sequence data. Existing analytic tools, such as tools for modelling a species climatic niche, are also wrapped for inclusion in the PSE. The data is linked by the PSEs tools to enable bioinformatics users to investigate scientific questions such as the biodiversity richness in regions of interest; the effect of climate change on the biodiversity of a region, and the usefulness of geographical data in refining phylogenetic hypotheses.

In parallel with the application projects in bioinformatics, the Open Grid Services Architecture - Data Access and Integration (OGSA-DAI) project [7] has been designing generic middleware to assist with access and integration of data from disparate data sources across the Grid, for use in a wide variety of e-Science projects. The first releases of OGSA-DAI implemented the Open Grid Services Infrastructure (OGSI) specification [8] and were built on the Globus toolkit (GT) [9] platform. Using the OGSA-DAI framework, external data resources can be incorporated within the OGSA framework and made accessible via a standard Grid service interface, offering uniform interfaces for accessing, querying and processing data stored in relational and XML databases as well as flat files. Figure 1 gives a basic example of using OGSA-DAI OGSI grid services to access a database. The software has since evolved from OGSI to the WS-RF [8] and WS-I [11] specifications.

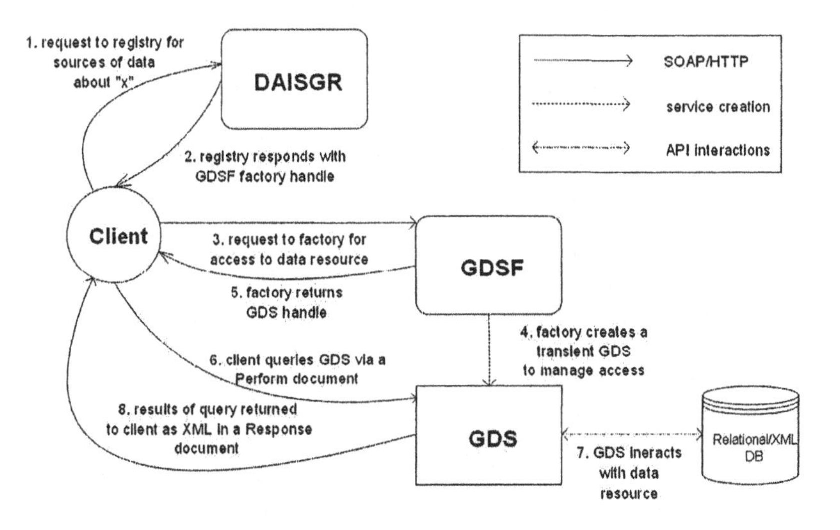

Figure 1. Basic data access using OGSA-DAI OGSI Grid services.

In spite of the functionality offered by OGSA-DAI, it became clear that the middleware was not being used in bioinformatics projects to any great extent. In discussions with investigators from various projects we found that this was mostly due to reluctance on their part to use emerging prototype software part-way through their projects. These projects were high risk developments because of the large scale collaborations involved and the utilisation of immature Grid software. Thus the staff of these projects did not want to add another unknown factor into their development strategies. It should also be remembered that the start of the OGSA-DAI project coincided approximately with the start of these projects.

The Bioinformatics and DAIT (BioDA [12]) project is a one-year study funded by the UK Biotechnology and Biological Sciences Research Council to investigate the benefits of using OGSA-DAI in bioinformatics Grids. The project aimed to establish communication between bioinformatics projects and DAIT (the team continuing OGSA-DAI development), to elicit requirements from bioinformatics projects, and to collate case studies involving existing bioinformatics projects. The latter includes prototyping an OGSA-DAI exemplar for BDWorld to access remote web databases. BDWorlds database handling is characterised by the diversity of the types of database used, the heterogeneity of the data with respect to its representation, and the variety of data being held and used in the analysis environment. This makes it an ideal test bed for OGSA-DAI as it will present many of the problems that such database middleware should be able to overcome more easily than traditional approaches to interoperability

In this paper we will highlight the generic data integration requirements gathered from the bioinformatics community, and examine some specific data integration issues arising from introducing OGSA-DAI to the BDWorld Grid.

2. Generic Bioinformatics Data Access and Integration Requirements

The first BioDA workshop brought together architects and infrastructure developers from the bioinformatics domain and DAIT project to examine the communitys data access and integration needs with particular reference to OGSA-DAI.

The workshop identified 17 key requirements and these were refined through a survey of 8 bioinformatics projects at various stages of development [13]. Our findings indicate that these projects are particularly keen to see OGSA-DAI offering more support for the following features.

1 schema integration;

2 schema mapping;

3 mixed language query;

4 complex join across databases;

5 provenance data;

6 flexible resource discovery facilitated by a richer metadata registry;

7 RDF database access.

The first four requirements map directly to data integration functionalities. The remaining three items reflect implicit needs for better metadata which will facilitate the selection and the location of distributed data resources via a metadata-driven two-step access to data [14]. These priorities are a conseqeunce of the nature of bioinformatics, where data sources typically have large, complex structures which reflect the richness of the scientific concepts that they model. Many of these data sources are related and cover roughly the same domain, eg. genes, sequence annotations, digital protein models [15]. The ability to integrate related but heterogeneous data will greatly facilitate the task of scientific discovery. The OGSA-DAI interfaces expose heterogeneous data sources as a single logical one and allow a client application to access the data in a uniform manner. But OGSA-DAI on its own does not make a data grid. Client programmers will still need to be aware of the types of data resources being accessed and accounts for the structural heterogeneities and the differences between query dialects.

The DAIT team may see many of the listed items as outside its original remit, and, therefore, as features which could be provided elsewhere. For instance, schema mapping has been implemented by projects such as GridMiner [16] as part of a higher-level mediation service layered over OGSA-DAI. We recognise this argument, but these requirements are highly desirable to bioinformatics project practitioners and their implementation would greatly enhance OGSA-DAIs appeal to potential users in this domain.

Apart from the calls for more functionality, our findings show that bioinformatics projects with commercial users/partners are very anxious about the security of their data. They have sought reassurance over the security of the data delivery mechanisms and even the latency of the subsequent footprint that the data leaves on the server. The issue is further complicated by the lack of coherent security models with the evolving WS-RF and WS-I specifications which OGSA-DAI now supports. This issue needs to be resolved, if bioinformatics projects with commercial users/partners are not to be deterred from adopting the product despite its utility.

OGSA-DAIs recent migration to Globus WS-RF, WS-I and OMII WS-I+ [17] platforms has also affected users confidence in the product. Infrastructural changes are disruptive and perceived as risky to project development. Our respondents have highlighted the need for OGSA-DAI to provide backward compatibility and to minimise the effects of migration on current client users. On the issue of support, we suggest that an official policy relating to the establishment of a medium to long-term support service, i.e. beyond the current funding lifetime of the OGSA-DAI/DAIT project, would help reassure potential users that the product is not going to become unusable through the lack of continued maintenance.

In this section, we have highlighted the principal data access and integration requirements gathered via the BioDA workshop and survey. Further details may be found in the BioDA Final Report [13]. The information gathered has been fed back to the OGSA-DAI/DAIT team to assist with the development of their product.

3. BDWorld Data Integration Issues

In this section, we outline the design and some data access and integration issues encountered while developing an OGSA-DAI (R5) exemplar for BD-World. The exemplar is based on the bio-climatic and ecological niche BDW use case and focuses specifically on the retrieval of geo-spatial locality data from globally distributed databases. The bio-climatic exemplar uses the known localities of a species and cross-references these with present day climate data to derive the species climate preference profile. This profile is then used to locate other geographical areas where such a climate exists and would be suitable habitat for the target species [3].

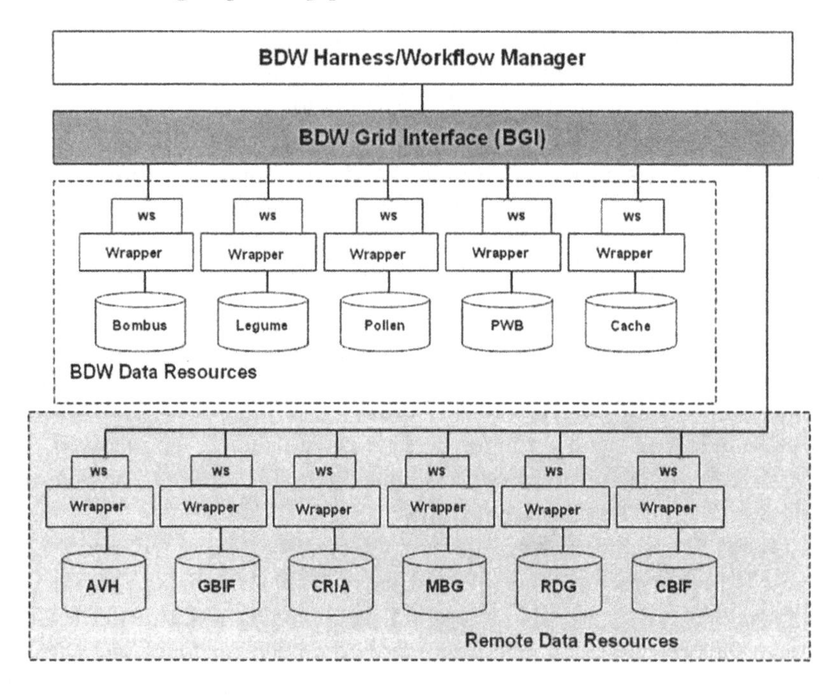

Figure 2. BDWorld locality data resource layer

First we review the distinctive characteristics of the BDWorld Grid that have influenced the design. A particular feature of BDWorld is its use of heterogeneous, legacy data resources with diverse structures and data standards. Many of these are Internet information resources only accessible via the HTTP protocol in XML format, or even as HTML pages, in which case screen scraping techniques are required. BDW currently has 11 locality data resources, comprising five local databases under the BDW administrative domain and six globally distributed data providers (see Figure 2). The remote data resources are autonomous web data servers exposed through different frameworks, eg.

HTML/CGI, JSP and web services. OGSA-DAI does not currently support access to these types of resources.

The user interface to BDWorld is provided through the Triana [18] workflow management system, BDWorld has also taken the position that any computationally intensive tasks within a scientific workflow, such as a data access, will be carried out within a single node, rather than distribute tasks across a number of steps [2]. This has influenced the design of the BDWorld architecture to focus on achieving resource inter-operability rather than maximising performance. It includes an abstraction layer (the BDWorld-Grid Interface (BGI)), which provides a syntactically uniform interface with a uniform resource invocation mechanism to all BDWorld resources (Figure 3), both databases and analytic tools. Resources are wrapped to conform to this interface; wrapped resources are then able to interact with various Grid or Grid-like implementations via an adaptor specific to the Grid infrastructure currently in use. Other BDWorld components are designed to use the same mechanism, and in particular Triana has been extended to act as a BGI client.

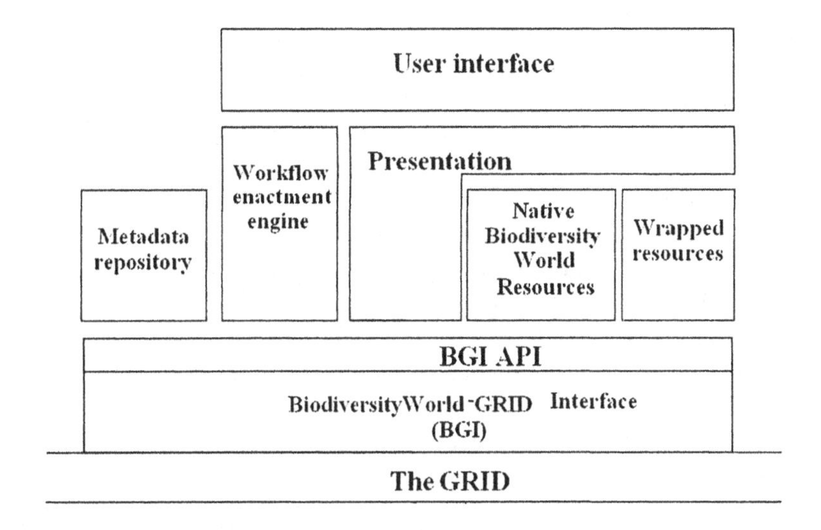

Figure 3. BDWorld architecture overview

To tap into these global repositories on biotic and abiotic information, BDWorld still needs the knowledge to discover and uses them correctly. As highlighted in the requirements survey above, metadata is crucial to facilitate the selection and the location of distributed data resources. To this end, BDWorld is building a metadata repository connected to an ontology in order to manage resource heterogeneity. This component is designed to support semantic equivalence testing when locating, and in particular, integrating datasets from autonomous data providers which, for example, may employ non-standard species names to index their data, or may use an unusual data representation.

To access and harvest data from the remote data resources, BDWorld resource wrappers must publish metadata on their capabilities and implement the BGI. This includes implementing the uniform resource invocation method: `invokeOperation`. This method takes three string parameters: the target resource handle; the name of the operation; and the serialized operation-specific input wrapped in a standard BDWorld communication object. An implication of this uniform resource invocation mechanism is that BGI data calls are not expressed in terms of standard SQL queries. Another feature is that data passing to and from the resources is communicated over the BGI as an XML document or a simple string. This permits the transmission of either the data or, if the volume is large, the handle for the data.

There are two main ways we could introduce OGSA-DAI into BDWorld, bearing in mind the BGI specifications and communication protocol. One possibility is to augment the BGI to make it possible for queries to be included in workflows and to be sent directly to OGSA-DAI enabled databases. Distributed query processing facilities could be developed to the point where they could assist in planning the execution and distribution of data-orientated parts of a workflow. However, this would be a very major revision to the BDWorld protocols, and does not take account of the fact that many of the resources of interest are simply not exposed as databases. The other option is to provide facilities within individual wrappers that benefit from OGSA-DAI. We opted for the latter approach in building our exemplar.

Before embarking on our building own custom solution, we first verified if it is possible to leverage existing OGSA-DAI based solutions, such as OGSA-DQP [19] and OGSA-WebDB [20]. The latter is developed by the Japan AIST to Grid-enable existing web database resources via OGSA-DAI. OGSA-WebDB may just be the right tool for BDWorld as it needs to access autonomous web data sources. However, both DQP and WebDB accept queries in formally structured query languages (e.g. SQL, OQL), which we feel would not be compatible with the BGI architecture without significant customization.

4. The BioDA Exemplar

Figure 4 gives the UML class diagram of our exemplar, which is developed with OGSA-DAI R5 OGSI. It has two main components: the custom OGSA-DAI activities and the data resource wrappers. The wrappers support custom interactions with the data resources being wrapped. These wrappers are simplified versions of the existing BDWorld localities data wrappers, and have been modified to remove non-essential dependencies on BDWorld components. We

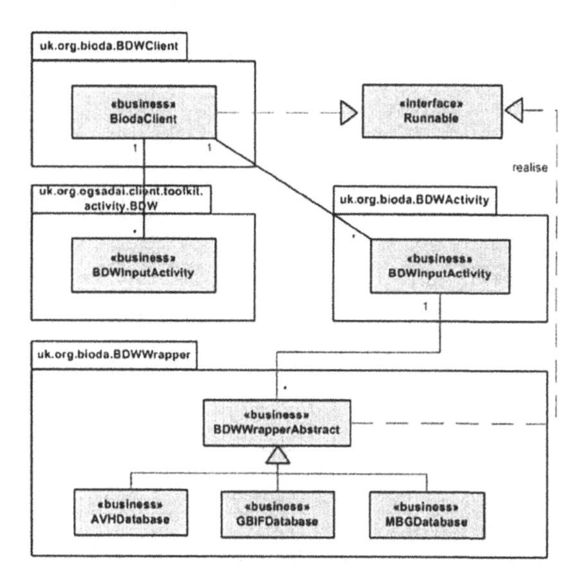

Figure 4. UML diagram of the BioDA exemplar

have implemented three wrappers which we feel are sufficiently representative of the remote localities data resources used by BDWorld.

To make the OGSA-DAI Grid Data Service (GDS) accessible to the current BDWorld Grid implementation, which is based on web services, we have configured the exemplar as a web service, using the Axis library [21] (see Figure 5). Note that we have opted to use a single virtual GDS instead of deploying separate GDSs for each resource. Our virtual GDS is configured for a postgresql database, which is the chosen database platform for BDWorld internal data resources. We adopted this strategy for the following reasons. Firstly, none of the data source specific capabilities exposed or provided by OGSA-DAI activities, eg. data resource mediators, SQL/XML operations, are applicable to our remote web data resources. There is no particular advantage in maintaining a one-to-one relationship between a GDS and a particular data resource. Secondly, there are various overheads associated with starting up an OGSI GDS [22–23]. We could minimize the overhead cost by sticking to one single GDS. Thirdly, this virtual GDS could potentially be extended to handle interactions with all BDWorld data resources, including the local postgresql resources.

Apart from delivering existing BDWorld functionalities, our exemplar also provides additional features which could be adopted with minor adjustments to the BDWorld workflow. In the existing design, the BDWorld workflow issues a synchronous data request to each resource wrapper. It also aggregates the

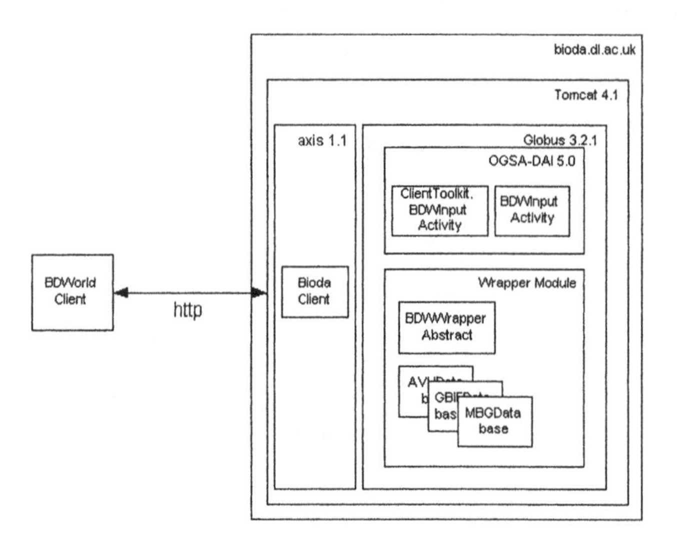

Figure 5. Principal software components of the BioDA exemplar

results and passes them onto the next workflow unit. We feel that we could add value by enabling one or more resources to be queried via a single data call to OGSA-DAI. We could also minimize unnecessary transfer of data by using a separate channel for data delivery, for instance to a compute node within the Ganglia Cluster that BDWorld is building. In fact, third party delivery may become necessary. If the exemplar is used to query several data resources concurrently, the aggregated result set could well exceed the size limit for SOAP. OGSA-DAI does not currently support SOAP with attachment. Our exemplar returns the gridFTP handles to the cache data files in addition to the actual data. Should BDWorld change its data delivery channel from SOAP to third party mechanisms, we could simply switch off the codes in our exemplar that package the data for SOAP delivery.

4.1 Usage of the BioDA Exemplar

Figure 6 shows the usage of the exemplar which goes through the steps as follows.

Step 1: We use an Axis web service (BioDaClient) to expose the OGSA-DAI OGSI GDS to non-GT clients. This web service supports the BGI uniform resource invocation mechanism.

Step 2: The web service contacts the OGSA-DAI Grid Data Service Factory and requests a GDS to perform the required database searches (for clarify, Figure 6 does not show this GDS instantiation process). Our exem-

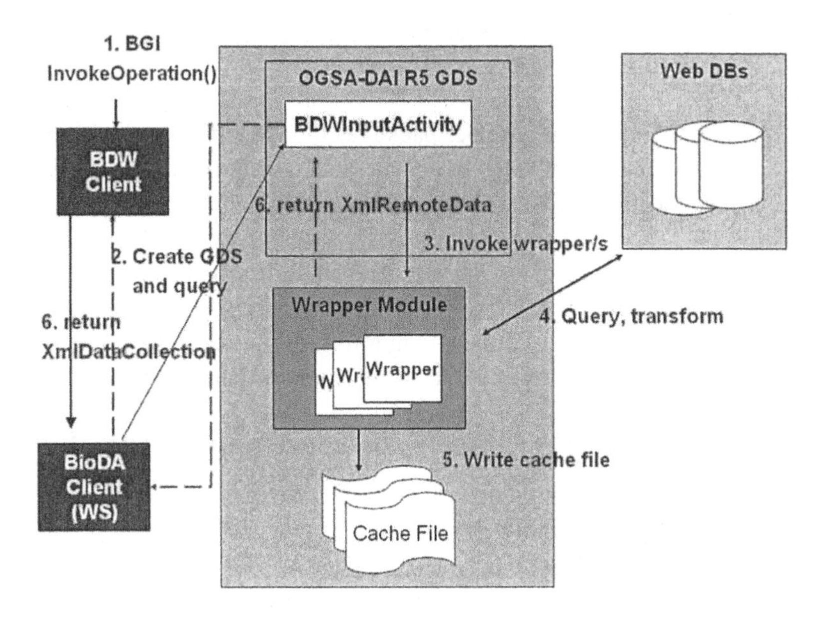

Figure 6. Principal software components of the BioDA exemplar

plar uses the OGSA-DAI client toolkit API and a custom client activity (BDWInputActivity) to generate the Perform Document and to manage the interactions with the GDS. It would be possible to bypass the use of client activities and submit a Perform Document directly to the GDS. Using the client toolkit introduces additional coding on the client side, however, the client toolkit provides ready-made components for use as basic building blocks to speed up application development, and, importantly, the API protects developers from changes in the OGSA-DAI specifications.

Step 3: The GDS processes the Perform request and instantiates the required activity. Our exemplar, in fact, uses two separate Perform documents: one to orchestrate the asynchronous delivery of input and one to manage the database searches. Our BiodaClient uses threads to explicitly orchestrate the execution of these documents. Newer OGSA-DAI releases provide client toolkit support for sequence and control flow. This moves the complexity of managing the operations from the client to the server, and simplifies the process of using OGSA-DAI.

Step 4: The individual database wrapper searches the remote data resource that it represents concurrently, downloads the results (if any) and performs the required data transformation.

Step 5: The individual wrapper writes the formatted localities data to a cache file on the local server.

Step 6: The individual wrapper packages the data into a standard XML document. The activity aggregates the results and returns the XML document to the BioDaClient via the web service to the BGI.

We have tested the exemplar with the BDWorld workflow and successfully used it in place of the existing BDWorld database wrappers. The next logical step is to amend the workflow manager to generate a single data call for multiple localities data resources and test the extended capability of the exemplar.

4.2 OGSA-DAI Usage Experience and Lessons Learnt

Our experience in implementing the BDWorld use case has demonstrated that OGSA-DAI is highly flexible and extensible. Even though web data resources are not supported as standard by OGSA-DAI, we have been able to leverage the framework to build a workable solution. Compared to GT3.2.1, the hosting container, OGSA-DAI 5 is relatively easy to install and use. OGSA-DAI offers helpful on-line documentation and there are both community-based and official support to ease the learning process.

In the exemplar, we have layered OGSA-DAI between the data wrappers and the BGI. This arrangement provides a degree of location transparency but also adds extra levels of indirection. Location transparency facilitates the exposure of data resources in a global context as data resource product and connection information is centralized in the OGSA-DAI server. Changes in these parameters need only affect the server. In our case, BDWorld is the data consumer rather than data provider. The lack of location transparency can be seen as a limitation of the current prototype; we are also concerned that the extra levels of indirection will increase the round-trip data access time as the BGI data calls have to be channelled via the web service interface and communicated through the OGSA-DAI specific layers to the data wrappers. Migrating to the new OGSA-DAI WS-I specification will help simplify our exemplar architecture and minimize the levels of indirection. As the current BDWorld Grid is implemented on web services, using OGSA-DAI WS-I will allow us to expose the OGSA-DAI services directly as web services and remove GT3.2.1 which serves no other purpose than to provide a hosting framework for the OGSA-DAI OGSI services.

In our exemplar, we are retro-fitting OGSA-DAI to a system with well-defined architecture and data handling strategies, which constrained our scope of applying OGSA-DAI. For instance, the workflow data handling does not provide for interaction between the data resources. Neither do the localities data queries require any interaction between data retrieved from the different resources. Our queries simply ask for all localities data associated with a particular taxon search string. Consequently, we feel we have not made much use of the data integration functionalities offered by OGSA-DAI and OGSA-DQP.

BDWorld is re-factoring its architecture to improve interoperation with third party components. This opens up possibilities for further usage of OGSA-DAI, and maybe OGSA-DQP, particularly with respect to minimizing unnecessarily data movement and moving computation to the data. These include leveraging third party data deliveries and the use of complex declarative queries to improve the filtering of results at source.

5. Conclusion

We have briefly summarised the common data access and integration requirements raised by the bioinformatics community and reviewed our OGSA-DAI exemplar for aggregating locality data for the BDWorld bio-climatic and ecological niche use case. We have highlighted other key data integration solutions based on OGSA-DAI and commented on their suitability for BDWorld. We have noted a range of features which, if incorporated into OGSA-DAI, would be beneficial to the bioinformatics projects surveyed by BioDA.

OGSA-DAI is an evolving software and has gone through many iterations since its first release just under three years ago. We feel that the lack of take up of the earlier versions could be due to a variety of reasons, both technical and non-technical. From our dialogues with various e-Science project stakeholders, it became clear that many e-Science projects such as BDWorld are building bioinformatics Grid applications from existing tools and data resources, filling in gaps where necessary with new components. In one way, OGSA-DAI could potentially facilitate the creation of a loosely coupled data grid. Yet in reality, there are many existing considerations which may limit its application. These include: the types of data resources typically used in bioinformatics; the nature of bioinformatics analyses; the types of infrastructure Grid middleware used; OGSA-DAI's previous confinement to the GT platform; OGSA-DAI functionalities; a lack of programmatic access to key public data resources.

The first releases of OGSA-DAI only offered support for database resources. Support for semi-structured resources were added later on to meet user demands. Secondly, many existing analytical tools take in whole data files without the need to interact with the data or filtering of the file contents. Other Grid access mechanism may seem more appropriate for working with file resources at the file level.

In the bioinformatics domain, public data repositories generally do not provide generic database access to their data, as is the case for most of the BDWorld locality data providers [24–25]. Consequently, we could not apply OGSA-DAI in a straightforward manner to access these autonomous data providers. Nevertheless, our exemplar illustrates that there are still scenarios in which OGSA-DAI may be usefully employed.

We feel that OGSA-DAI is primarily a framework for enabling a uniform, service-based access to disparate, heterogeneous and distributed data resources. It offers a subset of the JDBC functionalities and it exposes data resources without hiding their underlying models. Users would still need to know the data and how they are represented to use the information correctly. As highlighted elsewhere in this paper, OGSA-DAI relies on domain knowledge or other third party tools to provide the data integration capabilities. Projects concerned with data interoperation and requiring fast data access simply do not see enough advantages in OGSA-DAI.

As highlighted in Section 3, the lack of programmatic access to key public bioinformatics data repositories is also a factor that potentially limits the application of OGSA-DAI in bioinformatics Grids. Warehousing the databases locally is a solution, but this arrangement reduces the advantage of using OGSA-DAI as the data is under local administration and can be easily accessed directly. To facilitate the development of bioinformatics data Grids using community standards such as OGSA-DAI, public repositories may consider providing an OGSA-DAI interface to support public read access in addition to specialised web services.

Acknowledgments

The authors wish to thank all those who took part in our survey. We are particularly grateful to colleagues in BDWorld, DAIT, OGSA-DQP, CCLRC e-Science Centre, GeneGrid and GridMiner.

References

[1] M. Atkinson, Data Access and Integration. In *Ercim News* no. 59, p 34-80. 2004.

[2] A.C. Jones, R.J. White, W.A. Gray, F.A. Bisby, N. Caithness, N. Pittas, X. Xu, S. Sutton, N.J. Fiddian, A. Culham, M. Scoble, P. Wiliams, O. Bromley, P. Brewer, C. Yesson, and S. Bhagwat, Building a Biodiversity Grid. In *Grid Computing in Life Science* (Konagaya, A. and Satou, K., eds.), LNCS 3370, p. 140-151. Springer-Verlag, 2005. (Biodiversity World: http://www.bdworld.org/)

[3] R.J. White, F.A. Bisby, N. Caithness, T. Sutton, P. Brewer, P. Williams, A. Culham, M. Scoble, A.C. Jones, W.A. Gray, N.J. Fiddian, N. Pittas, X. Xu, O. Bromley, and P. Valdes, The Biodiversity World Environment as an Extensible Virtual Laboratory for Analysing Biodiversity Patterns, In *Proceedings of the Second UK e-Science All Hands Meeting*, pp. 341-344, 2003,.

[4] A.C. Jones, R.J. White, N. Pittas, W.A. Gray, T. Sutton, X. Xu, O. Bromley, N. Caithness, F.A. Bisby, N.J. Fiddian, M. Scoble, A. Culham, and P. Williams. Biodiversity World: An Architecture for an Extensible Virtual Laboratory for Analysing Biodiversity Patterns. In *Proceedings of the Second UK e-Science All Hands Meeting*, pp. 759-765, 2003

[5] A.C. Jones, X. Xu, N. Pittas, W.A. Gray, N.J. Fiddian, R.J. White, J.S. Robinson, F.A. Bisby, and S.M. Brandt. SPICE: a Flexible Architecture for Integrating Autonomous Databases to Comprise a Distributed Catalogue of Life. In *Proceedings of the 11th International Conference on Database and Expert Systems Applications*, LNCS 1873, p. 981-992, Springer-Verlag 2000. (SPICE: http://www.systematics.reading.ac.uk/spice/)

[6] Species 2000. http://www.sp2000.org .

[7] OGSA-DAI. http://www.ogsadai.org.uk/

[8] Open Grid Services Infrastructure Specifications, https://forge.gridforum.org/projects/ogsi-wg/document/Final_OGSI_Specification_V1.0/en/1

[9] Globus Toolkit. http://www-unix.globus.org/toolkit/

[10] WS-Resource Framework. http://www.globus.org/wsrf/

[11] Web Services Interoperability. http://www.ws-i.org/

[12] BioDA. http://isegserv.itd.rl.ac.uk/BioDA/pages/default.htm

[13] S.Y. Crompton, B.M. Matthews, W.A. Gray, A.C. Jones, R.J. White. Bioinformatics and OGSA-DAI (BioDA) Final Report, 2006 http://isegserv.itd.rl.ac.uk/BioDA/documents/BioDA_finalRep1_2.pdf

[14] P. Watson. Databases and the Grid. In *Grid Computing: Making the Global Infrastructure a Reality*, Wiley, p. 363-384, 2003

[15] B. Eckman, Z. Lacroix, L. Raschild. Optimised Seamless Integration of Biomolecular Data. In *IEEE International Conference on Bioinformatics and Biomedical Engineering*, pp. 23-32, 2001.

[16] GridMiner. http://www.gridminer.org/

[17] M. Atkinson, D. DeRoure, A. Dunlop, G. Fox, P. Henderson, T. Hey, N. Paton, S. Newhouse, S. Parastatidis, A.Trefethen, P. Watson, and J. Webber. Web Service Grids: An Evolutionary Approach. *UK e-Science Technical Report*, ISSN 1751-5971, 2004. (http://www.nesc.ac.uk/technical_papers/UKeS-2004-05.pdf)

[18] Triana. http://www.trianacode.org/

[19] OGSA-DQP. http://www.ogsadai.org.uk/about/ogsa-dqp/

[20] I. Kojima and S.M. Pahlevi. Design and Implementation of OGSA-WebDB a service based system for making existing web databases grid-ready. In *Proceedings of the The GGF10 Workshop*, Berlin, Germany, 2004. (OGSA-WebDB: http://www.gtrc.aist.go.jp/dbgrid/ogsa-webdb/)

[21] Apache Axis http://ws.apache.org/axis/

[22] K. Qi. Data Integration Scenarios in OGSA-DAI. *MSc dissertation*, The University of Edinburgh, 2004.

[23] M. Jackson, M. Antonioletti, N. Chue Hong, A. Hume, A. Krause, T. Sugden. Performance Analysis of the OGSA-DAI Software. *In Proceedings of the Third UK e-Science All Hands Meeting*, pp. 340-347, 2004.

[24] Richard O. Sinnot, Micha Bayer, D. Houghton, Dave Berry, M. Ferrier. Development of a Grid Infrastructure for Functional Genomics. *In Proceedings of the Third UK e-Science All Hands Meeting*, 2004.

[25] S.Y. Crompton, B.M. Matthews, W.A. Gray, A.C. Jones, R.J. White, J.S. Pahwa, OGSA-DAI and Bioinformatics Grids: Challenges, Experience and Strategies. *In Proceedings Sixth IEEE International Symposium on Cluster Computing and the Grid (CCGRID'06)*, Singapore, 2006.

FAILURE RECOVERY ALTERNATIVES IN GRID-BASED DISTRIBUTED QUERY PROCESSING: A CASE STUDY

Jim Smith and Paul Watson
Newcastle University
Newcastle upon Tyne, UK
Jim.Smith@ncl.ac.uk
Paul.Watson@ncl.ac.uk

Abstract Fault-tolerance has long been a feature of database systems, with transactions supporting the structuring of applications so as to ensure continuation of updating applications in spite of machine failures. For read-only queries the perceived wisdom has been that support for fault-tolerance is too expensive to be worthwhile. Distributed query processing (DQP) is coming to be seen as a promising way of implementing applications that combine structured data and analysis operations in dynamic distributed settings such as computational grids. Accordingly, a number of protocols have been described that support tolerance to failure of intermediate machines, so as to permit continuation from surviving intermediate state. However, a distributed query can have a non-trivial mapping onto hardware resources. Because of this it is often possible to choose between a number of possible recovery strategies in the event of a failure. The work described here makes an initial investigation in this area in the context of an example query expressed over distributed resources in a Grid and shows that it can be worthwhile to make this choice between recovery alternatives dynamically, at the point a failure is detected rather than statically beforehand.

Keywords: distributed query processing, fault-tolerance, parallel query processing, rollback-recovery.

1. Introduction

Much work [13] has been done to support access to multiple distributed, autonomous databases, particularly addressing issues relating to heterogeneity, consistency and availability. However, systems have tended to gather data to a central site for inter-site joins. As described in [19], the emergence of computational grids [5] provides support and motivation for the evolution of the more open query processing espoused in [4] where participants contribute not just data but also function and cycle providers. In such an environment, many widely distributed and autonomous resources may be utilized in the execution of a particular query. Furthermore, it seems likely that the applications will often be demanding, so that resource failures may be not only likely but also costly. It is then better to tolerate the fault rather than throwing away the work done already unless the resources required for completion are not available.

Previous work [21] describes a basic implementation of support for fault-tolerance in a publicly-available distributed query processing system for the Grid, OGSA-DQP [1]. In that work, the enhanced system is evaluated through measurements of overhead and recovery cost to show that significant gains can be made through recovering and continuing after a failure. However, that earlier work considered only a single recovery scenario, where a failed machine is replaced by an equivalent. In continuation, the work reported here demonstrates for an example scenario suited to the Grid-based nature of the system that there is in general a range of alternative recovery strategies and that it can be desirable to make the choice between these alternatives dynamically on the occurrence of an actual failure.

The rest of this paper is structured as follows. Section 2 discusses related work. Section 3 describes a mapping of an example query onto distributed computational resources and identifies a number of alternative recovery strategies which can be employed following machine failure during query execution. Section 4 reviews the support for fault-tolerance provided in an enhanced version of OGSA-DQP, emphasizing features not described in earlier work. Section 5 presents initial experimental demonstration of the use of alternate recovery strategies in practice. Section 6 concludes.

2. Related Work

Transactions [9] are widely used to structure applications which need to ensure consistent access to persistent data, especially when updates to the data are required. Typically, operations which update persistent state are recorded in a site log so that they can be undone and/redone during recovery from a failure to get back to a consistent state. A commit protocol, typically two phase commit is employed to ensure updates to distributed databases are either all committed or all aborted. Checkpointing database state in such settings reduces the cost of recovery since log entries prior to the checkpoint do not need to be redone. Such recovery techniques aim to ensure the persistent databases can be brought to a consistent state. The application issuing updates can be coded to retry any aborted transaction. Otherwise, or if its own internal state is lost, the application must restart. This is undesirable if the application is expensive.

Workflows [10] for instance can be structured using internal transactions and maintaining intermediate state in a database to ensure that work already committed need not be redone during recovery. This state can then be replicated to achieve high availability [12]. An individual stateful application which might be called by a workflow can be recovered by logging interactions with the application to support re-creation of the internal application's state after a failure [3].

Like workflow, distributed queries are evaluated through a directed graph structure, but while workflow execution is likely to be event driven, queries typically follow a pipelined data flow pattern. This pipelined nature, the typically wide area distribution and the high level expression of queries, has motivated the exploitation of recovery protocols built into the query algebra rather than at a lower, system, level. Example approaches include: [18, 11] implemented in stream processing [2]; [14] targetted at data warehouse loading; and [21] implemented in the Grid-based distributed query processing system OGSA-DQP. While it is important first to implement a protocol that can support some degree of fault-tolerance in such pipelined computations, it is also important to examine the use of that protocol in practice. The contribution of this paper is to consider practical recovery strategies in an example scenario. It transpires that even in this simple case, there are typically multiple possible strategies and that it can be beneficial to choose between the alternatives dynamically at run-time.

Distributed query processing is being increasingly seen as an important tool for expressing complex distributed Grid-based computations in a conveniently high level way. For instance, SkyQuery [15] supports DQP over Grid resources with Web Services (WSs) being represented as typed user defined functions. GridDB-lite [16] supports access of large scale scientific data from large parallel repositories via SQL queries. In the context of Grid oriented query processing systems, Polar* [19] and OGSA-DQP [1] are distinguished in supporting placement of parts of the query plan on machines which don't hold data, rather like the compute servers of ObjectGlobe [4], and then using established parallel query processing techniques to seek a benefit through data parallelism. In Figure 1 for instance, a simple query which accesses some expensive operation "F" is evaluated through exploitation of three copies of the WS hosting that operation, in order to reduce the response time. Work in Polar* demonstrated that speedup of an example query in the field of bioinformatics access-

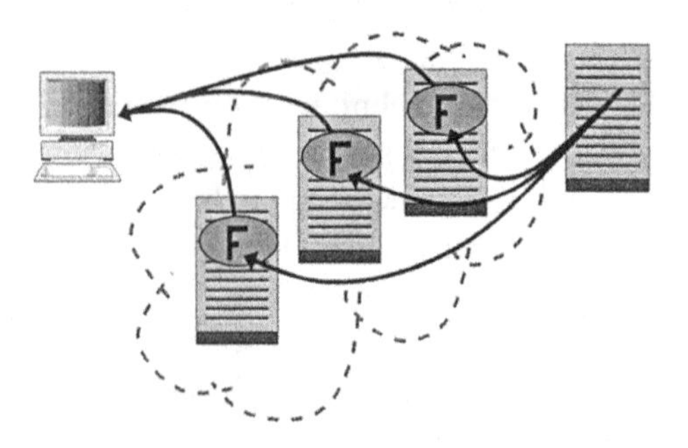

Figure 1. An example query initiated at a user's workstation, accessing data from a remote machine and using three copies of a web service hosting an expensive operation "F" to exploit data parallelism.

ing an expensive analysis function could be beneficial even in a heterogeneous environment [20]. The work described here focuses on the requirements for fault-tolerance arising in such query evaluations. Equally however, a query requiring a large join might profit through parallelization over dynamically acquired resources by being able to use a single phase algorithm, e.g. [22].

3. Recovery Options

Figure 2 shows how an example query might be mapped onto distributed resources by the DQP compiler. The query, shown in Figure 2(a) applies an expensive function call which is hosted by a publicly available WS to data accessed from a remote source. The compiler has generated from the query text a parallel plan shown in Figure 2(b) which implements the query using three partitions, P0, P1, P2. It happens that at the time the query is executed, there are two copies of the WS instantiated on machines which are available to the DQP instance. The compiler has chosen to employ both these instances in its execution plan. Thus, query execution shown in Figure 2(c), is distributed between the user's machine M0, the machine hosting the data source M1, and the two machines M2, M3 hosting the WS which exports the analysis call. During query execution tuples are retrieved from the data source on M1 and divided between M2 and M3. The result tuples on M2,M3 containing the outputs of calls to analysis are forwarded to M0 where the whole result is returned to the user.

The component of the plan allocated to a specific machine is an instance of a partition defined in the parallel plan. The single partition containing the operation call has been replicated on two different machines. The tuples from upstream are divided between the replica partitions to achieve a speedup. In general, most partitions in a parallel plan can be replicated in this way; the root partition is an exception. In the following discussion, a horizontal slice of

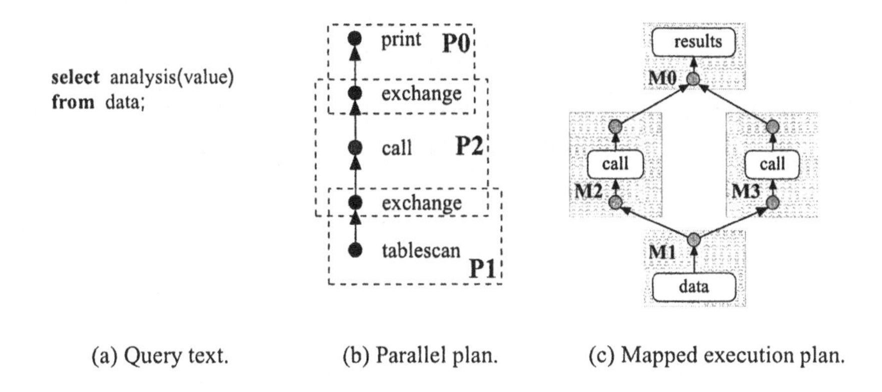

(a) Query text. (b) Parallel plan. (c) Mapped execution plan.

Figure 2. Mapping an example query.

a query plan formed by such replication is referred to as a replica set. Every partition of the parallel plan can be represented as a replica set, even if the cardinality of that replica set is restricted to 1. Thus, the example plan has three replica sets, of which two have cardinality 1 and one has cardinality 2.

During the course of the query execution, any of the machines participating could fail. In a failure, a machine might in practice disappear for good as far as the query execution is concerned; i.e. if the query completes before the machine becomes available. Alternatively, the machine might return to service swiftly, e.g. after a reboot. For the purpose of this work, responses addressing just a single machine failure at a time are addressed. A set of basic operations that can be used to respond to such single machine failures is described below.

restart(query, from) The simplest recovery strategy is to restart the query; this option can clearly be taken in response to failure of any machine. The restart could be from one of various stages. Thus, a second parameter is included to represent (in some way) the choice of where to restart from. For instance, starting from the compiled execution plan, avoids repeating the compilation stage and might be appropriate if for instance a required data source has failed transiently, i.e. has failed but quickly been restored. However, starting from scratch with the original query text offers greatest flexibility and might allow a query to be rerun correctly if a required resource has failed persistently. If the query plan has a point at which intermediate results are fully materialized, it is also possible to restart from that point, thereby saving the cost of repeating all work leading up to that point.

reduce(replica-set) *Reduce* is applied to a replica set to reduce its degree of parallelization by one. Where the failed machine is one of a set over which a partition of the parallel plan has been parallelized, *reduce* can effect recovery by re-parallelizing the partition over the same set of machines minus the one which had failed.

replace(partition) *Replace*, which is applied to a single instance of a partition, is least intrusive to other parts of the query plan. If a single machine fails the lost partition instance is recreated on a spare machine and the only impact on surviving machines is the need for reconnection of communications with neighbours.

An executing query encapsulates distributed intermediate state, e.g. buffers, hash tables etc. If such state is subject to losses or duplications due to actions of failure recovery, the answer returned will be incorrect. If a machine fails, whatever intermediate state was present on that machine just prior to the failure cannot be recovered from there. In a particular query, there may be a natural global materialization point upstream of where the failure occurs and then *restart* from that point is possible. By contrast, *reduce* and *replace* are both local operations which depend for their implementation on the services of an underlying recovery protocol. A recovery protocol maintains the capability for such transient state which is lost in a failure to be recovered after the failure. It achieves this through some form of replication. A common approach is to preserve remotely a snapshot of process state, but an alternative suited to query processing is to preserve copies of tuples in a machine while those tuples are sent for processing downstream [21].

In addition to the nature of the query plan and the point at which a failure occurs, recovery can also be constrained by the nature of the machines that are available. For instance, if the partition running on a failed machine contained a memory based join, a single replacement machine must have capacity to accommodate that join. In extension to the operations described above, it would be feasible to replace the single machine by two or more machines in parallel. If the failed machine was part of a replica-set running a join in parallel, then *reduce* is only possible if the surviving machines can accommodate the repartitioned join. If the failed machine was running an operation call in a WS hosted there, a replacement must host a similar WS.

4. Implementation

4.1 OGSA-DQP

OGSA-DQP [1] is a publicly available infrastructure which supports user submission of distributed queries over data and analysis resources, the former exposed as Grid Data Services (GDSs) via the OGSA-DAI infrastructure [17] and the latter as WSs. The infrastructure implements two Grid Services (GSs) [6], as follows.

- A GDQS (Grid Distributed Query Service) maintains the metadata catalogue describing the available computational resources and databases. A GDQS accepts user queries expressed in OQL over its global schema. It initiates compilation and optimization of queries to yield execution plans.

- A GQES (Grid Query Evaluation Service) is an evaluation engine that is capable of running a subplan of a distributed query plan generated by a GDQS. An instance of this service is created on each machine the optimizer decides should participate in the distributed query execution. Distributed query execution is therefore performed by a set of GQESs that communicate by exchanging tuples. The use of multiple GQESs allows exploitation of parallelism (e.g. parallelizing joins over a set of GQESs) and also fault-tolerance, as described in this work. The service comprises an execution engine which realizes the physical algebra, in the *iterator* style [8] and includes support for two key operations.

  - *perform* accepts a query subplan, specified as an XML document, and instantiates that plan within the query engine.

  - *putData* accepts a buffer full of tuples from another GQES which are intended for further processing in this GQES. This interface is employed within the exchange operator, after [7], to support the movement of tuples between GQESs.

4.2 Recoverable OGSA-DQP

In order to evaluate support for fault-tolerance in distributed query processing, an enhanced version of OGSA-DQP, is being developed. Many details of the enhancement are described in the earlier work [21]. This section gives only a brief summary and highlights differences. Figure 3 illustrates the structure of OGSA-DQP-REC.

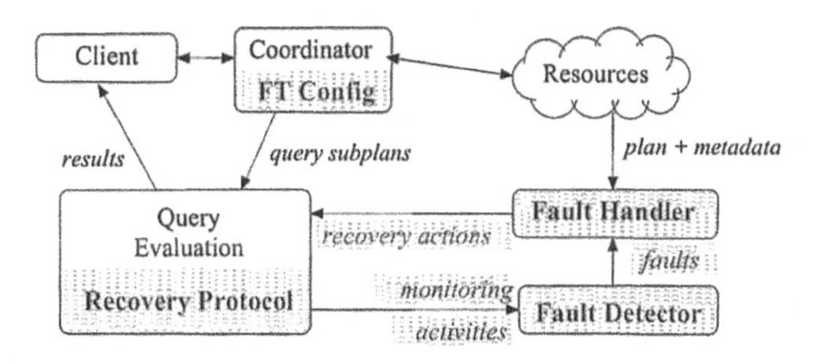

Figure 3. Components of OGSA-DQP-REC.

The client provides the means by which the user can specify a Quality Of Service (QOS) which can be translated into a requirement for fault-tolerance provision. Such a specification might for instance require tolerance to one machine failure during a query execution.

The coordinator takes a user query, generates a plan, and instantiates the required query evaluation environment. Based on the user's specification of the quality of service, the coordinator has to acquire the resources necessary to support the required provision of fault-tolerance. The optimizer has then to take account of the fault-tolerance requirements when generating a query plan, for instance when choosing the number of data source replicas and/or the scheduling of operators.

An enhanced algebra implements a recovery protocol which backs up tuples upstream till they are acknowledged as 'used' from downstream.

The Fault Detector (FD) monitors the running system so that it can notify the Fault Handler (FH) of failures. The FD aims; to impose low overhead; to give each monitored machine the best chance it can to indicate its correct running within a user-defined constraint; and yet to report any monitored machine which fails to indicate its correct running as fast as possible. To this end, the FD regards a sufficiently slow response from a cheap "heartbeat" call to any machine as grounds for deeming that machine as failed. The FD contains an array of counters, with one corresponding to each monitored machine, and each initialized to zero. At a regular interval, a thread (*probe*) per monitored machine makes a synchronous call on a null operation exported by lower level software on that machine, and decrements the corresponding counter by one on completion of each such call. At a defined interval, a single thread *probe-set* increments and tests the value of each of the counters. If any machine has failed, or is running slowly enough, then *probe-set* finds the value of the corresponding counter to exceed the maximum allowed value, whereupon the machine is reported as failed. If this maximum value is f, and both *probe* and *probe-set* employ the same interval I, a failure should be detected in approximately $f \times I$ seconds.

The FH acts upon notifications from the FD, deciding upon and effecting appropriate changes to the running system to exclude the reported machine, for instance substituting a suitable spare machine for one which has failed, or perhaps aborting the query and causing a suitable error indication to be returned to the user if there is no available resource. To perform this task, the FH uses a description of the plan allocated to the evaluators and metadata describing both the fault-tolerance provision and resources which are or may become available in order to support that fault-tolerance provision. The FH is divided into two parts. A Global Fault Handler (GFH) is responsible for deciding on the overall strategy to pursue for a distributed computation in the event of a failure notification and instructing relevant Local Fault Handlers (LFH). LFHs are responsible for performing reconfiguration operations locally.

In this work, two of the operations, *reduce* and *replace*, described in Section 3 are implemented in the FH. The operations are distributed between the GFH and the LFHs; the central GFH allowing coordination of what are inevitably distributed operations. The implementations are illustrated in Figure 4. The high level operation to redistribute retrospectively, employed in

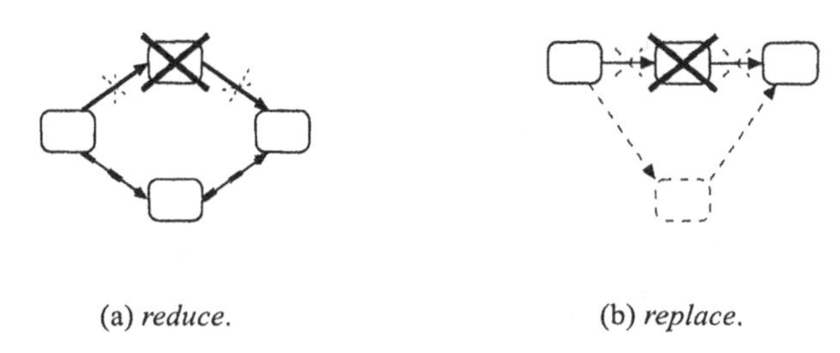

1 disable neighbours
2 redistribute retrospectively
3 reconnect survivors
4 enable neigbours
1 disable neighbours
2 install neweval
3 disconnect oldeval
4 connect neweval
5 enable neighbours

(a) *reduce*. (b) *replace*.

Figure 4. Implementation of recovery operations.

reduce, is responsible for reconciling neighbours up and downstream before changing the distribution of tuples specified in the upstream neighbours and also for ensuring that transient state distributed across the replica set is correctly distributed across the reduced replica set. In current OGSA-DQP-REC, this can be achieved by killing, recreating and reinstalling partitions to the surviving replicas. As part of normal restart processing, tuples backed up in the upstream neighbours are then replayed, but using the revised distribution policy. From an implementation point of view, this approach is clean and simple. It would be possible to avoid the overhead of a GS instance creation by implementing a suitable restart operation within the evaluator.

5. Experimental Results

The experiments are performed using OGSA-DQP-REC over a local area network comprising a cluster of 860MHz machines having 512MB main memory each, interconnected via a 100Mbps fast ethernet switch and a separate client 3GHz machine on a different subnet having 1GB main memory. An example dataset contains a single table with 10000 tuples, each containing a string attribute which serves as parameter to the analysis call. The latter is implemented in a web service which is hosted on two of the machines in the cluster. The query can be seen as a simplification of the bio-informatics example discussed in [19]. In these experiments, queries are submitted to the OGSA-DQP-REC system via a shell script. The OGSA-DQP-REC system compiles and runs a query using machines in the cluster and writes query results to a file on the client machine. The compiler maps the query onto the data source machine and either one or two of the machines hosting the web service, depending on whether *reduce* or *replace* is being tested. The execution time, measured from submission to completion of a query is saved to a database by the controlling shell script, which also injects faults where required simply by making an *ssh* call to the chosen machine in the cluster and there calling *killall -9 java* which has the effect of aborting the tomcat web server there.

Figure 5 shows the measured total elapsed time for query completion in both failure-free executions and executions where a fault is injected at some interval (Delay time) after the start of query execution and the fault-tolerant system recovers using either *replace* or *reduce*. In (FT-replace), the operation

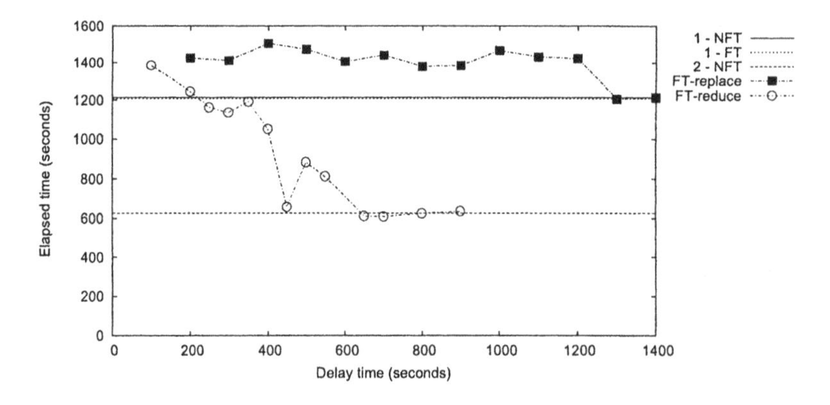

Figure 5. Measured results.

call is initially scheduled to just one of the machines hosting the web service, thereby leaving one spare and only the *replace* option is enabled in FH. In (FT-reduce) the operation call is initially scheduled to both these machines and just the *reduce* option is enabled in FH. The query performance is measured with the fault injection disabled, but using either one (1-NFT) or both (2-NFT) machines hosting copies of the web service and, in the former case, also with fault-tolerance support (i.e. recovery protocol and failure detector) enabled (1-NFT). These failure free executions are point measurements, at Delay time=∞, so for convenience horizontal lines are drawn at those values.

The failure free execution time is about 1200 and 600 seconds with parallelism of 1 and 2 respectively. These values are evident directly, but can also be seen by observing that when a fault is injected after query completion, the execution is failure free. The results show that the overhead of the fault-tolerance support is low (i.e. 1-NFT vs 1-FT) and that for this expensive function, the benefit obtainable through parallelization is very good. The results also show the usefulness of the *reduce* operation. In this example, if failure occurs very near the start of the query execution, there is little to choose between the two approaches, but when the failure occurs later during query execution, the overall response is improved through both machines having been actively participating in the query execution up to the time of the failure.

The experiments then suggest the best approach is always to use all available machines and then apply *reduce* to recover from each failure that occurs, up to the point that the last of the replicas has failed and *replace* (using a dynamically acquired machine) or restart is enforced. However, it is not always beneficial to use all available machines, so there may be some spare. In that case *replace* is preferable as execution continues with the original number of machines rather than dropping by one. In general, *reduce* may not always be applicable when there is more than one replica, for instance where the reduced replica set has insufficient memory to support a join which was parallelized over the set of machines. In response to failure of a machine participating in a complex parallel plan, it is possible to combine *reduce* of one replica set with *replace* of the original failed machine, for instance if the replica set containing the original failed machine doesn't support any reduction in parallelism. Even though a machine crash is in a sense a straight forward event, distributed queries can map onto distributed machines in complex ways so that responding to a machine crash is likely to entail some measure of choice between alternative options.

6. Conclusions

Distributed query processing is coming to be seen as a way of combining computational and database resources through a high level level expression that is convenient to the user. However, such a trend suggests that while individual queries will become more highly distributed and more demanding, individual machine failures will be more likely. In this setting it becomes preferable to recover from such an individual failure without having to start the interrupted query from scratch. This initial investigation of an example query suggests that there can be multiple recovery options available to a fault-tolerant DQP. While the set of basic operations identified here is not definitive, it appears unlikely that a single recovery operation would prove universally optimal. Instead it seems that one or more of a generalized set of basic operations might be applied dynamically to manipulate a running query plan so as to recover from a particular fault.

Acknowledgments

The work reported here has been supported by a grant from the Engineering and Physical Sciences Research Council; number RES/0550/7020 and has profited from discussions with Alvaro A. A. Fernandes, Anastasios Gounaris, Norman W. Paton and Rizos Sakellariou of the Information Management Group at Manchester University who are colleagues in the same project.

References

[1] N. Alpdemir, A. Mukherjee, A. Gounaris, N. W. Paton, P. Watson, and Alvaro A. A. Fernandes. OGSA-DQP: A grid service for distributed querying on the grid. In *EDBT*, pages 858–861, 2004.

[2] S. Babu and J. Widom. Continuous queries over data streams. *SIGMOD Record*, 30(3):109–120, September 2001.

[3] R. S. Barga, D. B. Lomet, S. Paparizos, H. Yu, and S. Chandrasekaran. Persistent applications via automatic recovery. In *IDEAS*, pages 258–267, 2003.

[4] R. Braumandl, M. Keidl, A. Kemper, D. Kossmann, A. Kreutz, S. Pröls, S. Seltzsam, and K. Stocker. ObjectGlobe: Ubiquitous query processing. *The VLDB Journal*, 10(1):48–71, August 2001.

[5] I. Foster and C. Kesselman, editors. *The Grid 2: Blueprint for a New Computing Infrastructure*. Morgan Kaufmann, 2003.

[6] I. T. Foster, C. Kesselman, J. M. Nick, and S. Tuecke. Grid services for distributed system integration. *Computer*, 35(6):37–46, June 2002.

[7] G. Graefe. Encapsulation of parallelism in the Volcano query processing system. In *SIGMOD*, pages 102–111, Atlantic City, NJ, USA, 1990. ACM Press.

[8] G. Graefe. Query evaluation techniques for large databases. *ACM Computing Surveys*, 25(2):73–170, June 1993.

[9] J. Gray and A. Reuter. *Transaction Processing: Concepts and Techniques*. Morgan Kaufmann, 1993.

[10] D. Georgakopoulos M. Hornick and A. Sheth. An overview of workflow management: From process modeling to workflow automation infrastructure. *Distributed and Parallel Databases*, 3(2):119–153, April 1995.

[11] J. Hwang, M. Balazinska, A. Rasin, U. Çetintemel, M. Stonebraker, and S. Zdonik. High-availability algorithms for distributed stream processing. Technical Report CS-04-05, Brown University, May 2004.

[12] M. Kamath, G. Alonso, R. Gunthor, and C. Mohan. Providing high availability in very large workflow management systems. In *EDBT*, pages 427–442, March 1996.

[13] D. Kossman. The state of the art in distributed query processing. *Computing Surveys*, 32(4):422–469, December 2000.

[14] W. Labio, J. Wiener, and H. Garcia-Molina. Efficient resumption of interrupted warehouse loads. In *SIGMOD*, pages 46–57. ACM Press, 2000.

[15] T. Malik, A. Szalay, T. Budavari, and A. Thakar. Skyquery: A web service approach to federate databases. In *CIDR*, 2003.

[16] S. Narayanan, T. M. Kurç, Ü. V. Çatalyürek, and J. H. Saltz. Database support for data-driven scientific applications in the grid. *Parallel Processing Letters*, 13(2):245–271, 2003.

[17] The OGSA-DAI project. http://www.ogsadai.org.uk, 2005.

[18] M. Shah, J. M. Hellerstein, S. Chandrasekaran, and M. J. Franklin. Flux: An adaptive partitioning operator for continuous query systems. In *ICDE*, pages 25–36. IEEE, 2003.

[19] J. Smith, A. Gounaris, P. Watson, N. W. Paton, A. A.A. Fernandes, and R. Sakalleriou. Distributed query processing on the grid. In *GRID*, pages 279–290, November 2002.

[20] J. Smith, A. Gounaris, P. Watson, N. W. Paton, A. A.A. Fernandes, and R. Sakalleriou. Distributed query processing on the grid. *International Journal of High Performance Computing Applications*, 17(4), November 2003.

[21] J. Smith and P. Watson. Fault-tolerance in distributed query processing. In *IDEAS*. IEEE Computer Society, 2005.

[22] X. Zhang, T. M. Kurç, T. Pan, Ü. V. Çatalyürek, S. Narayanan, P. Wyckoff, and J. H. Saltz. Strategies for using additional resources in parallel hash-based join algorithms. In *HPDC*, pages 4–13. IEEE Computer Society, 2004.

II

GRID DATA STORAGE

CONDUCTOR: SUPPORT FOR AUTONOMOUS CONFIGURATION OF STORAGE SYSTEMS

Zsolt Németh*
MTA SZTAKI Computer and Automation Research Institute
P.O. Box 63, Budapest, H-1518, Hungary
zsnemeth@sztaki.hu

Michail D. Flouris*
Department of Computer Science, University of Toronto,
Toronto, Ontario M5S 3G4, Canada
flouris@cs.toronto.edu

Renaud Lachaize and Angelos Bilas†
Institute of Computer Science (ICS), Foundation for Research and Technology - Hellas
P.O.Box 1385, Heraklion, GR 71110, Greece
{rlachaiz, bilas}@ics.forth.gr

Abstract Scalable storage systems are expected to scale to large numbers of physical storage devices and to service diverse applications without incuring high management costs. New storage virtualization architectures and techniques that are currently being proposed, aim at addressing these needs by providing the ability to configure storage systems to meet resource constraints and application requirements. However, this flexibility leads to a large number of options when configuring storage systems either statically or dynamically.

In this work we examine how this process can be automated. We present *Conductor*, a rule-based production system that is able to evaluate alternatives and minimize system cost, based on certain criteria. *Conductor* starts from a set of system resources and a set of application requirements and proposes specific system configurations that meet application requirements while minimizing resource costs. It captures human expertise in the form of rules to generate and evaluate configuration alternatives. In this work we focus on static configuration issues and examine various approaches for reducing complexity within a large configuration space. Our techniques manage to satisfy practical time and resource constraints.

Keywords: distributed storage architecture, virtualization, rule based management.

*Work performed while at FORTH-ICS, P.O. Box 1385, Heraklion, GR 71110, Greece.
†Also, with the Dept. of Computer Science, Univ. of Crete, P.O. Box 2208, Heraklion, GR 71409, Greece.

1. Introduction

As the amount of storage required increases, scalable storage systems provide a means of consolidating all storage in a single system and increasing storage efficiency (Figure 1). For this reason, storage system architectures are undergoing a transition from directly- to network-attached. This new architecture offers potential for flexible configuration of storage systems to better match application needs and thus, reduce system cost and improve efficiency. This is an important concern because distinct application domains have very diverse storage requirements; Systems designed for the needs of scientific computations, data mining, e-mail serving, e-commerce, search engines, operating system (OS) image serving or data archival impose different tradeoffs in terms of dimensions such as speed, reliability, capacity, high-availability, security, data sharing, and consistency.

Thus, storage consolidation leads to increased requirements for "flexibility" that will be able to serve multiple applications and their diverse needs. This "flexibility" refers to both storage management and application access issues and is usually provided through "virtualization" techniques: Administrators and applications see various types of virtual volumes that are mapped to physical devices but offer higher-level semantics through virtualization mechanisms.

Modern storage virtualization techniques aim at providing flexibility in configuring and accessing physical system resources. Storage virtualization may occur either at the filesystem or at the block level. Violin [5] is a kernel-level framework for building and combining virtualization functions at the *block* level. Violin targets commodity storage nodes and replaces the current block-level I/O stack with an improved I/O hierarchy that allows for (i) easy extension of the storage hierarchy with new mechanisms and (ii) flexible combining of these mechanisms to create modular hierarchies with rich semantics.

Figure 1(b) shows a virtual hierarchy that creates a virtual disk by aggregating three virtual devices: an aggregation of two encrypted disk, a pair of striped disks that is encrypted and an encrypted disk. Scenarios of more advanced virtualization semantics are discussed in [6].

Virtualization mechanisms, such as Violin, provide the means required for creating flexible configurations and exporting an abstract view of the actual storage resources to satisfy application requirements. However, such an approach results in a large number of alternatives that can match the application requirements. For instance, a certain capacity can be provided either with a single large disk or by aggregating many smaller disks; A required level of bandwidth may be reached either by a high-performance disk or by striping several lower speed disks; Encryption can be introduced at several levels of the hierarchy: at the topmost virtual device it could represent a centralized service, whereas at the level of physical disks it can be realized as many par-

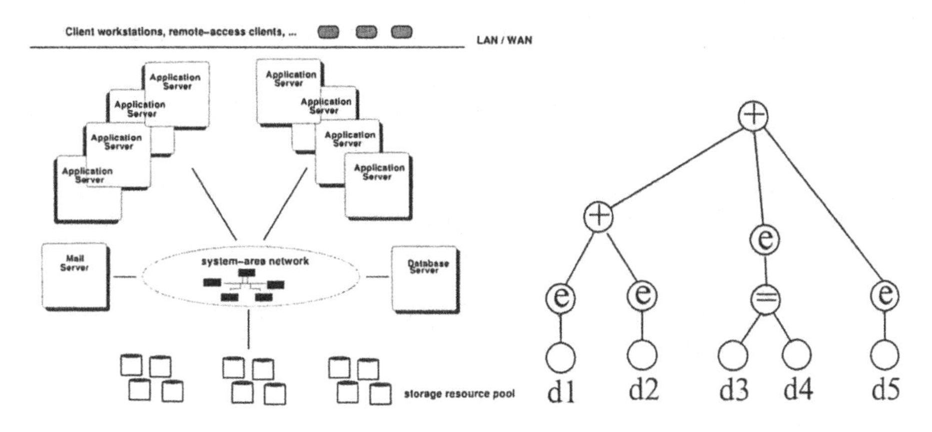

Figure 1. (a) Generic networked storage organization (left) and (b) example virtual hierarchy. ('+' represents an aggregation, '=' a striping, 'e' an encryption virtual device.) (right)

allel encryption services. Evaluating these alternatives usually requires human intervention that results in increased management costs. Beyond a certain complexity however, humans cannot survey and manage virtualization hierarchies.

In this work we present *Conductor* that is able to automatically evaluate configuration alternatives and suggest optimal solutions based on certain criteria. *Conductor* captures human expertise in the form of rules. Based on the rules, it builds various alternative configurations and makes suggestions about optimal ones. Configuration is essentially an exploration of a multi-dimensional search space and it is inherently of exponential complexity. The focus of this work is how the complexity of the search can be reduced so that it has acceptable running times for practical cases while the quality of the solution is not decreased.

We find that exhaustive search, i.e. trying all possible configurations is not feasible even for toy examples. Random reduction of the search space is a potential alternative but may exclude some of the optimal solutions. Heuristic search applies some additional information about the search space. We investigate two methods: (a) Zoned search, which enables or prohibits certain actions according to specific zones within the configuration space. (b) Clustered search, which creates clusters of similar devices and uses these clusters as the basis of the configuration space search. Both of these methods are able to deliver optimal solutions, have practically acceptable complexity and, in addition, can be combined.

The rest of this paper is organized as follows. Next section introduces related work. Section 2 presents an overview of *Conductor*. Section 4 discusses quality and complexity issues for various approaches to evaluating alternative system configurations. Section 5 presents our results and analysis of the overheads associated with each approach we examine. Finally, we draw our conclusions in Section 7.

2. Related work

Storage management involves many problems that are hard to formalize, involve multi-dimensional optimizations, exponential search, or ambiguous decisions. Even if there are explicit algorithms for certain problems, they quite often belong to the NP-hard class. Recent work tries to exploit "intelligent", heuristic-based, approaches for tackling some of these problems.

Polus [11] aims at mapping high level QoS goals to low level storage actions by introducing learning and reasoning capabilities. The system starts with a basic knowledge of a system administrator expressed as "rules of thumb" and it can establish quantitative relationships between actions taken and their observed effects to performance by monitoring and learning. To eliminate performance problems, the system finds an appropriate set of actions by backward reasoning in the generated knowledge base.

Ergastulum [2] is aimed at supporting the configuration of storage systems. It essentially helps with reducing the search complexity of possible design decisions by utilizing a best-fit bin packaging heuristics with randomization and backtracking. It takes into consideration workload characteristics, device specifications, performance models and constraints, and provides a near-optimal solution in practically acceptable time.

The work introduced in [3] assists in selecting the right data-redundancy scheme for disk arrays. It is a derivative of Ergastulum and explores and evaluates four methods for a specific problem: rule-based tagger, model-based tagger, and partially and fully-adaptive solvers.

A novel approach presented in [10] tries to predict the effect of certain actions and helps with making decisions at data distibution (encoding and placement). It has some similarities with the learning abilities of Polus. It establishes a set of *What... if...* statements where the hypothetical effect (what part) of a certain circumstance (if part) is stored. These relations are obtained by statistical, analytical or simulation methods. The accuracy of predictions were shown to be practically acceptable.

A main effort in both our as well as previous research is to capture aspects of human expertise. However, previous research has focused on different aspects and has applied different techniques. In our work we examine configuration of the virtualization hierarchy and consider disks themselves as black boxes, i.e. exclude low level physical aspects in the investigation. Polus mainly operates at the physical disk level and does not consider structural issues. Ergastulum and its derivative is similar to our work in a sense that it is also aimed at reducing the complexity of configuration. However, it supports initial system designs only and strongly relies on assumptions of the workload and performance models. Our intention is to extend Conductor so that it can manage dynamic reconfigurations therefore, initial configuration is carried out with limited assumptions about the workload and estimated performance figures. Also, the search methods used in each case are different: Ergastulum uses backtracking, whereas we apply forward chaining. At the current phase of work we do not apply any learning or predictive abilities nevertheless, these may be considered in the future.

3. System Overview

The aim of Conductor is to increase the degree of autonomy in storage systems by creating and maintaining virtual storage hierarchies (customized storage services) based on user and application requirements, without the intervention of system administrators. Thus, Conductor partly substitutes human system administrators and overtakes some of their tasks during the life-cycle of a storage system: (i) Initially configure new virtual hierarchies based on a prescribed specification. (ii) Monitor hierarchies to ensure they satisfy at runtime the prescribed specification. (iii) Detect where problems occur in hierarchies that deviate from specifications. (iv) Modify or rebuild, partly or entirely, such hierarchies.

In large-scale storage systems today, such tasks are performed by experienced personnel and thus, rely heavily on human expertise. As storage systems grow in size and their architectures leverage commodity components, it is projected [1] that the cost of maintaining them may dominate and eventually limit their scalability.

In this section we present the overall concept of Conductor. Although Conductor aims at addressing all issues above, this paper focuses on the first step, the creation virtual storage hierarchies based on prescribed specifications. This is the static part of the above tasks. The rest of the tasks constitute dynamic runtime management steps and are left for future work.

3.1 Conductor architecture

Conductor is built in the context of Violin [5], a storage virtualization framework. Our approach is to augment Violin with a rule-based, forward chaining production system for the following reasons: (i) Rule-based systems offer a straightforward way to express "common sense" and "rules of thumb" that are based on human expertise. These rules are declarative and specify the knowledge not the procedure to solve a problem. (ii) Data are represented as facts, i.e. abstract statements. This uniformity makes it possible to represent virtually all sort of information. (iii) Production systems apply highly efficient pattern matching mechanisms to select appropriate rules. Therefore, they are

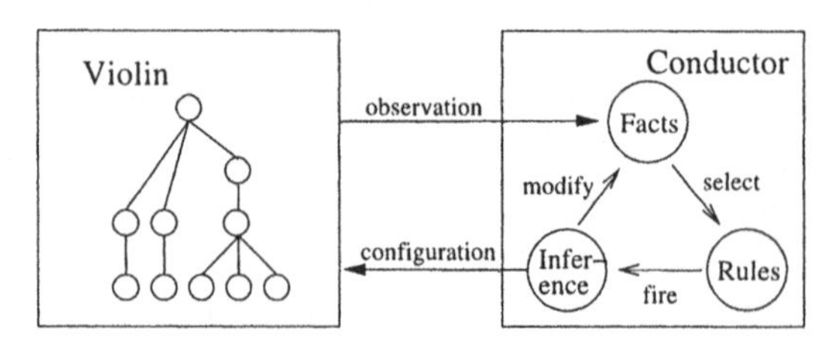

Figure 2. Conductor architecture.

able to capture information hidden in unrelated, unstructured, heterogeneous data by searching for certain patterns.

Figure 2 depicts the conceptual architecture of Conductor. Conductor communicates with the storage system (Violin) at two well defined points: it receives monitoring data from the storage system and sends configuration commands to it. Monitoring data are transferred between Violin and Conductor via a simple interface, such as the `/proc` filesystem in Linux. Commands that dictate configuration changes to Violin can also be sent through a similar interface, such as `ioctl` calls in Linux. All information is represented in Conductor as facts and rules:

Facts represent factual information about the system, that may be (i) static, which is basic information about system components, e.g. a directory of disks, network links, host nodes and their characteristics; (ii) dynamic, which is measured during system operation, e.g. throughput obtained from each virtual device, number of requests traversing a path; (iii) inferred, which is derived by Conductor during its working cycle.

Rules represent empirical knowledge about the system. They express actions that must be performed in a certain situation [4]. Such situations are described by the conditions of the rule that must be satisfied to enable the actions. Conditions involve the existence or non-existence of facts or certain patterns that facts must satisfy. From all applicable rules, i.e. where conditions are true, one is chosen and its actions are executed. Rules in Conductor essentially try to capture "rules of thumb" a human operator would perform in each case.

Conductor is implemented in CLIPS [4, 8], a production system framework, that realizes the production cycle [7] as depicted in Figure 2 : (i) Update factual information in the knowledge base. Facts activate rules as they are matched with the conditions of the rule. (ii) From the potentially many activated rules one is selected according to the conflict resolution strategy of the production system. (iii) As the selected rule fires, it may generate new (inferred) facts and update the knowledge base.

This simple cycle continues as long as there are activated rules. Note, that in each production cycle rules may be activated or deactivated and the execution order is governed by the conflict resolution strategy.

Conductor operates in two possible modes: (i) Initial configuration mode. This mode is used to configure virtual devices based on user requests and static facts. (ii) Diagnosis and dynamic reconfiguration mode, where it triggers diagnostic procedures and corrective actions. This work focuses on the initial configuration mode, which we describe next in detail.

4. Initial Configuration Mode

Initial configuration is a "bootstrapping" process that creates a new virtual hierarchy (target device) of devices from scratch according to a set of user and application requirements. Some of these requirements are related to the functionality of the target storage device and have static characteristics, whereas other requirements capture performance aspects and are dynamic. While static requirements can be guaranteed for the lifetime of the target device, the exact performance of a target device is hard to predict and guarantee. Storage performance is related to workload characteristics, such as access patterns that are typically unknown, difficult to predict, and dynamic in nature.

Rules used in the initial configuration mode satisfy all static requirements, whereas they only "try" to satisfy dynamic (performance) requirements based on estimated values for system components. One possible approach to improve this is to dynamically update estimated values with actual measured data as soon as they become available and trigger a full system reconfiguration, based on these measured values.

Conductor needs to explore a large configuration space with multiple dimensions. Each dimension corresponds to a property of the disks, e.g. capacity, bandwidth, level of redundancy. Some of these properties are continuous, whereas others are discrete. Any device is represented in this space by a vector: Each request for a target device is translated to a vector with components derived either from the user request or from desired system characteristics. Physical disks are represented as vectors with estimated values for their performance characteristics. Virtual devices that are created from combining other (virtual or physical) devices are represented as vectors with components derived by production rules. These rules express relationships and constraints between dimensions of device properties and guide configuration steps. Thus, we can define the problem of configuration as a search procedure in this multi-dimensional space that tries to produce a given target vector, the user request, using only appropriate combinations and modifications (rules) of initial vectors (devices). A solution to the problem consists of the set of initial vectors and the set of rules applied to transform them into the target vector.

Figure 3 shows an example with a configuration space of three dimensions. Initially, there are two disks d_1 and d_2 of a certain capacity and bandwidth and none of them are encrypted. If the rule of striping is activated by d_1 and d_2

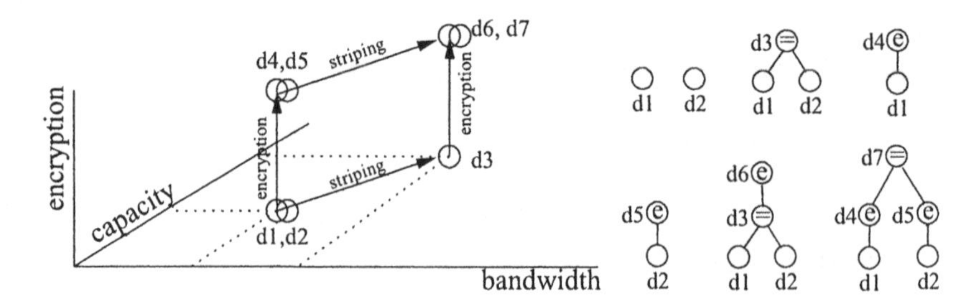

Figure 3. Configuration as exploration of the search space and the generated disks. (Empty circles are physical disks, = represents a striping, e represents an encryption virtual disk.)

and fires, it yields d_3 that has the added capacity of d_1 and d_2 and a bandwidth increased by factor α; for instance, assuming a linear access, α is around 2. When the rule of encryption is activated by d_3 and fires, it yields d_6 with the same capacity and bandwidth but with the added service of encryption. Rules are activated by disks and combinations of disks in an unspecified order if certain conditions are met. Thus, the rule of encryption can be activated by d_1 and d_2, yielding d_4 and d_5 that activate the striping rule yielding d_7 with the same characteristics as d_6. If any of these disks fall into a defined range of the required parameters then the search for a given configuration is successful.

Note however, that this example is simplified. There can be significantly more rules active simultaneously, e.g. aggregation, 3-, 4-, 5-way striping, mirroring, partitioning which combined would generate a huge disk population in the search space. Furthermore, only a few dimensions are taken into consideration in this example. For instance, encryption does not change capacity or bandwidth but it may increase response time. If mapping is also taken into consideration as a further dimension, d_6 and d_7 do not necessarily coincide. d_7 consists of two encrypted virtual disks that may work in parallel – depending on mapping options – giving better performance than the single encryption layer of d_6.

The search method may generate large numbers of possible disk configurations within an acceptable distance to the requested specification vector but one of them must be chosen, eventually. The specification can have more components than the required parameters. These additional components are related to the management of the device and may involve dollar cost, resource utilization, structural complexity, power consumption or other aspects; some are defined by the user, some others by the service provider. The specification vector may also give weights and annotations how these metrics can be evaluated. Based on these metrics a function is calculated that is a linear combination of certain scores how much the given component fits the specified one. For instance, the resulted capacity should be as close to the specified one as possible whereas the power consumption should be as little as possible furthermore, there are components, like encryption that requires an exact match. With appropriate weights the importance of these aspects can be tuned from don't care to uttermost. The calculated function is used to select the best vector among the resulted ones. Intuitively, we may say that we choose the closest vector to the specified one but the calculated function is not a distance metrics in a strict sense, hence we call it "cost". Smaller cost means better solution. In current experiments we use a simple dollar cost metrics; certain cost functions will be defined based on practical experience.

It is important to note that the search is non-monotonous: Virtual devices closer to the required specification vector are not necessarily better or more useful in generating the final solution. For instance, a given bandwidth can potentially be provided by two disks of 60% of the requested bandwidth whereas the same could not be fulfilled efficiently by two disks that have 90% of the requested bandwidth.

Also, the search is non-exact. Its aim is to find a target device with characteristics as close to the user requirements as possible. However, in most cases, the resulting device will not be an exact match, especially in cases where dynamic characteristics are considered.

4.1 Rules

Configuration is driven by rules that specify three aspects for creating a new virtual device from existing ones: (a) What properties the existing devices need to have, (b) Specifically how they should be combined, and (c) What are the projected property values for the new device.

There are different rules for various combinations and modifications of disks, e.g. aggregation, (n-way) striping, mirroring, partitioning, encryption. They incorporate conditions (disks eligible as targets of the operation), constraints (under what circumstances the operation is possible) and effects (new or modified parameters) of the given operation. For instance, the rule of striping picks two disks and check if (i) their capacities are the same, (ii) their bandwidths are similar, (iii) their latencies are below a certain limit and (iv) either both of them or none of them are encrypted. If these conditions hold, then striping is possible and results in a new disk that has doubled capacity, increased bandwidth, the same latency and encryption as the constituting disks.

As rules fire, they create new devices in the search space. These may fire other rules that, in turn, create new devices. This could continue infinitely therefore, rules incorporate conditions that limit the search, e.g. the height of the hierarchy or the distance from the requirements. When there are no more activated rules, the solutions are checked. If there are disks within an acceptable distance from the requested specification vector, one of them is chosen based on the cost function. Otherwise, some limiting conditions are changed

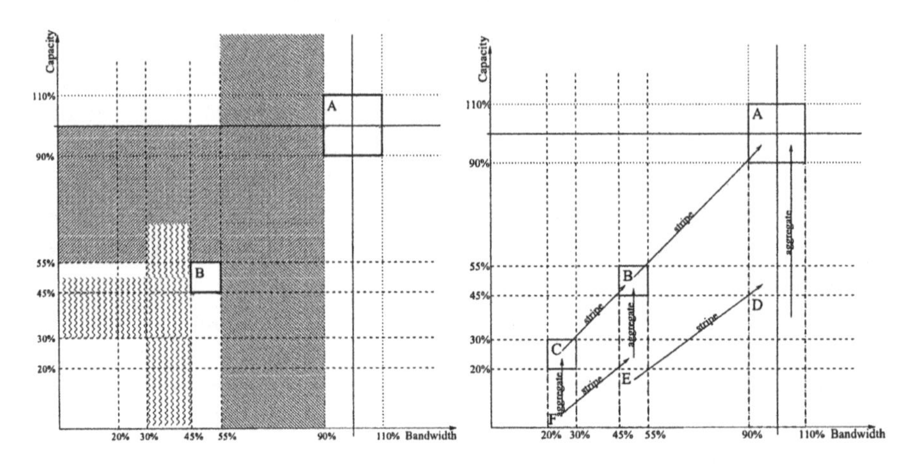

Figure 4. (a) Valid and invalid zones in the search space (left). (b) Operations are enabled one at a time so that zone A can be reached in the fewest steps (right).

that activate rules, e.g. one level higher hierarchy is allowed, and the search continues. It stops finally if either a solution is found or there are no solutions in a given number of iterations. To control the complexity of the search process we use certain heuristics. Next these are examined in details.

Exhaustive search. With exhaustive search all possible vectors are generated according to the rules. Some of these vectors will lead to the requested specification vector, whereas others will not. This approach will eventually generate the target device that is the closest to the requested specification at the least possible cost. However, this method has exponential complexity and is not realistic in practice.

A simple approach to reduce the complexity of the exhaustive search is to randomly omit generated vectors at the search. In our evaluation, we examine dropping one every 16, 8, 4, and 2 generated devices randomly. Although this simple approach significantly reduces the search space, it cannot guarantee that the generated disk will be acceptably close to the requirements and, even in this case, that it is the smallest possible cost.

Zoned search. Zoned search is heuristic, i.e. uses some additional information in order to omit irrelevant solutions and thus, decrease the search space. As rules define the projected properties, some disks can be combined so that they lead to the required solutions, whereas some others can not; they form certain zones in the search space. Zoned search divides the search space into zones and ignores those that cannot yield the required characteristics. As an example, consider a 2-dimensional search space in Figure 4(a). Assume the following: solutions are accepted with a 10% margin around the required vector (zone A in Figure 4(a)) and the rule of striping assumes an increase of bandwidth of 2. In this case no disks of bandwidth in the 55% – 90% region of the required can lead to a solution. They need additional bandwidth to be provided by striping. However, striping would arrange the new disk over the 110% range of the desired bandwidth. Similarly, disks with capacity above the 55% limit would not lead to the required solution. By striping these disks, the resulted capacity would be over the required. The idea can be followed in a recursive way, e.g. for zone B; in such a way the entire search space can be divided and classified into allowed and prohibited zones. This method can be generalized easily for other actions where the increase of bandwidth is other than 2.

It is important to note that zones are allowed or prohibited with respect to some action. For example, allowed zones for a 3-way striping mostly coincide with the prohibited zones of a 2-way striping. In the above example zones that may lead to capacity or bandwidth over 110% of the required are considered prohibited zones. However, if partitioning is an allowed action, these zones are allowed, since they can reach the target zone by creating a disk with much larger capacity and bandwidth and then use partitions of it.

Zoned search with random dropping. Zoned search may reduce search space significantly. However, within the allowed zones it still performs an exhaustive search. In the worst case scenario, when all disks can potentially lead to a solution, zoned search coincides with exhaustive search. Therefore, zoned search can also be combined with random dropping.

Fewest steps. The method of fewest step is also based on the zones. In this case however, combination actions are enabled one at a time. First, configuration checks if there are disks in the target zone (zone A in Figure 4(b).) If there are no disks then it checks those zones where zone A can be reached in a single step. Therefore, it enables aggregation for zone D and then 2-way striping for zone B. If there are still no solutions, it enables further rules that can lead to zones B and D in a single step: aggregation can put disks from zone E to zone B whereas 2-way striping can put disks from zone E to zone D. Obviously, more way striping can also be considered with different zones. As long as there are no solutions, it checks recursively, how these zones can be reached with the fewest steps. It cuts down large parts of the search space, however, with a high likelyhood of not finding the solution with the lowest cost.

Device clustering. The above search methods may assume a random disk population, i.e. they can be scattered evenly in the parameter space. In practice however, there are many disks of the same type and specifications. A clustering method puts these disks into groups and takes into consideration only one representative element of them. Groups are established dynamically as the configuration process goes on. The method significantly reduces search complexity. For instance, if there are n identical disks, the complexity of aggregation is $O(n^2)$ ($n * (n-1)/2$ potential pairs), whereas that of in case of clustering is $O(n)$ ($n/2$ pairs.) In general, complexity is proportional to the number of disk groups and not to the number of disks. While there may be hundreds or thousands of disks in a storage system, the number of groups is significantly lower. Note, that this method is orthogonal to the previous ones, i.e. it can be exhaustive but could be combined with zoning or random dropping. Its worst case scenario, when all groups have a single element, has the same complexity as its non-clustered version.

5. Evaluation

We have implemented the framework of Conductor using CLIPS [4, 8]. Our implementation currently provides rules for aggregation, 2-, 3-, 4-, 5-way striping, encryption and mirroring with all the search heuristics mentioned in the previous section. In this section, we evaluate the search heuristics with respect to run-time complexity. We first present results without disk clustering and then we consider the effect of clustering similar disks in groups. We run our experiments on PCs with Intel P4-grade CPUs at 3.0 GHz and 512 MBytes of memory.

Individual Disks. Figure 5 summarizes the search times without clustering. The system consists of a variable number of disks (x axis). Since in this experiment disks are taken individually, we assumed a random disk population where each disk has a capacity of 100, 200, 300, 400, and 500 GBytes and nominal bandwidth of 33, 50, 70 and 100 MBytes/s. Also, each has an initial cost, a one-dimensional integer metrics that is used to select the 'cheapest' solution among the functionally equivalent ones. For the sake of simplicity we may consider it as the dollar cost of the resource. A user asks for a virtual disk with 600-GByte capacity, 100-MBytes/s throughput, and a cost not exceeding 200. For the purpose of this experiment, Conductor is allowed to use only two actions: aggregation and striping. All other actions are disabled.

We see that although exhaustive search finds the best solution possible (minimum cost), it is in practice unable to deal with more than 24 physical disks. In this case it generates more than 200000 facts and fires nearly 120000 rules, which results in unacceptably long running times (and even sometimes crashes).

If we omit some of the intermediate virtual disks *randomly* and keep only one out of two, four, and eight (labeled as random 2, random 4, random 8 in Figure 5(a)), the search becomes viable both in compute time and memory capacity. This method, however, eliminates as expected some of the best solutions. Figure 5(b) compares the cost of the best solutions found. We see that

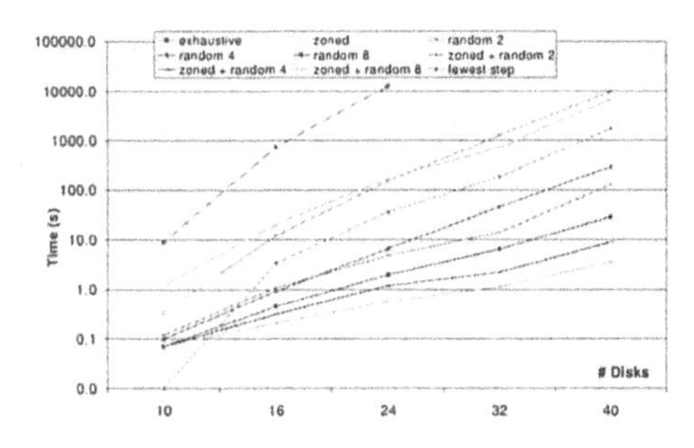

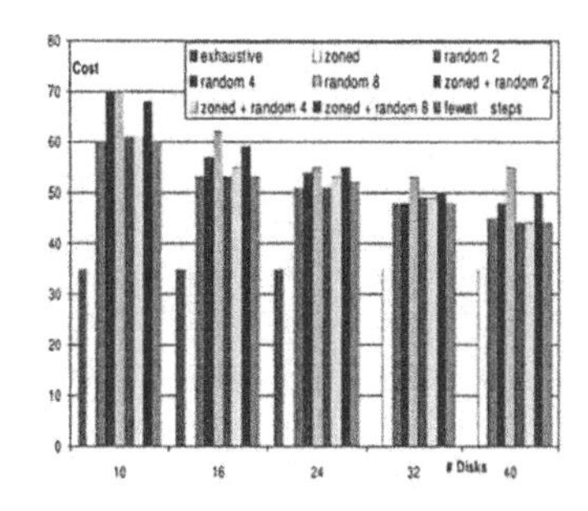

Figure 5. (a) Run times of different configuration search methods (left). (b) Comparison of the costs of the best solution found by different methods (right).

compared to exhaustive search, these methods result in disks with higher cost. However, the difference decreases as the number of disks grows.

Zoned search reduces the search space efficiently while it does not eliminate good solutions: It results in virtual disks with cost similar to exhaustive search and can handle significantly more disks. Furthermore, zoned search can be accelerated by applying random dropping and renders running times acceptable even for more than 40 physical disks.

Finally, it seems that fewest-steps is an interesting but not practically useful approach. Its running time is inconsistent: if it finds a solution in a small number of steps (1 or 2), as is the case with 10 physical disks, then it is significantly faster than other methods. Otherwise, its running time is close to zoned search, however, with potentially higher cost in the resulting virtual disk configurations.

Clustered Disks. In practice, hardware resources, such as disks, are often acquired and upgraded in bulk and exhibit similar characteristics. Thus, we can assume that, in most cases, a large system will consist of disks that can be clustered based on their characteristics to a smaller number of groups. As opposed to the previous experiment, where potentially all disks may be different, in this experiment we introduce 3, 5, and 7 different groups of disks. Since we anticipate that clustering will result in improved running times, we use a more complex example: A user requests a virtual disk with capacity of 1200 GBytes and throughput 140 MBytes/s. Moreover, we configure two versions of this disk, with and without encryption. To increase the size of the configuration space, we enable in Conductor rules associated to aggregation and 2- and 3-way striping. Finally, we only present results for exhaustive search to see the net effect of clustering.

Figure 6 shows that running times are approximately three orders of magnitude smaller compared to using individual disks. Even for 128 disks of 7

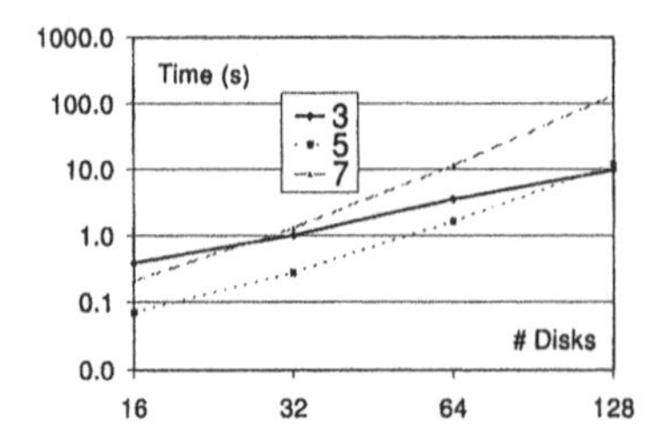

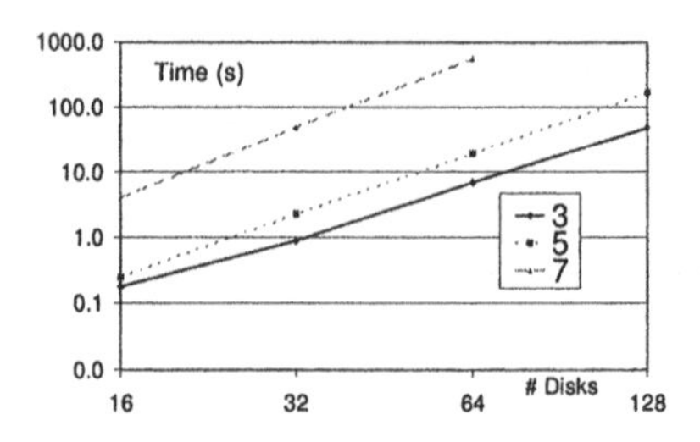

Figure 6. Run times of clustered disk search for 3, 5, and 7 groups of disks, without and with encryption.

different types the search is less than 2 minutes. When including encryption in the target virtual disk configuration, the number of groups that needs to be considered doubles. However, running time remains low.

6. Conclusions and future work

Future, large-scale storage systems are envisioned to offer a lot of flexibility in configuring virtual resources to meet user and application requirements. Configuration of large-scale storage systems that support such flexibility requires considering a large number of alternatives. For instance, a user request for a virtual volume of specific size, throughput, redundancy level, with encryption and compression capabilities over a system that consists of hundreds of physical disks will require considering millions of alternatives. Although this task is traditionally performed manually by experienced storage administrators that can quickly reduce this space, it is foreseen that human cost will not scale with system size.

In this work, we propose Conductor, a rule based system for evaluating configuration alternatives that meet user requirements and minimize system cost. Although Conductor is designed to deal with both static (initial configuration based on estimated performance values) and dynamic (run-time reconfiguration based on measured performance values) properties of storage systems, in this work we only explore initial system configuration. The main issue in this direction is to reduce search complexity.

Our design relies on heuristic rules that capture human expertise and various search methods that aim at reducing search complexity without compromising the quality (cost) of the resulting configurations. We implement Conductor as an extension to Violin [5] using CLIPS [4]. We find that although considering individual disks may be in practice prohibitive for real, large-scale systems, clustering disks in groups substantially improves overheads and results in a practical approach to exploring the configuration space.

The next step in our work is to explore dynamic system behavior, i.e. what is the quality of the proposed configurations at runtime, how far is it from user requirements in terms of dynamic features such as throughput and response time, and how we can incorporate more knowledge in system rules to allow for run-time reconfiguration actions that will result in improved configurations. Finally, besides dynamic configuration issues, future work should also consider mapping of virtual volumes to distributed physical resources and should take into account disk, CPU, memory, and network characteristics.

Acknowledgments

During this work Zsolt Nmeth was supported by the ERCIM Fellowship programme. Also, we thankfully acknowledge the support of the European FP6-IST program through the UNIsIX project and the FP6 Network of Excellence CoreGRID, and the support of the General Secretariat for Research and Technology, Greece through the MASC project.

References

[1] Gartner Group. Total Cost of Storage Ownership – A User-oriented Approach. September 2000.

[2] E. Anderson et al. Ergastulum: Quickly Finding Near-Optimal Storage System Designs. HP Labs SSP technical report HPL-SSP-2001-05 (2002)

[3] E. Anderson et al. Selecting RAID Levels for Disk Arrays. Proc. of the USENIX FAST Conference, January 28-30, 2002, Monterey, CA, USA.

[4] C Language Integrated Production System (CLIPS) http://www.ghg.net/clips/CLIPS.html and also CLIPS Reference Manual. Vol. 1, Version 6.24, 15 June 2006

[5] M.D. Flouris, A. Bilas. Violin: A Framework for extensible Block-level Storage. Proc. of the 22nd IEEE / 13th NASA Goddard Conference on Mass Storage Systems and Technologies (MSST 2005) April 2005, Monterey, CA, USA. IEEE Computer Society.

[6] M. Flouris, R. Lachaize, and A. Bilas. Violin: a Framework for Extensible Block-Level Storage. Book on Knowledge and Data Management in Grids, CoreGRID series, Springer Verlag, 3, 2006.

[7] D.Klahr, P. Langley, R. Neches (eds.): Production System Models of Learning and Development. MIT Press, 1987.

[8] W. Mettrey. A Comparative Evaluation of Expert System Tools. Computer 24, 2 (Feb. 1991), pp. 19-31.

[9] E. Riedel. Storage Systems. Not Just a Bunch of Disks Anymore. Queue, June 2003, ACM, pp. 32-41.

[10] E. Thereska et al. Informed data distribution selection in a self-predicting storage system. Proc. of the International Conference on Autonomic Computing, ICAC-06, Dublin, Ireland, June 2006.

[11] S. Uttamchandani et al. Polus: Growing Storage QoS Management Beyond a "Four-year Old Kid". Proc. of the USENIX FAST '04 Conference, March 2004, San Francisco, CA, USA.

VIOLIN: A FRAMEWORK FOR EXTENSIBLE BLOCK-LEVEL STORAGE

Michail D. Flouris*
Department of Computer Science,
University of Toronto,
Toronto, Ontario M5S 3G4, Canada
flouris@cs.toronto.edu

Renaud Lachaize and Angelos Bilas†
Institute of Computer Science (ICS),
Foundation for Research and Technology - Hellas
P.O.Box 1385, Heraklion, GR 71110, Greece
{rlachaiz, bilas}@ics.forth.gr

Abstract

The quality of virtualization mechanisms provided by a storage system affects storage management complexity and storage efficiency, both of which are important problems of modern storage systems. We argue that current storage systems provide limited flexibility and extensibility in virtualizing, managing and accessing storage.

In this work we address this problem by proposing Violin, a virtualization framework that allows easy extensions of block-level storage stacks. Violin allows (i) developers to provide new virtualization functions and (ii) storage administrators to combine these functions in storage hierarchies with rich semantics. Violin makes it easy to develop new virtualization functions by providing support for (i) hierarchy awareness and arbitrary mapping of blocks between virtual devices, (ii) an easily extensible I/O command set, (iii) explicit control over both the request and completion path of I/O requests, and (iv) persistent metadata management.

In this paper we present Violin's architecture and we show how simple Violin modules can be combined in more complex hierarchies. Finally, we demonstrate hierarchies with advanced virtualization functionality that is difficult to implement with monolithic drivers.

Keywords: storage virtualization, multi-layered storage, block-level I/O.

*Work partly performed while at the ICS-FORTH, P.O. Box 1385, Heraklion, GR 71110, Greece.
†Also, with the Dept. of Computer Science, University of Crete, P.O. Box 2208, Heraklion, GR 71409, Greece.

1. Introduction

Storage is becoming an increasingly important issue as more and more data need to be stored either for archival or online processing purposes. As the amount of storage required increases, scalable storage systems provide a means of consolidating all storage in a single system and increasing storage efficiency. However, storage consolidation leads to increased requirements for "flexibility" that will be able to serve multiple applications and their diverse needs. This flexibility refers to both storage management and application access issues and is usually provided through virtualization techniques: Administrators and applications see various types of virtual volumes that are mapped to physical devices but offer higher-level semantics through virtualization mechanisms.

We argue that the importance of virtualization at the block-level is increasing for two reasons. First, certain virtualization functions, such as compression or encryption, may be simpler and more efficient to provide on unstructured fixed data blocks rather than variable-size files. Second, block-level storage systems are evolving from simple disks and fixed controllers to powerful storage nodes [1, 8] that offer block-level storage to multiple applications over a storage area network [9]. In such systems, block-level storage extensions can exploit the processing capacity of the storage nodes, where filesystems (running on the application servers) cannot. For these reasons and over time, with the evolution of storage technology a number of virtualization features, e.g. volume management functions, RAID, snapshots, moved from higher system layers to the block level.

Today's block-level storage systems provide some flexibility in managing and accessing storage through I/O drivers (modules) in the I/O stack or through the filesystem. However, this flexibility is limited by the fact that current I/O stacks require the use of monolithic I/O drivers that are both complex to develop and hard to combine. As a result, current block-level systems offer predefined virtualization semantics, such as virtual volumes mapped to an aggregation of disks or RAID levels. In this category belong both research prototypes [2, 4, 7] as well as commercial products, such as EMC enginuity and Veritas VM. In all these cases the storage administrator can switch on or off various features at the volume level, but cannot extend them.

In this work we address the flexibility and extensibility problem by providing a kernel-level framework for (i) building and (ii) combining virtualization functions. We propose *Violin* (Virtual I/O Layer INtegration), a virtual I/O framework for commodity storage nodes that replaces the current block-level I/O stack with an improved I/O hierarchy that allows for (i) easy extension of the storage hierarchy with new mechanisms and (ii) flexible combining of these mechanisms to create modular hierarchies with rich semantics.

The main contributions of *Violin* are: (i) it significantly reduces the effort to introduce new functionality in the block I/O stack of a commodity storage node and (ii) provides the ability to combine simple virtualization functions into hierarchies with semantics that can satisfy diverse application needs. *Violin* provides virtual devices with full access to both the request and completion paths of I/Os allowing for easy implementation of synchronous and asynchronous I/O. Supporting asynchronous I/O is important for performance reasons, but also raises significant challenges when implemented in real systems. Also, *Violin* deals with metadata persistence for the full storage hierarchy, offloading the related complexity from individual virtual devices. To achieve flexibility, *Violin* allows storage administrators to create arbitrary, acyclic graphs of virtual devices, each adding to the functionality of the successor devices in the graph. In each hierarchy, blocks of each virtual device can be mapped in arbitrary ways to the successor devices, enabling advanced storage functions, such as dynamic relocation of blocks.

Violin was first introduced in [6], where its implementation and evaluation are presented. This paper presents more of a system overview and examples of how advanced storage functionality can be implemented as a set of *Violin* modules. For more details on implementation and evaluation please refer to [6].

The rest of the paper is organized as follows. Section 2 presents the design and implementation of *Violin*. Section 3 presents advanced virtualization modules, while Section 6 discusses related work. Finally, Section 7 draws our conclusions.

2. System Architecture

Violin is a virtual I/O framework that provides (i) support for easy and incremental extensions to I/O hierarchies and (ii) a highly configurable virtualization stack that combines basic storage layers in rich virtual I/O hierarchies. *Violin*'s location in the kernel context is shown in Figure 1, illustrating the I/O path from the user applications to the disks. The architecture of *Violin* is driven by four main concerns: (i) High-level virtualization semantics and mappings, (ii) Generic and extensible in-band command API, (iii) Simple in-band control over the I/O command path and (iv) Metadata state persistence. Next we discuss each of these aspects in more detail.

2.1 Virtualization Semantics

A virtual storage hierarchy is generally represented by a *directed acyclic graph* (DAG). In this graph, the vertices or *nodes* represent *virtual devices*. The directed edges between nodes signify *device dependencies* and *control flow* through I/O requests. Control in *Violin* flows from higher to lower layers. This

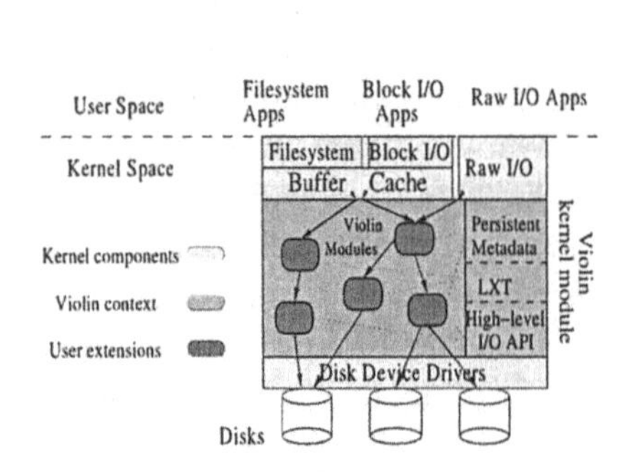

Figure 1. Violin in the operating system context.

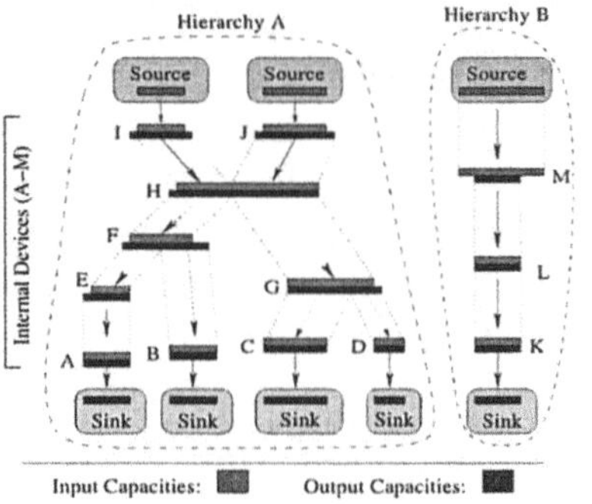

Figure 2. Violin's virtual device graph.

arises from the traditional view of the block-level device as a dumb passive device. Each virtual device in the DAG is operated by a virtualization module that implements the desired functionality. Virtual devices that provide the same functionality are handled by different instances of the same module. From now on, we will use the terms module and device interchangeably.

Figure 2 shows an example of such a device graph. Graph nodes are represented with horizontal bars illustrating the mappings of their address spaces and they are connected with directed vertices. There are three kinds of nodes and accordingly three kinds of I/O modules in the architecture:

- *Source nodes* that do not have incoming edges and are top-level devices that *initiate I/O requests* in the storage hierarchy. The requests are initiated by external kernel components such as file systems or other block-level storage applications. Each of the source devices has an external name, e.g. an entry in `/dev` for Unix systems.

- *Sink* nodes that do not have outgoing edges and correspond to bottom-level virtual devices. Sink nodes sit on top of other kernel block-level drivers (external to *Violin*), such as hardware disk drivers and, in practice, are the final recipients of *Violin*'s I/O requests.

- *Internal* nodes that have both incoming and outgoing edges and provide virtualization functions. These nodes are not visible to external drivers, kernel components, or user applications.

Violin uses the above generic DAG representation to model its hierarchies. A *virtual hierarchy* is defined as a set of connected nodes in the device graph that do not have links to nodes outside the hierarchy. A hierarchy within a device graph is a self-contained sub-graph that can be configured and managed independently of other hierarchies in the same system. *Violin* hierarchies are device container objects that are explicitly created before virtual devices (nodes) are added to them.

To manage devices and hierarchies, users may specify the following operations on the device graph: (i) Create a new internal, source, or sink node and link it to the appropriate nodes, depending on its type. (ii) Delete a node from the graph, or (iii) Change an edge in the graph (i.e. remap a device).

Violin checks the integrity of a hierarchy at creation time and each time it is reconstructed. Checking for integrity includes various simple rules, such as the presence of cycles in the hierarchy graph and lack of input or output edges in internal nodes. Creating hierarchies and checking dependencies reduces the complexity of each *Violin* module.

A hierarchy in *Violin* is constructed amd/or dynamically modified with simple user-level tools implementing the above graph operations and linking the source and sink nodes to external OS block devices.

2.1.1 Dynamic Block Mapping and Allocation. Nodes in a hierarchy graph do not simply show output dependencies from one device to another but rather map between block address spaces of these devices. As can be seen in Figure 2, a storage device in the system represents a specific storage capacity and a block address space, while the I/O path in the graph represents a series of translations between block address spaces. *Violin* provides transparent and persistent translation between device address spaces in virtual hierarchies.

Devices in a virtual hierarchy may have widely different requirements for mapping semantics. Some devices, such as RAID-0, use simple mapping semantics, where blocks are mapped statically between the input and output devices. There are, however, modules that require more complex mappings. For instance, providing snapshots at the block level, requires arbitrary translations and dynamic block remappings [5]. Similarly, volume managers [10] require arbitrary block mappings to support volume resizing and data migration between devices. Another use of arbitrary mappings is to change the device allocation policy, for instance, to a log-structured policy. The Logical Disk [3] uses dynamic block remapping for this purpose.

Violin supports dynamic block mapping through a logical-to-physical block address translation table (LXT) mapping between the input and output address spaces of a device [6]. Dynamic block mapping capabilities give to a virtual device the freedom to use its own disk space management mechanisms and policies, without changing the semantics of its input devices, higher in the I/O stack.

2.2 Generic In-band Command API

The second significant aspect of *Violin* is easy support for definition and handling of generic I/O commands on *Violin*'s devices. Every request in the system (internal or external) is serviced through a series of I/O commands which are handled by *Violin* devices. Control and data I/O requests are handled in the same manner, using the same in-band command mechanism for data and control propagation in virtual hierarchies.

The two main design goals for *Violin*'s I/O command definition were (i) to make commands as generic as possible and (ii) to allow arbitrary stacking of command-handling devices to create hierarchies. We believe that these are necessary properties for a flexible and extensible storage framework supporting a wide range of storage functionality. A command definition in *Violin* consists of three main parts: (i) a command opcode unique across all devices and used to specify the command type, (ii) a pointer to the command data in memory and (iii) a pointer to a block-map data structure. The purpose and usage of a block-map will be discussed later in this section.

2.2.1 Basic commands vs. extended commands. *Violin* I/O commands can be categorized, depending on their scope, to basic and extended. Basic commands, such as read and write, need to be defined, "understood", and serviced across the entire hierarchy by all devices in the I/O path, as well as by the core framework code for internal purposes. They do not need, however, to be implemented in the core framework itself, but are implemented by all *Violin* modules. The most obvious examples of basic commands are the common read and write commands, which perform block I/O through all devices in the system and need to be understood by every device in a hierarchy. They are also used by devices and by the framework code itself, for example to read and write metadata to disk. Note, however that every device has its own private handler of the basic I/O command, which in turn relies on the corresponding command handlers of lower devices in the hierarchy graph. Thus, even though each device is able to "see" and thus, reference only the block addresses of its directly-underlying device(s), as requests propagate in the hierarchy the addresses of the blocks they reference are translated, one device at a time. In this manner, every request corresponding to a basic command passes through a path in the graph following the chain of command handlers from every device in the graph to the next. In case of multiple output edges, edge selection is handled by the corresponding command handlers in the multi-output devices. Finally, for reasons of module simplicity, *Violin* allows the definition of default basic command handlers, which can be used by simple layers which need the default edge-selection and block-mapping behavior.

The second type of I/O commands, extended commands, are defined and handled only by individual devices and their modules. An extended command needs only to be understood by a subset of the devices in a hierarchy. A request concerning a private command will be issued only to specific devices in a hierarchy that are able to "understand" it. Thus, contrary to basic commands

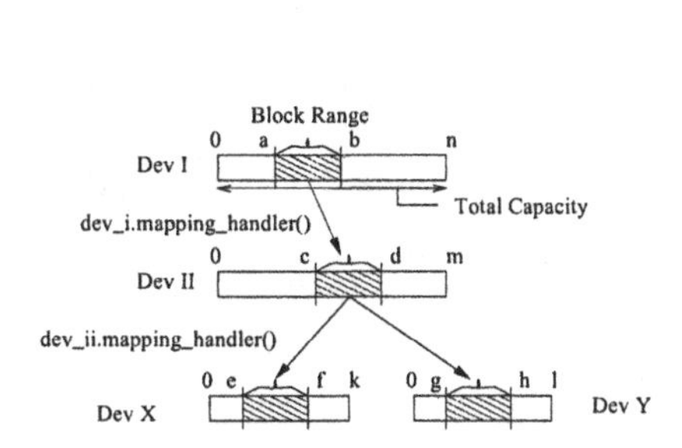

Figure 3. Block-range mapping process through a hierarchy.

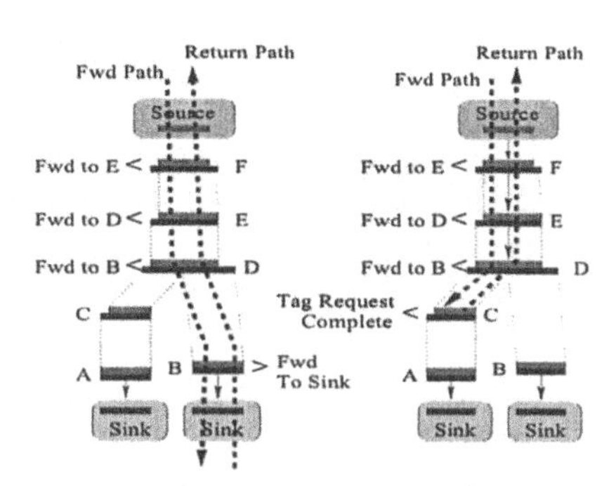

Figure 4. Example of request flows (dashed lines) through devices. Forward paths are directed downwards, while return paths upwards.

whose existence is inherently known by all devices, a device's extended commands need to register themselves to a *Violin* hierarchy at device initialization. Extended commands are much easier for the module developer to implement compared to basic ones, however they raise two important issues for the *Violin* hierarchy model: (i) routing decisions and (ii) block-mapping of arguments.

2.2.2 Handling extended commands. *Violin* allows arbitrary placement of devices when creating a hierarchy, let us consider a private command registered by a layer placed low in a hierarchy. External application requests issuing this extended command will have to traverse the graph passing through higher devices to reach the specific device. However, in contrast to basic commands, these higher devices do not know how to handle the extended command and are not able to make routing decisions for the next device in the graph (edge-selection). Furthermore, *Violin* is not able to translate the block addresses of a request directly to a low-level device, since each layer is able to reference only the block addresses of its directly-underlying layer(s). Thus, in the case when block addresses are necessary as command arguments in order to satisfy an extended command belonging to a lower-level device, the framework needs to map block addresses to the address-space of the corresponding device which may be placed anywhere in a hierarchy.

Violin's approach to both these issues is to provide block-mapping facilities to all devices in a hierarchy, independent of their location in the stack. More specifically, *Violin* allows layers to specify private commands as being either "block-mapped" or "regular" private commands. These two types of private commands have different routing and block-mapping behavior. Regular commands have two properties: (i) no dependence on block addresses and (ii) simple routing semantics, that is they simply need a graph traversal through edges to the target devices. To our experience, these properties can be found in the majority of extended commands defined in storage layers. *Violin* handles regular commands by traversing the device graph and using the command definition table to find the target device(s). If a path traversal reaches a "sink" node in the graph, and no target device has been found, *Violin* responds with an error to the command.

"Block-mapped" extended commands have more complex semantics. They need specific route selection through higher-level devices and/or block address translation since block addresses are part of the command's arguments. Such commands are subject to translation of arguments that represent block-ranges and device selection. This is achieved by augmenting each layer, i.e., extending the layer API, with a block-mapping API call, `block_map()`. This call is written by module developers for every module that is loaded in an *Violin* hierarchy and translates an input block-range to any output block-range(s) on one or more output devices as shown in Figure 3. Thus, *Violin*'s block-mapping API deals both with routing through the device graph and block address remapping.

2.3 Violin I/O Request Path

Another significant aspect of *Violin* is how the I/O request path works, that is how I/O commands are issued and how they flow through the framework. *Violin* is not only reentrant but also supports synchronous and asynchronous requests. I/O requests never block in the framework, unless a driver module has explicitly requested it. Moreover, since *Violin* is reentrant, it runs in the issuer's context for each request issued from the kernel. Thus, many requests can proceed concurrently in the framework, each in a different context.

A generic virtual storage framework must support two types of I/O requests:

- *External requests* are initiated by the kernel. They enter the framework through the source devices (nodes), traverse a hierarchy through internal nodes usually until they reach a sink node and then return back up the same path to the top of the hierarchy.

- *Internal requests* are generated from internal devices as a response to an external request. Consider for example a RAID-5 module that needs to write parity blocks. The RAID-5 device generates an internal write request to the parity device. Internal requests are indistinguishable from external ones for all but the generating module and are handled in the same manner.

Command requests in *Violin* move from source to sink nodes through some path in a virtual hierarchy, as shown in Figure 4. Sink devices are connected to external block devices in the kernel, so after a request reaches a sink device it is forwarded to an external device. As mentioned previously, when multiple output nodes exist, routing decisions are taken at every node, according to its mapping semantics. Virtual devices can control requests beyond simple forwarding. When a device receives an I/O request it can make four control decisions and set corresponding control tags on a request:

- *Error Tag* indicates a request error. Erroneous requests are returned through the stack to the issuer with an error code.
- *Forward Tag* indicates that the request should be forwarded to an output device. In this case, the target device and block address must also be indicated. Forwarding occurs to the direction of one of the output graph vertices.
- *Return Control Path Tag* indicates that a device needs return path control over the request. Some devices need to know when an asynchronous I/O request has completed and need control over its return path through the hierarchy (Figure 4). For instance, an encryption module requires access to the return path of a read request, because data needs to be decrypted after it is read from the sink device.
- *Complete Tag* indicates that a request is completed by a device. Consider the example of a caching module in the hierarchy. If a requested data block is found in the cache, the device loads the data in the request buffer and sets the "complete" tag. The completed request is not forwarded deeper in the hierarchy, but returns from this point upwards to the issuer as shown at the right of Figure 4 for device C.

A final issue with requests flowing through the framework, is dependencies between requests. For instance, there are cases where a module requires an external request to wait for one or more internal requests to complete. To deal with this, when an internal request X is issued (asynchronously) the issuer module may register one or more dependences of X to other requests (Y, Z, ...) and provide asynchronous callback functions. Requests X, Y, Z are processed concurrently and when each completes the callback handler is called. The callback handler of the module then processes the dependent requests according to the desired ordering (i.e. it may wait for all or a few requests to finish before releasing them). This mechanism supports arbitrary dependencies among multiple requests.

2.4 State Persistence

State persistence is an essential property of storage stacks. Storage layers that offer advanced functionality require dynamic block mappings with metadata of significant size. Thus, a generic extensible framework for layered storage such as *Violin* must support advanced metadata management facilities. The three main issues associated with metadata are: facilitating the use of persistent metadata, reducing memory footprint, and providing consistency guarantees.

2.4.1 Persistent Metadata. In *Violin*, modules can allocate and manage persistent metadata objects of varying sizes using a unique object ID and the requested object size, as it would allocate memory.

Violin's metadata manager automatically synchronizes dirty metadata from memory to stable storage in a lazy manner. The metadata manager uses a separate kernel thread to write to the appropriate device, all in-memory metadata. The user can also flush metadata objects explicitly using a flush call. This is for example necessary for the versioning layer, which needs to ensure metadata stability before creating new snapshots.

Internally, each metadata object is represented with an object descriptor, which is modified only by allocation/deallocation calls. During these calls metadata object descriptors are stored in a small index in the beginning of the metadata device. A pointer to the metadata header index is stored with each virtual device in the virtual hierarchy. Thus, when the virtual hierarchy is being loaded and recreated, *Violin* reads the device metadata and loads it to memory.

2.4.2 Metadata Consistency. In the event of system failures, where a portion of the in-memory metadata may be lost or partially written, application and/or *Violin* state may be corrupted. We can define the following levels of metadata consistency:

Lazy-update consistency, that is, metadata are synchronized on disk overwriting the older version every few seconds. This means that if a failure occurs between or during updates of metadata then metadata may be left inconsistent on-disk and *Violin* may not be able to recover. In this case, there is a need for a *Violin*-level recovery procedure (similar to `fsck` at the filesystem level), which however, we do not currently provide. If stronger guarantees are required then one of the next forms of consistency may be used instead.

Shadow-update consistency, where we use two metadata copies on disk and maintain at least one of the two consistent at all times. If during an update the set that is currently being written becomes inconsistent due to a failure, *Violin* uses the second copy to recover. In this case, it is guaranteed that *Violin* will recover the device hierarchy and all its persistent objects and will be able to service I/O requests. However, application data may be inconsistent with respect to system metadata.

Atomic versioned-metadata consistency, guarantees that after a failure, the system will be able to see a previous, consistent version of application data and system metadata. Thus, this is equivalent to a rollback to a previous point in time. In *Violin* this can be achieved by using a versioning layer [5] at the leaves of a hierarchy. Although such a layer is available in *Violin*, its current implementation would need slight modifications so that its own metadata are handled differently in this particular case.

Violin currently supports the first and second forms of metadata consistency. We expect that all three forms of consistency will be available in the future releases of the framework code.

2.5 Module API

Extending an I/O hierarchy with new functionality is an arduous task in modern kernels. The interface provided by kernels for block I/O is fairly low-level. A block device driver has the role of servicing block I/O `read` and `write` requests. Block requests adhere to the simple block I/O API, where every request is denoted as a tuple of `(block device,read/write,block number,block size,data)`. In Linux, this API involves many tedious and error prone tasks, such as I/O request queue management, locking and synchronization of the I/O request queues, buffer management, translating block addresses and interfacing with the buffer cache and the VM subsystem.

Violin provides to its modules high-level API calls, that intuitively support its hierarchy model and hide the complexity of kernel programming. The author of a module must set up a *module object,* which consists of a small set of variables with the attributes of the implemented module and a set of methods or API functions. More details on the module API can be found in [6].

2.6 System Implementation

We have implemented *Violin* as a loadable block device driver in the Linux 2.4 and 2.6 kernel versions, accompanied by a set of simple user-level management tools. Our prototype implements fully the I/O path model described in Section 2.5. *Violin* extension modules are implemented as separate kernel modules that are loaded on demand. However, they are not full Linux device drivers themselves but require the framework's core. Upon loading, each module registers with the core framework module, binding its methods to internal *module objects*. The overhead of *Violin* is relatively small: benchmarks results are always within 10% of those achieved by monolithic drivers [6].

3. Advanced Virtualization Scenarios

In this section we describe some advanced virtualization scenarios where using *Violin* would greatly reduce the time and effort to develop the required storage functionalities. Note that, currently, we do not have fully implemented all these usage examples, but we present their design as *Violin* modules. In particular we present three virtualization scenarios: (i) dual-path fail-over and

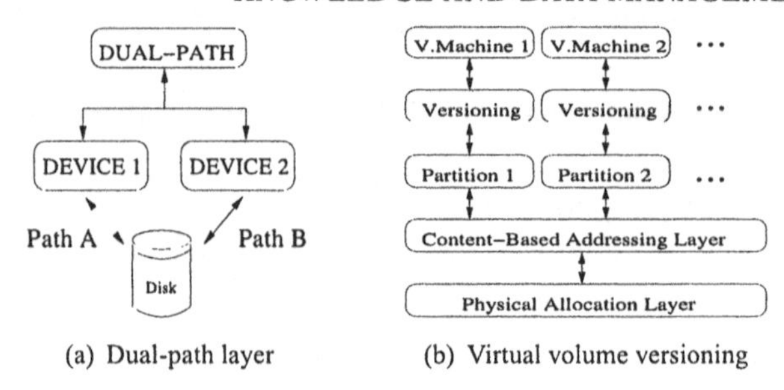

(a) Dual-path layer (b) Virtual volume versioning

Figure 5. A dual-path layer for fail-over and load-balancing and a volume versioning and consolidation layer for virtual machines.

dynamic load-balancing, (ii) volume sharing services: free-block allocation and locking, (iii) volume versioning for virtual machines.

3.1 Fail-over and Load-balancing

A dual-path module provides fault-tolerance and/or dynamic load-balancing functionality. As shown in Figure 5(a), the module has a single input and two output devices. Using internal metadata, which need not be necessarily persistent, this layer balances the load between two paths to the same device and in case one of the paths fails, it sends all requests through the working one. This is a very useful function for remote storage devices (accessed for instance through iSCSI), where each path passes through an independent network path (switches, cables, etc.). In the event of a network failure this layer easily performs fail-over to the working path. Such a layer is very easy to implement using *Violin*, since the path configuration functionality is built in. Thus the fail-over operation of the module amounts simply to selecting a different device in case it receives errors through one of the paths. Load-balancing functionality is also simple to implement, keeping some response statistics to make routing decisions for sending requests through the two paths.

3.2 Volume Sharing

Sharing virtual volumes between many user applications requires coordinating (i) accesses to data and, as mentioned above, metadata via mutual exclusion and (ii) allocation and deallocation of storage space. To facilitate such sharing, *Violin* can incorporate block-level locking and allocation mechanisms, designed and implemented as optional, separate virtual modules. This essentially makes locking and allocation in-band operations, eliminating out-of-band services that are commonly used in file systems. The locking mechanism is integrated in the virtual hierarchies as an optional virtual module and may be used by *Violin* devices to lock shared metadata or by applications that share data at the block-level. Both kinds of modules can be inserted at various (and possibly multiple) places in a virtual hierarchy according to the needs of a given application.

3.2.1 Block-range locking. *Violin* can provide support for block-range locking over a block volume. The main metadata in the locking layer is a free-list that contains the *unlocked* ranges of the managed virtual volume. When a lock control request arrives, the locking layer uses its internal metadata to either complete or block the request. At an unlock request the locking layer updates its metadata and possibly unblocks and completes a previous pending lock request. The locking API should support multiple-reader, single-writer locks in both blocking and non-blocking modes.

To achieve mutual exclusion, locks for a specific range of blocks should be serviced by a single locking virtual layer. This is achieved by placing locking layers at specific points in the hierarchy. Multiple layers may be used for servicing different block ranges. Thus, load balancing lock requests across multiple devices is simplified.

Lock and unlock requests are block-mapped commands (see Section 2.2). This allows us to distribute the locking layers to any desirable serialization point in a hierarchy. Note that the metadata of a locking layer does not need to be persistent. Instead, we use a lease-based mechanism to reclaim locks from a failed application.

3.2.2 Block allocation. The role of a block allocator module is to handle block management in a consistent manner for applications sharing the same block volume. The allocator distributes free blocks to the applications and maintains a consistent view of used and free blocks. All such block-liveness information is maintained by the allocator, offloading all the potentially complex free-block handling code from higher system and application layers.

The allocator metadata for managing free blocks consist of free-lists and bitmaps to handle blocks of various sizes, which are kept consistent by using the persistent metadata locking primitives. Frequent locking at fine granularity will result in high allocation overheads. To address this issue we can amortize the overhead associated with locking metadata by dividing the available (block) address space of a shared volume in a sufficiently large number of allocation zones. Each zone is independent and has its own metadata, which can be locked and cached in memory when using this particular zone.

The metadata of locked zones are automatically synchronized to stable storage, similarly to all other module metadata in *Violin*, in two occasions: (i) periodically every few seconds and (ii) when a zone is unlocked and its metadata released from the cache.

3.3 Optimized storage support for virtual machine images

Nowadays, there is a growing resort to (system-level) virtual machines (VM) in the context of data centers. They have proven to be a useful tool to address needs such as server consolidation, interoperability, and flexible administration (e.g. time and space mobility). As a consequence, a farm of servers may now host thousands of different operating system images, which raises concerns regarding the scalability of the underlying (shared) storage system.

It has been observed that a VM image store exhibits a set of specific properties [11]. In particular, (i) there is no write sharing for a given image, (ii) block-level snapshots are used extensively, and (iii) different VM images (and different snapshots of a given image) have many blocks in common.

By combining modules implementing different features such as versioning, content-based addressing and (virtual and physical) space allocation, we could obtain such a suitable VM image block store. Figure 5(b) illustrates the structure of such a storage system on a single node. The modular nature of Violin facilitates the integration of multiple virtualization semantics. In this example, copy-on-write techniques are used both at the level of the per-VM versioning layer and at the level of the (shared) content-based addressing module, to achieve good performance and space efficiency.

4. Related Work

Violin is related to previous on (a) extensible filesystems, (b) extensible network protocols, and (c) block-level storage virtualization. In the latter area, the two most advanced open-source volume managers currently are EVMS and GEOM. EVMS [4], is a user-level distributed volume manager for Linux, which supports user-level plugins. However, it does not offer persistent metadata or block remapping primitives to these plugins. Moreover, EVMS focuses on configuration flexibility with predefined storage semantics (e.g. RAID levels) and does not easily allow generic extensions (e.g. versioning). GEOM [7] is a stackable BIO subsystem for FreeBSD. The concepts behind it are, to our knowledge, the closest to *Violin*. However, GEOM does not support persistent metadata which, combined with dynamic block mapping are necessary for advanced modules such as versioning [5]. *Violin* has all the configuration and flexibility features of a volume manager coupled with the ability to write extension modules with arbitrary virtualization semantics.

For a detailed discussion of all related work, please refer to [6].

5. Conclusions

In this work we present *Violin*, a virtualization framework for block-level disk storage and the motivation behind it. *Violin* allows easy extensions to the block I/O hierarchy with new mechanisms and flexible combining of these mechanisms to create modular hierarchies with rich semantics.

To demonstrate its effectiveness we implement *Violin* within the Linux operating system and provide several I/O modules. In previous work [6], we have showed that *Violin* significantly reduces implementation efforts. For instance, in cases where user-level library code is available, new *Violin* modules can be implemented within a few hours. Finally, the performance overhead of *Violin* over traditional, monolithic drivers and driver-based hierarchies, is within 10% of their counterparts [6].

Overall, we find that our approach provides adequate support for embedding powerful mechanisms in the storage I/O stack with manageable effort and small performance overhead. We believe that *Violin* is a concrete step towards supporting advanced storage virtualization, reducing storage management overheads and complexity, and building self-managed storage systems.

Acknowledgments

We thankfully acknowledge the support of Natural Sciences and Engineering Research Council of Canada, Canada Foundation for Innovation, Ontario Innovation Trust, the Nortel Institute of Technology, Nortel Networks, the General Secretariat of Research and Technology, Greece and the support of the European FP6-IST program through the SIVSS project and the CoreGRID Network of Excellence.

References

[1] A. Acharya et al. Active Disks: Programming Model, Algorithms and Evaluation. In *Proc. of the 8th ACM ASPLOS Conference*, San Jose, CA, 1998.

[2] M. de Icaza et al. The linux raid-1,-4,-5 code. In Proc. of *LinuxExpo*, Apr. 1997.

[3] W. de Jonge et al. The Logical Disk: A New Approach to Improving File Systems. In *Proc. of 14th ACM Symp. on Operating Syst. Principles*, 1993.

[4] Enterprise Volume Management System. http://evms.sourceforge.net.

[5] M. D. Flouris et al. Clotho: Transparent Data Versioning at the Block I/O Level. In *21st IEEE Conference on Mass Storage Systems and Technologies*, Apr. 2004.

[6] M. D. Flouris and A. Bilas. Violin: A Framework for Extensible Block-level Storage. In *Proc. of 13th IEEE Conf. on Mass Storage Systems and Technologies*, Apr. 2005.

[7] FreeBSD: GEOM Modular Disk I/O Request Transformation Framework.

[8] G. A. Gibson et al. A Cost-Effective, High-Bandwidth Storage Architecture. In *Proc. of the 8th ACM ASPLOS Conference*, San Jose, CA, 1998.

[9] B. Phillips. Industry Trends: Have Storage Area Networks Come of Age? *Computer*, 31(7):10–12, July 1998.

[10] D. Teigland et al. Volume managers in linux. In *Proc. of USENIX Tech. Conference*, June 2001.

[11] A. Warfield et al.. Parallax: Managing Storage for a Million Machines In *Proc. of the USENIX Workshop on Hot Topics in Operating Systems*, June 2005.

CLUSTERIX DATA MANAGEMENT SYSTEM (CDMS) – ARCHITECTURE AND USE CASES *

Konrad Karczewski and Lukasz Kuczynski
Institute of Computer and Information Sciences
Czestochowa University of Technology
{xeno, lkucz}@icis.pcz.pl

Abstract Nowadays grid applications process large volumes of data. This creates the need for an effective data-management solutions. For the ClusteriX project the CDMS (ClusteriX Data Management System) is being developed. Analysis of user requirements and existing implementations of a Data Management System have been the foundations for its creation. Special attention has been paid to make the system user-friendly and efficient.

Taking into account grid specific networking conditions, for example different bandwidth, current load and network technologies, between geographically distant sites, CDMS tries to optimize data throughput via replication and replica selection techniques. Another key feature to be considered during grid service implementation is fault-tolerance. In the CDMS modular design and distributed operation model assures single point of failure elimination. In particular multiple instances of Data Broker are running simultaneously and their coherence is assured by a synchronization subsystem.

Keywords: data management, data safety, replication, fault-tolerance, GRMS.

*This work has been supported by the Polish Ministry of Science and Information Society Technologies under grant 6T11 2003C/06098 "ClusteriX - National Cluster of Linux Systems".

1. Introduction

Data management issues are amongst the most important in modern grid environment [1, 13]. As the applications being run on grids become more real-life oriented, they generate or depend on data sets of growing importance and confidentiality.

One of the principal goals of data management systems in grids is to provide transparent and efficient access to globally distributed data [1]. Among the most important issues that need to be solved are: optimization of the data transfers over the WAN, reliability and security of data access and ease of use [8].

The most frequently encountered approach to solving these problems is based on application of metadata and mechanism of data replication [2, 11]. Metadata are used, e.g., for the translation of a logical filename to its physical location. The replication mechanism should provide optimization of data access and reliability. An example of a modern data management system based on the above-mentioned mechanisms is the Reptor system [10], developed as a part of the EU DataGrid Project. Being one of the most advanced grid data management systems, it still does not provide full transparency, and is difficult to use. Its other shortcomings are: the lack of mechanisms of adaptation to the network infrastructure, and presence of single points of failure, e.g., single Metadata Repository.

ClusteriX (National Cluster of Linux Systems) is a distributed national computing infrastructure with 12 sites (local Linux clusters based on 64-bit Itanium2 processors) located across Poland [3, 14]. ClusteriX sites are connected by the Polish Optical Network PIONIER providing a dedicated communication infrastructure. This paper presents our experience in building the ClusteriX Data Management System (CDMS) its architecture and use cases [9].

The paper is organized as follows. In Section 2, we introduce the base requirements placed on the Data Management System while the CDMS architecture minutes are presented in Section 3. Section 4 is devoted to system interface, while Sections 5 and 6 describe respectively the integration of CDMS with end-user applications and the GRMS Resource Broker. The paper finishes with conclusions in Section 7.

2. Data Management System

A modern Data Management system should be implemented with the following features in mind: transparent access, reliability, security and safety of transferred and stored data, access control, possibility of transparent data compression and access optimisation.

The development of an intuitive and effective data access and system administration toolkit was seen as an equally important task. It is particularly necessary when the end-user is not expected to be aware of the low-level mechanisms and in the CDMS an Virtual File System (VFS) abstraction layer was implemented, creating an illusion of working with a local file system.

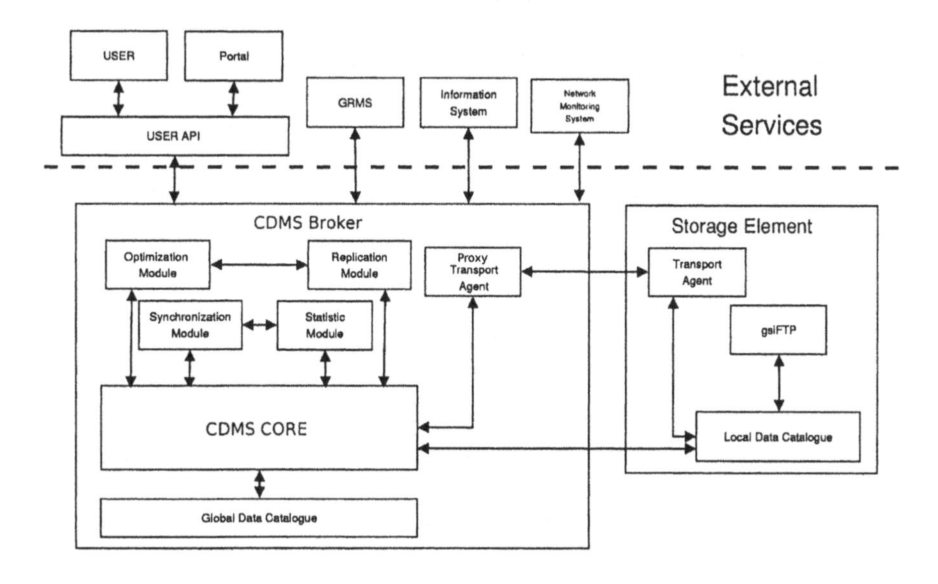

Figure 1. Architecture of the CDMS.

2.1 Transparent Data Access

Data access mechanisms should be implemented as a layer between client application and Data Management System. Such an approach allows to hide low–level mechanisms and improve them without the need for rewriting end–user application. This, in addition to a well–designed API, provides developers and scientists with a stable platform for Grid–oriented development. Moreover, the end–users can utilize latest functionality without any modifications to their software.

Moreover, this approach allows for modular design of the Data Access System which in turn makes possible fast delivery of a basic functional version of the system and further development of its parts with no disturbances to the functional part. For example this may allow for implementation of "intelligent data access" functionality and "plugging it in" on selected distributed systems which will provide the necessary infrastructure (e.g. multiple, geographically distant Data Storage Elements).

2.2 Data access optimisation

A modern Data Management System should provide data access optimisation mechanisms. The main task of this subsystem is choosing the most suitable data location to use, taking into account multiple factors, such as:

- available resources on the storage elements
- network properties:
  - bandwidth
  - topology
  - current throughput
- user access permissions

Additionally to improve effectiveness and minimise data access time data partitioning mechanism (splitting into smaller parts) could be used. In such case Data Broker would decide on partitioning of the file and then it would search optimal locations for the parts. Every part would be replicated in several locations to minimise chance of losing the data in case of a failure. Such solution, besides improving the system fault-tolerance, would as well improve data access time by copying several parts in parallel from different locations. Not without value is fact that this storage method increases security of the stored data. To provide correct data reconstruction metadata stored in the metadata server would have to contain information allowing proper rebuilding of a file.

2.3 Reliability

Reliability is one of the most important aspects of the Data Management System. The following basic functionalities are required:

- improving fault–tolerance of the system by providing Data Replication mechanism
- automation and control by the Data Broker assures maximum transparency

Increase of reliability level could be accomplished by elimination of the single–point–of–failure. The basic way of achieving this is implementation of a distributed Data Broker Service. This implies:

- automated control takeover in case of failure
- metadata replication and synchronisation
- distributed metadata server
- heartbeat mechanism

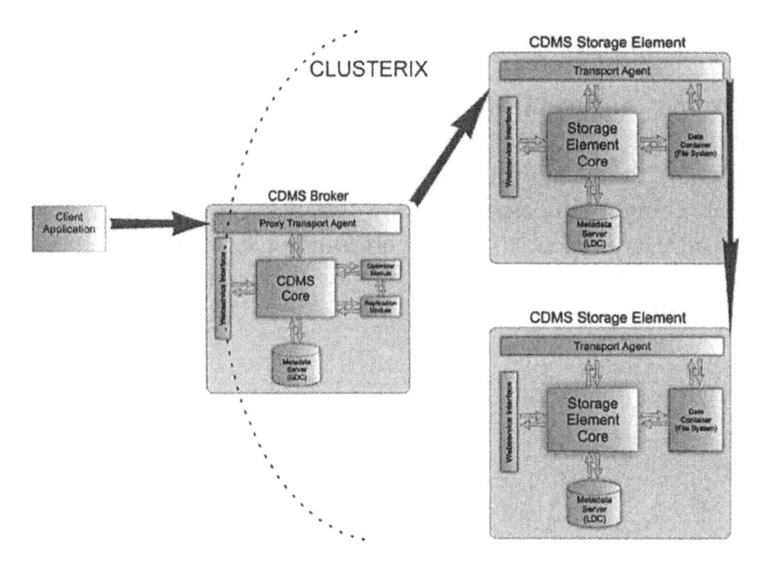

Figure 2. Chain Transfer

2.4 Security and Safety of Data

To provide required level of security, the Data Management System must include:

- user authentication and authorisation (e.g. GSI based)
- data encryption possibility
- permissions delegation (single–sign–on)

To improve data safety the following mechanisms could be implemented:

- Access Control Lists embedded in the metadata
- Data partitioning (only a part of data is available on each storage element)
- dataset name transformation (e.g. md5)

2.4.1 Access Control Lists. Access Control Lists allow to manage access to resources, constrain users' rights and manage visibility of data. When every part of the Data Management system will be capable of using ACLs the security of the stored data can be managed according to user demands. The data available to every member of a given community or even every user of the Grid would be advertised and visible to everyone requesting it. This may include scientific papers, results of community founded research, conference materials, tutorials and such. Data considered available for anyone willing to pay for it may be advertised, but it will be accessible only to users authorised by its owner. Finally the confidential data would be invisible for anyone but its owner and the authorised users.

To allow for such a functionality the ACLs must be included in the metadata and properly understood by the Metadata Server. The Data Broker uses delegated user credentials while performing user–requested operations. This allows to control the metadata operations commited by the Data Broker on users behalf.

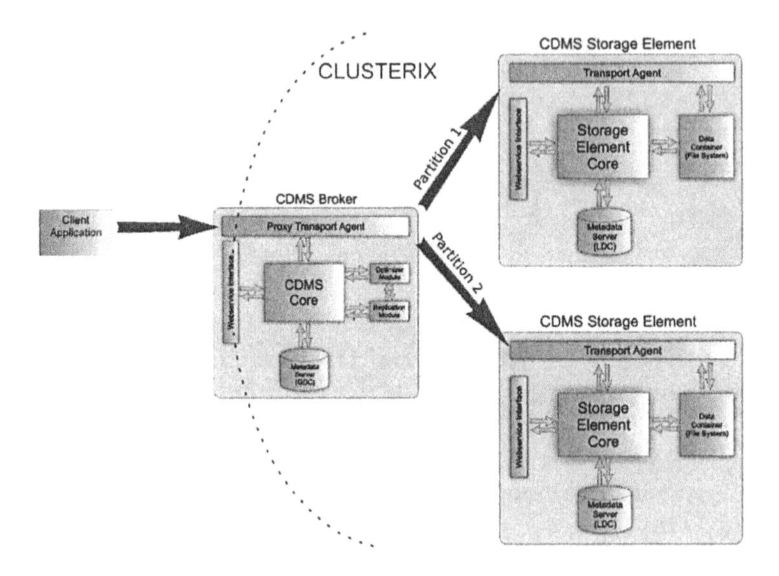

Figure 3. Data Partitioning

2.4.2 Data Partitioning. Data Partitioning enables increased data security, since no Storage Element holds complete data and the partitioning information is available only to Data Broker. Furthermore it is possible to accommodate part size to the space available to the user on a given storage element which provides for better usage of the storage space.

In addition to the improvement in data security, data partitioning increases the performance of the Data Management system by allowing parallel transmission of multiple parts of the data set from different Storage Elements. Moreover it enables load balancing between Storage Elements and eliminates bottlenecks that would occur if data were not partitioned and a single Storage element received a request for a large data set. Currently such a request will be directed to multiple Storage Elements storing parts of the data.

Data Partitioning Mechanism functioning consist of two parts: storing the data in the system and its retrieval on user's demand. The first part consists of the following steps:

- client authenticates and authorises in the GSI subsystem
- new dataset is registered in the Data Broker
- Data Broker:
  - decides on partitioning of the dataset and searches for the optimal locations
  - digests the dataset name
  - encrypts and splits the data (if required) and stores the parts on the Storage Elements
  - updates the Metadata Server information

Upon successful completion of this sequence user's data is stored in the system and by default visible only to its owner. This prevents the possibility of accidentally leaving data prone to unauthorised retrieval by a forgetful user or by a network failure preventing the owner from finishing the access control setup. Access permissions may be specified in the data storage request if necessary.

Data retrieval operates in a reverse manner from the data storage process:

- Client authenticates and authorises in the GSI subsystem and requests data retrieval using dataset name
- Data Broker:
  - digests the dataset name and checks user's rights in the Metadata Server
  - retrieves the partitioning information and chooses the optimal Storage Elements for data retrieval
  - retrieves parts of the dataset, reunites files, decrypts and transfers it to the requested location

2.5 Distributed Data Broker

To ensure stable operation of the Grid environment the elimination of a single–point–of–failure is a critical task. Data Management System as one of its most important subsystems must be well–protected from the possibility of a breakdown in case of a computer system or network failure. Implementation of a distributed Data Broker service is crucial to achieving such an immunity.

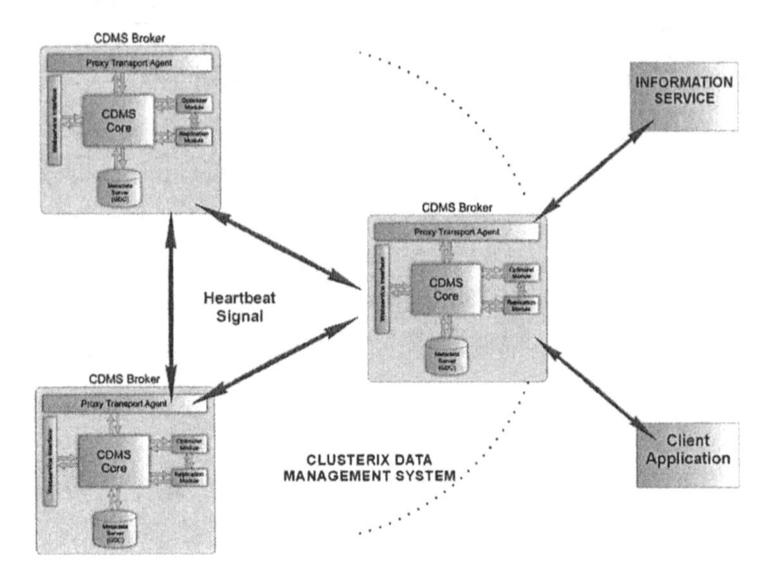

Figure 4. Distributed Broker Architecture

The proposed solution makes use of an Information System. The user agent queries IS for the Data Broker location, receives current Primary Data Broker address and continues communication with the Data Broker.

When the Primary Data Broker becomes unavailable because of a system or network failure the Synchronisation Subsystem detects the problem and the Secondary Data Broker takes over Primary Broker functions and updates IS record about its parameters. When the original Primary Data Broker gets reconnected it starts operation as the last one in the hierarchy and rebuilds its information by querying the up–to–date systems.

3. System Architecture

The architecture of the ClusteriX Data Management System was introduced in [9]. It has a modular design and consists of (Fig. 1):

- Main Management Module (CDMS Core)
- Global Data Catalogue (GDC)
- Local Data Catalogue (LDC)
- Transport Subsystem
- Synchronization Module
- Statistic Module

– Optimization Module

– Replication Module

The main part of the system is the CDMS Core responsible for data collections management, data coherence, running the Optimizer and Replicator processes and data transfer initialization. Using data stored in the Global Data Catalogue, the Main Management Module performs the mappings of logical filenames to the Storage Element holding the data. Proper functioning of the GDC is crucial for reliable operation of the CDMS, which makes replication of this data vital for the entire system.

The responsibility of the Replication Module is to perform data replication on the CDMS Core request. It currently allows for the initial and automatic replication.

The initial replication process consists of three stages: choice of the suitable Storage Elements, replication planning, and the replication itself. Accepting a request for an incoming data transfer – from a user into the CDMS – the Main Management Module queries the Optimization Module for possible locations for the incoming data. Next it takes the first two entries from the returned list, and initiates the parallel data transfer.

The automatic replication is carried out by the Replication Module when the system load is low. It decides upon decreasing or increasing the number of replicas using information provided by the Statistic Module. When the demand for a given dataset increases, the number of replicas is increased as well. When the data are no longer needed, the number of replicas is decreased accordingly by removing the least accessed copies [12].

The main task of the Optimization Module is determining the best data location from available replicas. The application of this module decreases delays in data access and balances the load between Storage Elements. The Optimization Module uses such statistical data as network throughput and performance of Storage Elements, as well as measured values like current network load, system load and available disk space on Storage Elements.

The Transport Subsystem has been introduced to increase the CDMS performance during data transfers. It consists of the Proxy Transport Agents (PTAs) and the Transport Agents (TAs). The PTA is responsible for transferring data between the user and the CDMS. It runs as a standalone process, accepting data transfer requests from the CDMS Core. Such a solution allows the CDMS Core to select the agent located closest (in networking terms) to the served user.

The main task of a TA is transferring data between Storage Element and the Proxy Transport Agents. Data sent by the user to PTA are directed to a suitable TA. The CDMS Core asks the Optimization Module for the suggested data locations, and then it requests the proper TA to perform the required operations.

An important feature of the Transport Subsystem is parallel data transfer between the Proxy Agent and the Transport Agents. It enables data replication in the very moment they enter the Data Management System. Taking into account that the network infrastructure inside ClusteriX core has considerably greater thoroughput than the external network, the overhead generated by the replication is negligible.

3.1 Implementation

The CDMS has been implemented in the C language (Optimisation an Replication Modules excepted) using the gSOAP package [4]. An adequate data transmission security, x509 certificates infrastructure and gsiftp protocol support have been achieved using Globus Toolkit 3.x libraries [5].

In the grid infrastructure based on the Globus Toolkit, users are identified using x509 certificates, which have unique subjects. This fact is the foundation of user namespaces introduced in CDMS, which are named after the subject of an user certificate. This approach eliminates possibility of collisions in file and directory names. Every user in the CDMS system has his own file system root (/) located in his namespace. The Universal Resource Locator (URL) for the CDMS system is defined as follows: `cdms://[user-namespace]/url-path`. The user-namespace part can be omitted, in such case the subject of the certificate used to access the data will be used automatically.

4. System Interface

The access to the system resources is possible via a WebService interface using the SOAP protocol. Such a solution allows to make client applications independent from the operating system and programming language. An example of a CDMS client application is the administrative toolkit implemented in the C language for the Linux/UNIX platform. Another example is the GridSphere portlet, offering a rich user-level access functionality, implemented in the Java language [6].

Every interface function returns a message which consists of two parts. The first one contains the error code and the error message. The second part is strictly dependent on the called function, and contains the relevant data, for example, directory listing. The system interface consists of the end-user and the administrator parts.

The basic functionality of the CDMS is accessible by a set of functions belonging to the end-user interface. They allow user applications to create and remove directories, copy data between CDMS and local file system, list contents of directories, etc. The basic set of user utilities is a part of the CDMS package. They have been deliberately implemented to resemble standard Unix utilities. For example, `clx_ls /` displays contents of a user home directory.

A package of administration utilities has been provided as well. They use the WebService interface to communicate with the CDMS broker. The provided functionality includes: creation and removal of user account, quota manipulation and modification of access control lists.

The CDMS administration will be greatly simplified by a GridSphere portlet which is currently under development. It will allow the system to be administered via a web browser, making this task completely independent from the operating system.

5. Integration of End-User Applications with CDMS

Computational applications can use CDMS directly or indirectly. The most common situation is when an application works with files stored on a local file system. In such case, input files of the application can be staged in from the CDMS, and the results stored in the CDMS during the stage-out phase. This is the "indirect" use, and does not require any modification of the application itself.

Another case is when the application is modified to use the CDMS directly. This involves use of the WebService interface via the SOAP protocol. Additionally any interaction with the CDMS must be authenticated and later encrypted via the GSI layer, so support for this feature is another requirement for the application. After satisfying these requirements, the end-user would be able to request data transfer to and from CDMS during computations.

The general scheme of the application execution is very similar in both cases. First the user places a request to the Resource Broker, e.g. GRMS, specifying resource requirements, input and output data, and providing it with a credential, allowing it to interact on the user behalf with CDMS as well as the local jobmanagers. The Resource Broker selects an appropriate computational resource, requests input data transfer and commits the application to a local job manager. After the computations are finished, the obtained results are retrieved from the local file system and placed in the CDMS. The sole difference is that the CDMS-aware application can fetch additional data during run-time, for example, after assessing results obtained at a specific point of computations. Also, such an application can place partial results in the Data Management System allowing the user to check on the application progress periodically, or use them as the input data for another application.

6. Integration with GRMS

A very important part of the CDMS development was to implement mechanisms of cooperation with the Resource Broker. The final result is almost a complete transparency of this cooperation from the user point of view. The only difference is a modification of the URL. In a basic grid infrastructure data management is based on a ftp server accessed via the gsiftp protocol, and the URLs point to such a server. In a CDMS-enabled infrastructure URLs point to logical file names (Fig.5), which are further resolved by the Data Broker.

```
<grmsjob appid = "demo">
  <simplejob>
     <executable type="single" count="1">
        <file name="exec-file" type="in">
          <url>cdms:///demo.pl</url>
        </file>
     </executable>
  </simplejob>
</grmsjob>
```

Figure 5. Sample job description including CDMS URL. The `demo.pl` file is located in the root directory of the user running this job

The GRMS analyses the job description, and decides whether an initial data transfer is necessary. When the application specifies a remote source of data in a standard grid infrastructure, GRMS is responsible for copying the data via a third-party transfer to a computational resource. With CDMS such a scenario is not possible because the physical data location is unknown. In this case, the GRMS connects to the CDMS Broker and requests the data to be transfered on the designated node.

In the CDMS WebService interface, multiple functions for copying data to computational nodes are defined. For the integration with Resource Brokers, the following functions are designated:

```
1)  enum CopyStatus { COPYING, FINISHED, FAILED };

2)  CopyStatus copyToCEBlocking( string lfn, string url );
3)  CopyStatus copyFromCEBlocking( string lfn, string url );

4)  string copyToCE( string lfn, string url );
5)  string copyFromCE( string lfn, string url );
6)  CopyStatus getCopyStatus( string sid );
```

The blocking functions (2 and 3) require as the parameters the logical file name (URL in CDMS), and external data locations, e.g., URL pointing to the computational resource storage. They return the status of copy operation (FINISHED or FAILED). The non-blocking functions (4 and 5) accept exactly the same parameters as their blocking versions, but they return an unique data transfer session identifier (SID). It can be used to check the current status of a data transfer via the `getCopyStatus` function. It may return one of the states defined in the `CopyStatus` enum. Such an approach allows for the CDMS integration with any Resource Broker.

6.1 Stage-In Scenario

The sequence diagram (Fig.6) presents the CDMS actions during a data transfer request from the Resource Broker.

In the first step, the GRMS decides upon the resource assignment, and requests a data transfer to be performed. At the moment, GRMS uses blocking functions so the `copyToCEBlocking` function will be called (1).

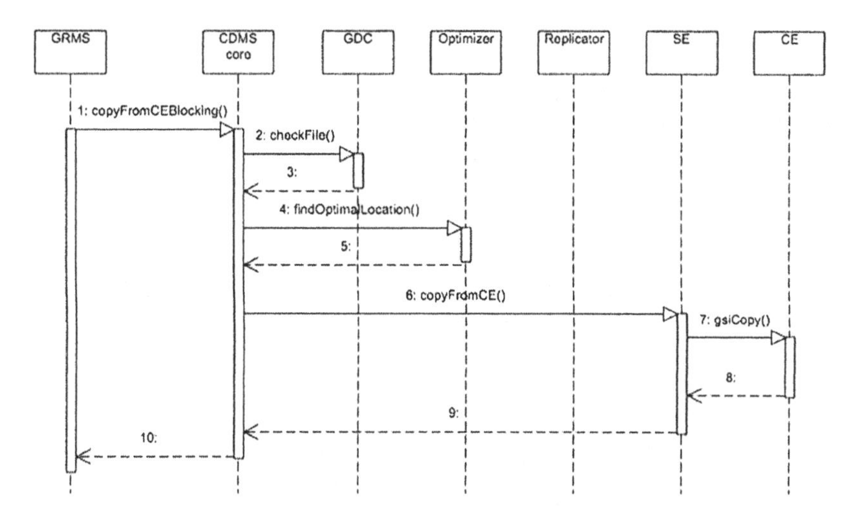

Figure 6. Stage-in sequence diagram

The Management Module of CDMS verifies if the requested file exists in CDMS (2), and calls the Optimization Module to determine the best physical data location to be used (4). The Optimization Module requires, as its input, the destination of requested data, list of Storage Elements holding replicas of the file, and file size. Using these parameters and querying the Network Resource Manager, the Optimization Module orders the list of Storage Elements by feasibility and returns it to the Management Module. The CDMS Broker delegates user credentials (obtained from the GRMS) to the selected Storage Element, and requests it (6) to perform data transfer to a computational resource (7). When this data transfer is finished (or it has failed), the `copyToCEBlocking` function returns (10) with a proper status code, and the GRMS continues with the job preparation and execution.

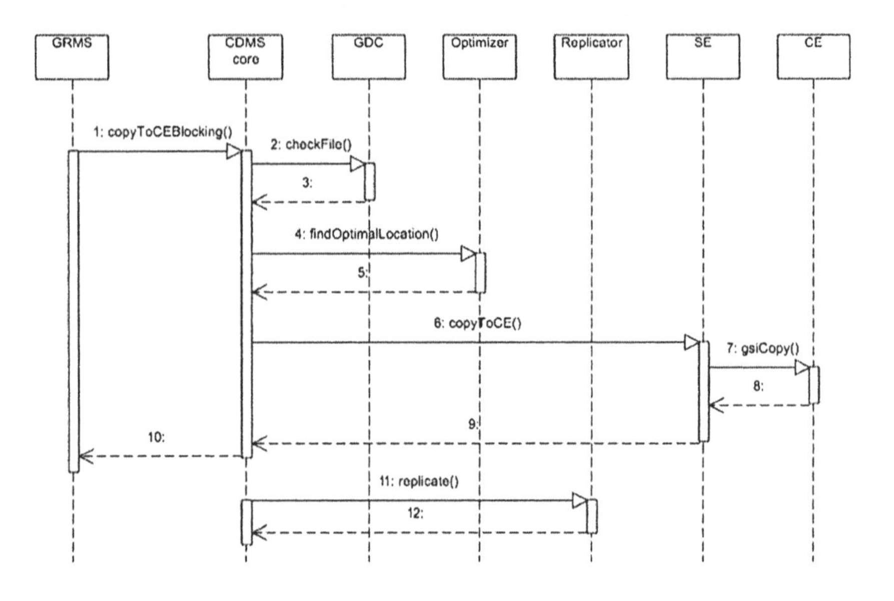

Figure 7. Stage-out sequence diagram

6.2 Stage-Out Scenario

After the job is finished, the results have to be retrieved from the computational resource. If the user requested them to be placed in the CDMS, the GRMS again contacts the Data Broker to request data transfer. In Fig.7 the sequence diagram for such a scenario is shown.

First the GRMS calls (1) a blocking function `copyFromCEBlocking` with the proper parameters (logical file name and physical data location). The CDMS Broker checks whether such a file exists (2). If so, all the replicas will be updated to the new version and if it is a new file, CDMS creates its logical instance in the Global Data Catalogue, and starts the optimization process (4). In this case, the Optimization Module requires only the file size and physical data location as parameters. The Management Module receives an ordered list of feasible Storage Elements, then delegates user credentials and requests the data retrieval to be performed (6), using the WebService interface of Storage Element. After the transfer is finished, the `copyFromCEBlocking` function returns (10), and GRMS continues with the job finalizing procedures, while CDMS initiates the replication process for the newly received data (11).

7. Related work

Because the idea of Data Management encompasses databases, distributed filesystems, remote file access protocols as well as local filesystems and HMS solutions we decided to focus on a subset of available systems. Taking into account that the CDMS is designed to work in a Globus Toolkit based grid infrastructure we will treat this feature as the common denominator for discussed solutions.

7.1 Data movement in the Globus Toolkit

The Globus Toolkit offers a basic set of grid services. Among them there are Data Management related ones, namely GridFTP, RFT, RLS and DRS[5].

The GridFTP is an extension to the standard FTP. Added are GSI based authentication and authorisation mechanisms and the basic, fast and effective file transfer protocol is preserved. Although globus-url-copy and the GridFTP are in general very powerfull tools they have some limitations. Most important is the fact that while globus-url-copy can recover from remote failures – server and network outages – a problem on the client side means that the recovery is not possible. To address this issue a service preserving the data transfer state is needed. Such a solution is offered by the Reliable File Transfer (RFT) service.

The RFT is a service based on the Web Service Resource Framework (WSRF), which provides the functionality encountered in resource brokers – user can submit a data transfer request via a webservice interface, specifying data source and destination. Later the transfer status may be controlled via the same interface. Similar features are available in CDMS as well, but the CDMS was developed with Globus Toolkit 3.x in mind and the RFT was introduced in the 4.x series.

The Replica Location Service (RLS) is a tool providing simple, distributed registry for keeping track of replicas on physical locations. Logical file namess (unique identifiers for contents of a file) are mapped to physical file names on a storage system.

The Data Replication Service ensures that a specified set of files exists on a storage site. It is based on the RLS and RFT and provides WSRF interface. It was introduced in Globus Toolkit 4.0.

The CDMS provides automated data replication based on independent mechanisms.

7.2 Alternative implementations

Data Management System (DMS) is a data management solution developed in the frame of the PROGRESS project[7]. It's main goal was to provide a data storage mechanism for the PROGRESS system and data access via a broad gamut of network protocols. The system architecture is quite similar to the CDMS architecture, but obviously it is aimed at a very narrow user group so a feature comparison is not really possible.

In general there are different data management solutions available, but usually they are either developed for a specific user group or aimed at specific task. Moreover in many projects an intuitive user interface was not considered as an important goal and they require a fair amount of network protocol or grid knowledge from the end-user. The CDMS strives to fill the gap providing intuitive user interface to a complex data management solution.

8. Conclusions

The CDMS is an advanced grid data management system, providing the end-user with efficient mechanisms for data transfer and storage. A very important feature of this system is its near complete transparency to users and seamless integration with the Resource Manager. On the other hand, advanced users are able to efficiently utilize the CDMS for inter-application data transfer, and to implement modules adapting CDMS to their needs.

References

[1] Allcock, B., et al.: Data Management and Transfer in High Performance Computational Grid Environments. Parallel Computing Journal **28**, **5** (2002) 749–771

[2] Bruin, R.P., Dove, M.T., Calleja, M., Tucker. M.G.: Building and Managing the eMinerals Clusters: A Case Study in Grid-Enabled Cluster Operation. Computing in Science & Engineering **7**, **6** (2005) 30–37

[3] ClusteriX Project Home Page, http://clusterix.pcz.pl

[4] gSOAP Project Home Page, http://www.cs.fsu.edu/ engelen/soap.html

[5] GLOBUS Toolkit Homepage, http://www.globus.org/toolkit

[6] GridSphere Project Home Page, http://gridsphere.org

[7] http://www.man.poznan.pl/coe/documents/Data_Management_WP.pdf

[8] Karczewski, K., Kuczynski, L., Wyrzykowski, R.: Secure Data Transfer and Replication Mechanisms in Grid Environments. Proc. Cracow Grid Workshop - CGW'03, Cracow, 2003, 190–196

[9] Karczewski, K., Kuczynski, L., Wyrzykowski, R.: CDMS - ClusteriX Data Management System. Proc. Cracow Grid Workshop - CGW'04, Cracow, 2004, 241–247

[10] Kunszt, P., Laure, E., Stockinger, H., Stockinger, K.: Advanced Replica Management with Reptor. Lect. Notes in Comp. Sci. **3019** (2004) 848–855

[11] SDSC Storage Resource Broker, http://www.sdsc.edu/srb/

[12] Slota, R., Skital, L, Nikolow, D., Kitowski, J.: Algorithms for Automatic Data Replication in Grid Environment (this volume)

[13] Valentin, O., Lombard, P., Lebre, A., Guinet, Ch., Denneulin, Y.: Distributed File System for Clusters and Grids. Lect. Notes in Comp. Sci. **3019** (2004) 1099–1104

[14] Wyrzykowski, R., Meyer, N., Stroinski, M.: Concept and Implementation of ClusteriX: National Cluster of Linux Systems. Proc. LCI Int.Conf. on Linux Clusters: The HPC Revolution 2005, Chapel-Hill, NC, April 2005

III

SEMANTIC GRID

ARCHITECTURAL PATTERNS FOR THE SEMANTIC GRID *

Ioannis Kotsiopoulos, Paolo Missier, Pinar Alper, Oscar Corcho, Sean Bechhofer, and Carole Goble
School of Computer Science
The University of Manchester
United Kingdom
{ioannis, pmissier, penpecip, ocorcho, seanb, carole}@cs.man.ac.uk

Abstract The Semantic Grid reference architecture, S-OGSA, includes *semantic provisioning services* that are able to produce semantic annotations of Grid resources, and *semantically aware Grid services* that are able to exploit those annotations in various ways. In this paper we describe the dynamic aspects of S-OGSA by presenting the typical patterns of interaction among these services. A use case for a Grid meta-scheduling service is used to illustrate how the patterns are applied in practice.

Keywords: Semantic Grid, Grid services, architectural patterns.

*This work is supported by the EU FP6 OntoGrid project (STREP 511513) funded under the Grid-based Systems for solving complex problems, and by the Marie Curie fellowship RSSGRID (FP6-2002-Mobility-5-006668)

1. Introduction

The Grid aims to support secure, flexible and coordinated resource sharing by providing a middleware platform for advanced distributed computing [6] . Grid middleware architectures aim to allow collections of any kind of resourcescomputing, storage, data sets, digital libraries, scientific instruments, people, etc to easily form Virtual Organizations (VOs) that cross organizational boundaries in order to work together to solve a problem. However, existing Grid middleware architectures and the standards on which they are based on, fall short of addressing some of the original vision of configurable, self-healing, adaptive, and interoperable middleware [6]. This is due mainly to the following reasons:

Knowledge burial. Knowledge and metadata regarding Grid entities is currently generated and used in an ad hoc fashion, much of it buried in the middleware's code libraries and database schemas. This esoteric expression and use of knowledge hinders interoperability when it comes to building open, interoperable and adaptive systems. Existing Grid middleware is therefore considerably affected by syntactic changes in protocols and representations, and it becomes highly dependent on human intervention during its operation.

Dominance of XML-based vocabularies and protocols. The Grid community has developed a number of specifications and standards that aim to increase interoperability among middleware components. XML has become the de-facto language not only for expressing these specifications, but also for describing Grid entities and their behaviour. However, XML-based specifications do not provide a complete solution to the problem of knowledge burial due to the lack of a shared formal interpretation of XML documents.

Lack of models for Grid processes. Many aspects of the Grid are still not formally defined, therefore it becomes difficult to identify the challenges and even more difficult to find solutions. Take as an example the formation of Virtual Organizations (VOs); creating a model for forming VOs can help setting-up a community-wide terminology, highlight differences among existing systems and bring about previously unforeseen issues to be solved for interoperability. This model should be the product of a knowledge acquisition process, similar to those being undertaken by the Web [4], Web Services [3]and Semantic Web Services communities [9, 14]. The outcome of the modeling process can be used for the development of interoperable metadata based on explicit semantics.

The Semantic Grid is an extension of the current Grid in which information and services are given well defined and explicitly represented meaning, better enabling computers and people to work in cooperation [8]. In the Semantic Grid, the goal of sharing virtualized computational and data resources is extended to include explicit metadata and knowledge. During the last few years, several projects have embraced this vision and there are already successful pioneering applications that combine the strengths of the Grid and of semantic technologies [15]. As a result of some of these efforts, the S-OGSA reference architecture has been recently proposed [5], with the aim of providing a systematic approach for designing Semantic Grid applications.

This paper is focused on the dynamic aspects of semantic Grid. We begin by presenting a summary of S-OGSA ("semantically enhanced OGSA"); then introduce a use case for Semantic Grid, namely semantic meta-scheduling of Grid resources [11]. With the help of the use case, we present two service interaction patterns that demonstrate the key aspects of Semantic Grid dynamics in S-OGSA. Finally, we provide some conclusions and future research directions.

2. Semantic Grid concepts

In this section we provide a summary of the fundamental properties of S-OGSA; a more comprehensive discussion can be found in [5]. S-OGSA consists of (i) an information model of semantic resources, which extends the OGSA model, and (ii) two new types of Grid services, *Semantic Provisioning Services* and *Semantically Aware Grid Services*.

2.1 A Semantic Grid Information Model

Two types of entities are at the basis of the information model:

Grid Entities (*G-Entities*) are anything that carries an identity on the Grid, including resources and services [19];

Knowledge Entities are special types of Grid Entities that represent or could operate with some form of knowledge. Examples of Knowledge Entities are ontologies, rules, knowledge bases or even free text descriptions that encapsulate knowledge that can be shared. Knowledge services are those that provide access to or operate over those knowledge resources, e.g. rule engines and automated reasoners.

Semantic Bindings (*S-Bindings*) are the entities that come into existence to represent the association of a Grid Entity with one or more Knowledge Entities. The existence of such an association transforms the subject Grid entity into a **Semantic Grid Entity**. Semantic Bindings represent metadata assertions on web resources. In our model, Semantic Bindings are first class citizens as they are modelled as Grid resources with an identity and manageability features as well as their own metadata.

Semantic Grid Entities are those Grid Entities that are either the subject of a semantic binding, are themselves a semantic binding, or a Knowledge Entity. In keeping with our design principles, Grid entities can simultaneously be associated with zero or multiple knowledge entities of different forms and capabilities, and can acquire and discard associations with knowledge entities through their lifetime. It should be noted that S-OGSA does not prescribe any specific technology for the realisation of these.

2.2 Semantic Provisioning Services

These are services that provision semantic entities. These Semantic Services are themselves Grid Services. Following the aforementioned classification of semantic entities, two major classes of services are:
Knowledge provisioning services (*KPS*), which can produce (and in some cases store) knowledge resources, and that can be used to manage knowledge resources. KPS support the creation, storage and access of different forms of knowledge resources. For example: ontology services (a major form of knowledge) and reasoning services.

Semantic Binding provisioning services, which can produce (and in some cases store) S-Binding resources, and that can be used to manage S-Binding resources. For example: semantic binding index services, for accessing and storing metadata associating Grid entities with knowledge entities; and annotation services for generating metadata from different types of information sources, like databases, files or provenance logs. S-Bindings are stateful, so they are subject to soft state processes; i.e. they will time out, get deleted or be removed. A typical way of producing S-Bindings is by annotating Grid entities as is shown in the Grid entities annotation pattern (Section 4).

2.3 Semantically Aware Grid Services

This class of Grid Services are able to exploit semantic technologies to consume semantic bindings in order to deliver their functionality. Their role is complementary to the role of *Semantic Provisioning Services* since they consume the semantic entities held by **Knowledge provisioning services** and **Semantic Binding provisioning services** and use their services. The combination of *Semantic Provisioning Services* and *Semantically Aware Grid Services* can address the knowledge burial problem discussed in Section 1 since explicitly shared knowledge can be consumed by third party services. Semantically

Aware Grid Services are able to exploit explicit semantics, and therefore can benefit from the additional context it provides for service operation. Examples include:

- A **VO Manager service** that can perform semantics-aware service access authorization;

- A **Grid resource catalogue** that supports semantic searches;

- An **ontology service** that is capable of incorporating new concepts into an ontology.

3. The Grid scheduling use case

We illustrate the use of semantic grid concepts in practice, by describing an existing Grid service that is currently being enhanced as a semantics-aware service. The service addresses a real and common problem in the area of resource co-allocation on the Grid. The problem of resource co-allocation emerges when dealing with complex workflows that require multiple data, computing and network resources; these resources are commonly highly distributed, and are subject to autonomous and independent management by different organizations.

We are specifically interested in resources whose usage is controlled by schedulers on the Grid, either at the local or the cluster level; allocating multiple such resources and orchestrating their access requires the introduction of a new type of Grid service, called a *meta-scheduler* (MS) or *super-scheduler*. The MS is responsible for the co-scheduling [17] of resources in order to assemble, on demand, a virtual machine that enables the execution of distributed jobs consisting of many parallel tasks. In particular, the MS provides higher-level resource management by implementing a consistent interface into various Grid scheduling systems, and thus hides much of the heterogeneity of the local schedulers that control the actual underlying resources.

For our use case, we focus on the generic meta-scheduler recently proposed by Wäldrich et al [20], whose design attempts to generalize on the type of resources that can be scheduled. This MS interfaces with multiple local schedulers, negotiating with them *advance reservation* of resources based on user requirements that may include time and QoS constraints. The goal of the negotiation is to determine time slots where the required resources are available for the requested start times of the application or workflow parts. The meta-scheduler implements two main functionalities: (i) allocation of a single resource for a single application for a fixed period of time, and (ii) co-allocation of multiple resources for the same fixed period of time for single or multiple applications.

In order to be able to participate in the negotiation, schedulers must satisfy at least the first of the following requirements:

1 provide advance reservation of resources by offering job execution start and stop times;

2 allow at least partial access to the local schedules, e.g. the available timeslots;

3 allow for some control on existing reservations, e.g. by handling requests for cancellation, or time extensions.

Thus, meta-scheduling includes the following main steps:

- discover schedulers that (i) manage resources that are compatible with the requirements of the Grid workflow, and (ii) satisfy (at least) the first of the remaining two requirements above;
- negotiate suitable timeslots with the pre-selected schedulers;
- commit to the advance reservation, and interact with the schedulers to handle any subsequent change in the agreed-upon reservation.

The meta-scheduler interacts with local schedulers through dedicated adapters that hide the heterogeneity of the schedulers' native interfaces. These adapters offer a uniform set of abstract operations to the meta-scheduler, which include requesting available start time slots for jobs, submitting scheduling requests for a specific time slot, and requesting the state of the current reservation.

The meta-scheduler described in [20] negotiates with the local adapters using the WS-Agreement framework [1]. It has been integrated into the UNICORE Grid system, and its functionality has been demonstrated on the VIOLA testbed for advanced network services [12]. The meta-scheduler is accessible through UNICORE client plugins, which allow users to specify requests for co-allocated resources to run a distributed job on VIOLA.

3.1 Limitations of the current meta-scheduling model

The focus of the current implementation is on the meta-scheduling algorithm, rather than on the discovery and pre-selection of the eligible schedulers, and on the design of the adapters. However, the latter is a serious issue for the scalability of the proposed approach. Our study of meta-scheduling as a promising Semantic Grid use case stems from the observation that, while the adapters provide a uniform set of operations, no shared data model is available to describe a scheduler's set of capabilities. For example, there is no explicit and shared definition of scheduling concepts like *timeslot* or *schedule queue*, or of capabilities like *timeslot reservation change*. Instead, these concepts are left implicit in the implementation of the adapters, which only expose a simple set of scheduling operations.

This arrangement results in an architecture that is vulnerable to changes. Firstly, when the schedulers' capabilities change, they are not easily reflected in the adapters, which leave this knowledge implicit within their code. Secondly, when the meta-scheduler requirements for the required capabilities change, eg due to changes in the meta-scheduling negotiation strategy or allocation decision algorithm, there is no shared vocabulary to describe the new requirements.

Motivated by these observations, we have proposed [11] a semantic approach to meta-scheduling on the Grid, which improves upon the current design by:

- introducing a shared, explicit and lightweight but extensible semantic model to describe a scheduler's set of capabilities as well as its current state (which the meta-scheduler will need to query, see requirement 2). This is known as the *Grid Scheduling Ontology*;
- enhancing the adapters so that they can generate metadata regarding the schedulers' capabilities;
- enhancing the existing meta-scheduler as a Semantic Grid service, which is (i) aware of the available schedulers' semantics annotations, and (ii) able to exploit them to perform scheduler discovery and pre-selection.

3.2 The Grid Scheduling semantic model

The design of the enhanced meta-scheduler is based on a semantic model of Grid scheduling concepts. A detailed presentation of the model can be found in [11]; what follows is a brief summary.

At the core, the model includes concepts for schedulers, scheduler capabilities, scheduler reservation, and additional concepts to represent the state of a local schedule; each of these classes is the root of an extensible hierarchy. Furthermore, relationships amongst these root classes are established using *object properties*, used for instance to associate sets of capabilities to a scheduler.

The model is defined as an ontology in OWL DL [12]; using the OWL DL operators, scheduler classes can be defined to contain all and only schedulers with a defined set of capabilities. For example, a limited-disclosure-scheduler, a subclass of scheduler, is the class of all schedulers that allow their local schedule to be queried.

These intensional definitions provide a focused way to add *semantic annotations* to individual schedulers, which are instances of one or more of the scheduler classes. In their simplest form, annotations include capabilities metadata, which may state for instance that that "a scheduler is both capable of offering advance reservation, and allows queries on its current schedule".

These annotations facilitate the schedulers' pre-selection by a meta-scheduler. More precisely, they allow a Description Logic reasoner [2] for the type of DL supported by OWL, to automatically classify a scheduler whose semantic annotations are known, as a member of one or more scheduler classes, defined intensionally as shown above. Once this classification has taken place, it is easy to show that scheduler discovery using this model amounts to (i) selecting from the ontology a scheduler class whose definition satisfies the selection criteria, and (ii) querying the ontology class to retrieve all the individual schedulers in the class.

Casting this discovery pattern within the Semantic Grid context is straightforward: local schedulers (LS) are Grid entities, and their semantic annotations can be defined as knowledge entities using the terminology introduced earlier; they are maintained in a metadata store as first-class Grid Entities themselves. Semantic bindings in this case embody the association between schedulers and their annotations; the bindings are exploited by the meta-scheduler, which becomes a semantically -aware and -capable Grid service.

Figure 3 shows how the meta-scheduler may make use of the S-OGSA semantic services suite presented in Section 4. In the next section, S-OGSA style interactions are described in a principled way, using the Grid meta-scheduling case study as an example.

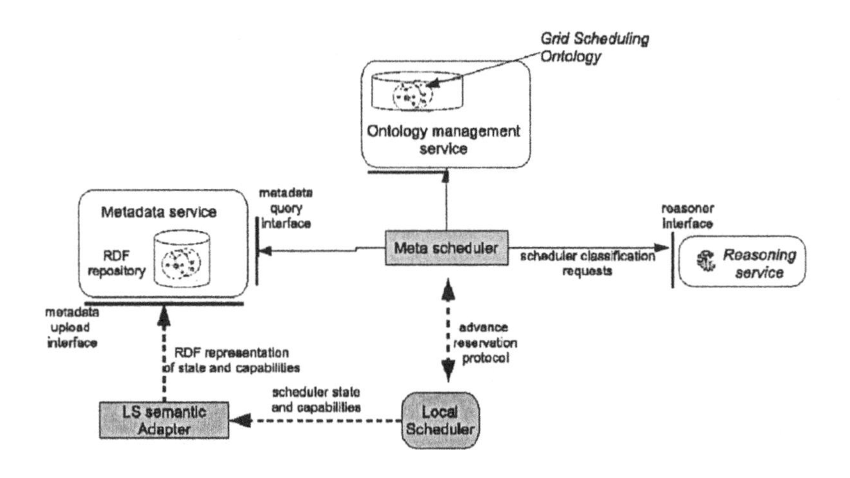

Figure 1. Casting meta-scheduling in the S-OGSA context

4. Service interaction patterns for the Semantic Grid

The description given in Section 2 provides a static view of the S-OGSA architecture. Ultimately, however, the goal of provisioning and consuming semantics in the Grid is realized when S-OGSA services interact with one another and with Grid entities. We now present the two most relevant service interaction patterns that define these dynamic aspects of the Semantic Grid. The patterns follow the main steps in semantic information processing in S-OGSA, namely:

- Producing semantic annotations, i.e., ontology-referenced metadata for some Grid entity (resources or services), and representing those annotations as persistent knowledge entities. Grid entities and their annotations are thus both first-class Grid citizens, and can participate in a semantic binding;
- Resolving the semantic bindings in order to retrieve annotations for given Grid entities.

These patterns describe the preparatory actions that any semantically-aware Grid service, such as the meta-scheduler and the adapters that are responsible for producing the metadata, would carry out before semantics can be exploited.

The patterns are presented according to the well-known format discussed in [16]. The dynamics of each pattern are explained with UML sequence diagrams while additional comments are used inside the sequence diagrams wherever the interaction is complex or needs some clarification, so as to make the diagrams as self-contained as possible.

4.1 Grid entity annotation pattern

Definition: The Grid entity annotation pattern encapsulates the functions needed to annotate Grid data resources or services, producing either raw or semantic metadata and store them persistently. By *raw metadata* we mean any annotation that can be associated to a piece of data, or, more generally, to a Grid entity. *Semantic metadata*, on the other hand, is metadata that carries explicit references to the semantic models, i.e., reference ontologies, required for its interpretation. In this work, we are only interested in the latter. When annotations are stored in a Metadata store they become Grid Resources since they are given a unique identifier. From this set of annotations, those that link Grid Entities with Knowledge Entities are called Semantic Bindings.

Example: The capability profile of a scheduler can be expressed using terminology from a Grid Scheduling Ontology (GSO), so that any user who has access to the ontology may be able to interpret the profile. The LS (Local Scheduler) Semantic Adapter shown in Figure 3 supervises and monitors one local scheduler and produces semantic annotations regarding its capabilities and state changes. Annotations are used by the metascheduler for service pre-selection.

Context: Generation and storage of semantic metadata for Grid entities.

Problem: The use of intelligent reasoning mechanisms requires semantic metadata.

Solution: The annotation process can be either done manually, semi-automatically or on-demand without any user interaction. This pattern is concerned with automatic and semi-automatic annotations according to which an Annotation Service is able to fetch reference ontologies from an Ontology Service, and use them to create semantic annotations that can be interpreted using those ontologies. The outcome of the annotation is persistently stored using the Metadata Service.

Dynamics: The annotation process is triggered by a requestor that wants to annotate a piece of data. First, the annotation service needs to obtain a reference to a suitable ontology. For this, it invokes the Ontology Service which returns a handler to this ontology. During the annotation process this handler is used to retrieve ontology *concepts* and *properties* from the Ontology Service. Optionally, the Annotation Service may also retrieve existing annotations from the Metadata Service, for reference or for updating purposes. When the annotation process finishes, the annotation is persistently stored in the Metadata Service and assigned a unique identifier. The annotation has now become a special type of Grid Entity that links Knowledge Entities (i.e. the ontology) to Grid Resources. This Grid Entity is called a *Semantic Binding* and can be retrieved from the Metadata Service using the aforementioned unique identifier: the Semantic Binding ID.

Associated to the annotation is also, potentially, its provenance metadata, describing the annotation process itself (when it was performed, by whom, the external resources it is based on, and so forth). Note that this pattern is only concerned with S-OGSA service interactions, rather than with the specific annotation process, which may vary depending on the domain of the Grid resource and the purpose of the annotation.

4.2 Metadata and Knowledge querying Pattern

Definition: This pattern allows an application to retrieve semantic bindings and/or query the semantic metadata associated to a set of Grid Entities, with

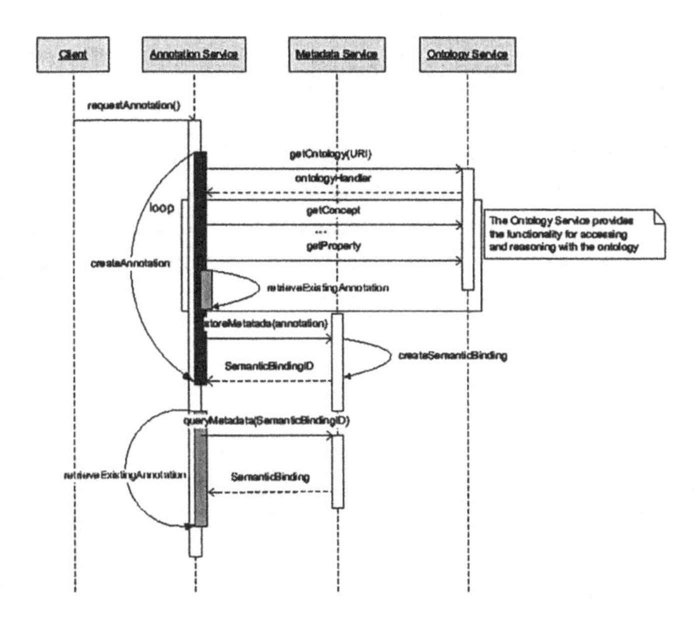

Figure 2. Data annotation interaction patterns

the help of the metadata and ontology services.

Example: The capabilities required for a scheduler to participate in advance reservation are represented by one or more scheduler classes in the ontology. As we have shown, eligible schedulers are all and only the instances of those classes. Retrieving those instances may require reasoning capabilities, as well as access to the metadata storage.

Context: Semantically aware Grid services that need to retrieve semantic bindings in order to perform their function.

Problem: Exploiting semantic bindings involves retrieving semantic metadata associated to some Grid entity.

Solution: Since semantic metadata can be implemented in a formal language (e.g., RDF Schema, OWL), reasoning techniques can be used in order to retrieve the metadata. Depending on the reasoning mechanisms available for the formal language in which the metadata is implemented, different types of inferences will be available, from the retrieval of subclasses or ancestors of a given class to the classification of sets of individuals according to their most specific class. During the query answering process, we can exploit the reasoners capabilities in order to infer new facts by aggregating knowledge already stored in the Metadata Service.

Dynamics: The behaviour of the Metadata Querying Pattern is shown in Figure 3. Retrieving raw metadata is straightforward. For semantic metadata, the metadata service uses the ontology service for expanding or restricting the queries that are sent in the message, such as adding subclasses of the concepts used in the query, or detecting inconsistencies in the query before they are issued to the metadata service.

5. Discussion

In this paper we have provided a dynamic view of the Semantic Grid by focusing on some of the most common interaction patterns among the semantic middleware components identified in S-OGSA. Our coverage of patterns here is far from being exhaustive and there are several variations to undertaking the two core Semantic Grid functionalities covered in this paper, namely annotation and metadata querying.

The annotation (or metadata generation) pattern that we have covered displays the case, where metadata for grid entities is generated semi-automatically and on-demand, which in the illustrative scenario corresponds to the LS Semantic Adapter's annotation of a scheduler that has recently joined the VO, or to a scheduler that has just changed its state. On-demand and semi-automatic characteristics require the metadata generation pattern to include phases for discovery of annotation resources (e.g. ontologies).

Annotation could also be done automatically and initiated dynamically as Grid entities come into existence. Cases where VO membership of Grid entities change frequently; where most middleware activities heavily rely on existence of grid entity metadata, or where metadata represents historical/contextual information of a Grid entity (e.g. provenance), all necessitate annotation to be a sustained activity. In the sustained annotation case, the resource discovery phase is generally skipped, and the annotation tooling is configured to use a specific set of resources and methods.

The metadata querying patterns we have covered demonstrated capabilities ranging from simple retrieval of raw metadata to expansion of semantic metadata via ontological inference.

The patterns are intended to be the building blocks of more complex interactions that build-up **activities** of middleware and applications in the Semantic Grid ecosystem. For instance, in our illustrative scenario, the motivation for

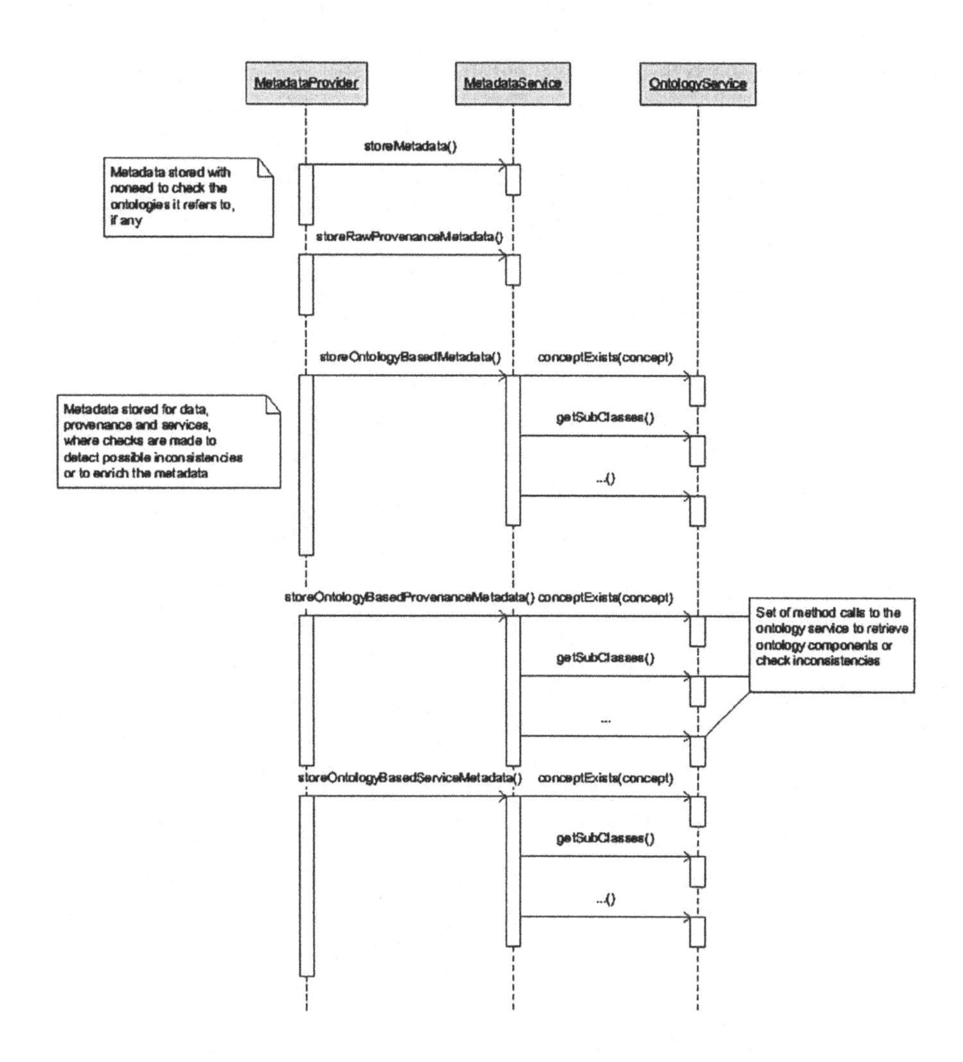

Figure 3. Metadata storage interaction patterns

providing semantic descriptions for local schedulers came from the need for the Semantic Discovery activity.

Such semantically-enhanced activities are also currently being investigated in fields such as the Semantic Web (SW) and Semantic Web Services (SWS). Work in these areas investigates *i)* suitable technologies and models for semantically describing resources in their respective distributed environment (e.g., the Web or the Web services) and *ii)* how these semantic descriptions can be exploited in the context of a particular activity with special focus on discovery, negotiation and composition. There are certain aspects of the Grid that appear to have higher priority when compared to other distributed environments. These aspects and their effect on semantics can be summarized as follows:

Dynamism and Dependency Management. Unlike other distributed environments, the resources in the Grid are very dynamic. Resource state changes frequently, and information regarding the state of the system has a definite lifetime. Grid information systems aggregate resource state information (generally represented as XML based resource properties) into index services in order to provide an aggregate system snapshot and enable discovery of resources based on their properties. To the extent that semantic metadata adds to resource state information, managing the lifetime of the semantic bindings becomes important. These issues, which have so far attracted little research attention in the semantic web (SW) and semantic web services (SWS) communities, need to be addressed in the Grid context.

Trust and Consistency. Building a well-controlled resource sharing environment is the main aim in the Grid. Introduction of metadata and knowledge into the Grid brings about the issues of trust-ability and consistency of these. These issues are also under investigation in the SW and SWS communities [7]. The uptake of semantics in the Grid depends on existence of usable models and frameworks in this area.

6. Future Directions

Our current S-OGSA architectural descriptions, including their static and dynamic aspects, do not prescribe any semantic technology and content for the realization of semantic entities and services in the Grid. We are aware that the guidance of S-OGSA would increase if it is accompanied with some generic content and experience reports (e.g. best practices) on particular technology choices. Therefore, as part of our future work we will be providing:

Meta-models for knowledge and metadata. In order to facilitate interoperable use of the S-OGSA entities in a Grid environment we need to provide minimal information on what they are. This will be done by modelling the different types of realizations for Semantic Bindings (e.g., RDF, natural language) and Knowledge Entities (e.g., ontologies, rule bases).

Profiles for S-OGSA. In this chapter we have demonstrated S-OGSA with a scenario where Description Logic based knowledge and RDF based metadata representations have been used to provide semantic capability descriptions for schedulers and their discovery through use of a DL classifier. The choice of realization technology for knowledge and metadata modelling depends on many factors including the nature of the problem at hand, the characteristics of the candidate semantic technologies and the availability and maturity of their associated tools/services. Returning to our example in this chapter, the use of an open-world based DL classifier proved suitable for discovery of distributed resources. This however should not imply that these particular technologies are fit for the solution of other Grid problems (e.g. policy reconciliation, agreement negotiation). In fact closer investigation of such problems [7]has shown that semantic technologies other than DL and RDF could be ideal for tailoring solutions to these problems. Based on this observation we would like to provide profiles for S-OGSA that demonstrate exploitation of different semantic technologies for the solution of different Grid problems.

References

[1] A. Andrieux, K. Czajkowski, A. Dan, K. Keahey, H. Ludwig, T. Nakata, J. Pruyne, J. Rofrano, S. Tuecke, and M. Xu. Web services agreement specification. Technical report, Global Grid Forum, July 2005. https://forge.gridforum.org/projects/graap-wg/document/WS-AgreementSpecification/en/16.

[2] Franz Baader, Diego Calvanese, Deborah L. McGuinness, Daniele Nardi, and Peter F. Patel-Schneider, editors. *The Description Logic Handbook: Theory, Implementation, and Applications*. Cambridge University Press, 2003.

[3] D. Booth, H. Haas, F. McCabe, E. Newcomer, M. Champion, C. Ferris, and D. Orchard. Web services architecture. Available at http://www.w3.org/TR/ws-arch/, 2004.

[4] D. Brickley and R. V. Guha. Rdf vocabulary description language 1.0: Rdf schema. Available at: http://www.w3.org/TR/rdf-schema/, 2004.

[5] O. Corcho, P. Alper, I. Kotsiopoulos, P. Missier, S. Bechhofer, D. Kuo, and C. Goble. An overview of s-ogsa: a reference semantic grid architecture. *Journal of Web Semantics*, 4, 2006.

[6] I. Foster, H. Kishimoto, A. Savva, D. Berry, A. Djaoui, A. Grimshaw, B. Horn, F. Maciel, F. Siebenlist, R. Subramaniam, J. Treadwell, and J. V. Reich. The open grid services architecture, version 1.0. Technical report, Open Grid Services Architecture WG, Global Grid Forum, 2005.

[7] R. Gavriloaie, W. Nejdl, D. Olmedilla, K.E. Seamons, and M. Winslett. No registration needed: How to use declarative policies and negotiation to access sensitive resources on the semantic web. In *1st European Semantic Web Symposium (ESWS2004)*, pages 342–356. Springer-Verlag, 2004.

[8] C. A. Goble, D. D. Roure, N. R. Shadbolt, and A. A. Fernandes. *In The Grid 2: Blueprint for a New Computing Infrastructure Second Edition*, chapter Enhancing Services and Applications with Knowledge and Semantics. Morgan Kaufmann, i. foster and c. kesselman, edition, 2003.

[9] D. Martin, M. Paolucci, S. McIlraith, M. Burstein, D. McDermott, D. McGuinness, B. Parsia, T. Payne, M. Sabou, M. Solanki, N. Srinivasan, and K. Sycara. Bringing semantics to web services: The owl-s approach. In *First International Workshop on Semantic*

Web Services and Web Process Composition (SWSWPC 2004), San Diego, California, USA, 2004.

[10] D. L. McGuinness and F. v. Harmelen. OWL Web Otology Language Overview, February 2004. W3C Recommendation.

[11] P. Missier, P. Wieder, and W. Ziegler. Semantic support for Meta-Scheduling in Grids. Submitted.

[12] Online. VIOLA - Vertically Integrated Optical Testbed for Large Application in DFN, 2005. Project web site: http://www.viola-testbed.de/.

[13] L. Pouchard, L. Cinquini, and G. Strand. The earth system grid discovery and semantic web technologies. In *Workshop for Semantic Web Technologies for Searching and Retrieving Scientific Data, at the 2nd International Semantic Web Conference*, 2003.

[14] D. Roman, U. Keller, H. Lausen, J. d. Bruijn, R. Lara, M. Stollberg, A.Polleres, C. Feier, C. Bussler, and D. Fensel. Web service modelling ontology. *Journal of Applied Ontology*, 1:77–106, 2006.

[15] D. De Roure, Y. Gil, and J. A. Hendler. Guest editors' introduction: E-science. *IEEE Intelligent Systems*, 19:24–25, 2004.

[16] D. C. Schmidt, M. Stal, H. R., and F. Buschmann. *Pattern-Oriented Software Architecture: Patterns for Concurrent and Networked Objects*, volume 2. John Wiley and Sons Ltd, 1 edition, 2000.

[17] J. Schopf. Ten Actions When Grid Scheduling – The User as a Grid Scheduler. In J. Nabrzyski, J. Schopf, and J. Weglarz, editors, *Grid Resource Management – State of the Art and Future Trends*, pages 15–23. Kluwer Academic Publishers, 2004.

[18] N. Sharman, N. Alpdemir, J. Ferris, M. Greenwood, P. Li, and C. Wroe. The mygrid information model. In *UK e-Science All Hands Meeting*, 2004.

[19] J. Treadwell. Open grid services architecture glossary of terms. Technical report, Open Grid Services Architecture WG, Global Grid Forum, 2005. Available at: http://forge.gridforum.org/projects/ogsa-wg.

[20] O. Wäldrich, P. Wieder, and W. Ziegler. A meta-scheduling service for co-allocating arbitrary types of resources. In *Proc. of Sixth International Conference on Parallel Processing and Applied Mathematics (PPAM 2005)*, 2005.

A METADATA MODEL FOR THE DISCOVERY AND EXPLOITATION OF SCIENTIFIC STUDIES

Shoaib Sufi
CCLRC, Daresbury Laboratory, Warrington WA4 4AD, United Kingdom
s.a.sufi@dl.ac.uk

Brian Matthews
CCLRC, Rutherford-Appleton Laboratory, Didcot, Oxfordshire OX11 0AX, United Kingdom
b.m.matthews@rl.ac.uk

Abstract A general model for the representation of scientific study metadata does not exist. The e-Science enablement of the data holdings of CCLRC requires such a model to allow access to the data resources of the facilities in a uniform way. By proposing a model and an implementation, the adoption of such a system would aid interoperability of scientific information systems in the organisation and form a specification of the type and categories of metadata that studies should capture about their investigations and the data they produce inside and outside of CCLRC. This allows further exploitation of scientific Studies and associated datasets, ease citation, facilitate collaboration and allow the easy integration of pre-Grid metadata into a common Grid/e-Science enabled scientific information platform. In this paper, we describe a science metadata model developed at CCLRC, with its motivation, overall design, usage and future development.

Keywords: metadata, e-Science, data curation, data integration, search, browsing.

1. Introduction

Scientific research projects have two major outputs: publications, in journals and other forms of literature; and the data sets generated during the course of observations and experiments. These are then subject to analysis and visualisation to generate the results reported in the literature. Traditionally, science has concentrated on the former output as the major means of disseminating the results of research, whilst access to the latter has been restricted to small groups of individuals closely associated with the original researcher. However, modern distributed information systems offer the opportunity to provide access to both outputs to a wider audience. This allows other researchers to verify the results of the analysis, and also to reuse the data-sets to carry out secondary analysis, possibly in combination with results from elsewhere, to produce new insights without the cost of repeating the original experiment.

These data resources are typically stored in many file systems and databases physically distributed throughout organisations with, at present, no uniform way of accessing or searching them to find what data is available. It is often necessary to open and read the actual data files to find out what information they contain. There is little consistency in the information which is recorded for each data-set held and sometimes this information may not even be available on-line, being recorded only in experimenters' logbooks. This situation creates the potential for serious under-utilisation of these data resources or for wasteful re-generation of data. It also hinders the development of cross-discipline research, as this requires the location and combination of data across traditional disciplinary boundaries.

Metadata is seen as a key factor in the archiving and distribution of scientific data. Through the use of good metadata models, defined at the appropriate level, scientists can publish and share data, and allow the results of experiments and studied to be browsed and searched. Appropriate metadata thus encourages reuse of data within and across scientific disciplines.

The CCLRC Scientific Meta-Data Model (CSMD) is a study-data orientated model [1]. It seeks to capture the high level information pertaining to scientific studies and the data that they produce. As a base minimum the CSMD forms a specification of the types of information a scientific study should maintain in order to be useful to parallel and follow on studies as well as to the researchers themselves in later years (e.g. loss of original data, check previous results and perform some new form of analysis). The CSMD supports indexing at various levels of granularity from the study to investigations inside the studies to data collections and atomic data objects (e.g. files and databases, including query tables). The indexing mechanism supports keywords and taxonomic classification while including support for reference to controlled vocabularies. The latest version is version 2 [2].

The CSMD is being used as the core metadata carrier for the Grid enabling of the world class large scale scientific facilities at CCRLC covering area such as Neutron Science, Lasers and Synchrotron Science. A generic model covering all these requirements did not previously exist, and therefore CSMD was developed as a core component of any facility Data Grid aiding collaboration, exploitation and citation of scientific studies across the virtual organisation.

In this paper, we briefly describe the notion of a Science Data Portal as developed in CCLRC. We go on to describe the metadata model used in the data portal, both in its overall structure, and some of the details, including an example. In future developments, we discuss how this metadata model can be related to metadata formats for cataloguing publications.

2. A Science Data Portal

The concept of a data portal [8–11]has been developed as a tool for browsing and searching the contents of distributed scientific data sources across a variety of scientific domains. Such a system has potentially a wide spectrum of users from scientists working in related fields wanting to find information on a topic, through experimenters interested in accessing and analysing their own data, to the data curators based at the facilities themselves who want to use the portal as a data management tool.

A data portal system has been developed within CCLRC [8–9] to enable researchers to access and search metadata about data resources held at the ISIS and SRS facilities within CCLRC. The system being developed has three main components: a web-based user interface; a metadata catalogue; and generic data resource interfaces, integrated using standard Web protocols. The system can offer a distributed interface to scientific data resources both inside and outside CCLRC.

The data resources accessible through the data portal system may be located on any one of a number of data servers. Interfaces between these existing data resources and the metadata catalogue are being implemented as web services based wrappers that will present the relevant metadata about each resource to the catalogue so it appears to the user to be part of the central catalogue.. These wrappers are implemented as XML encoding of the specific metadata relating to that resource using the metadata model schema; wrappers are an established technique for providing such interfaces [15].

2.1 A Metadata Catalogue

In order to construct a generic data portal, including mechanisms for cataloguing, browsing and accessing data resources across a wide number of scientific domains, a generic metadata model for scientific data is needed.

There are many metadata formats supporting specific data sources and domains such as CERA which has been developed for earth observation data [13] and the NERC Datagrid metadata model for environmental data [14]. Also, there are general models of metadata such as the Dublin Core [12] for discovery information for library resources. However, there has been few attempts to provide a metadate model to cover the generic nature of the scientific data holdings, similar to the Data Documentation Initiative [16] developed for the social sciences. Such a metadata for science has the requirement of being both more specialised than general metadata models , whilst being more general than metadata formats for specific domains in science, and covering a large range of metadata types, as defined classifciations of metadata such as [17]. The CSMD is designed to be such a generic model for science data holdings.

When the metadata model is used in a particular domain, more detailed metadata may be provided. A mechanism is needed to access such metadata in an interoperable way from the generic scientific metadata while preserving the meaning, and allows deeper searches into the domain specific metadata. Thus the CSMD is designed to be extensible for particular domains of interest.

The logical structure of the metadata in the catalogue is based on the scientific metadata model. Figure 1 gives a breakdown of the metadata model into its six major components. The study metadata corresponds to associative descriptive metadata, the access condition to associative restrictive metadata, data description to a form of schema metadata (describing how the data is laid out in the file structure), data location to navigational metadata, and related material to associative supportive metadata. Additionally, keywords can be assigned from controlled vocabularies for topic based browsing. These components are considered in more detail in later sections of this paper.

The model is necessarily very generic to cater for a large range of differing types of data. Specialisations of this metadata format will be used for each domain, and generic queries can be then devised to search over the common views on the metadata. The model uses a hierarchical model of the structure of scientific research programmes, projects and studies, and also a generic model of the organisation of data sets into collections and files. This allows a flexible structure to be developed, relating different data sets and their components together. For example related sets derived from one another from raw data through data reduction and analysis to a final result; alternative and failed analyses can also be recorded, as well as calibration data sets, against which results are measured.

The metadata catalogue is implemented using a standard relational database. Once the specific data sets required by the user have been identified using the available metadata, the catalogue provides links to the files holding the actual data. Users can then use these links to access the data with their own applications for analysis as required.

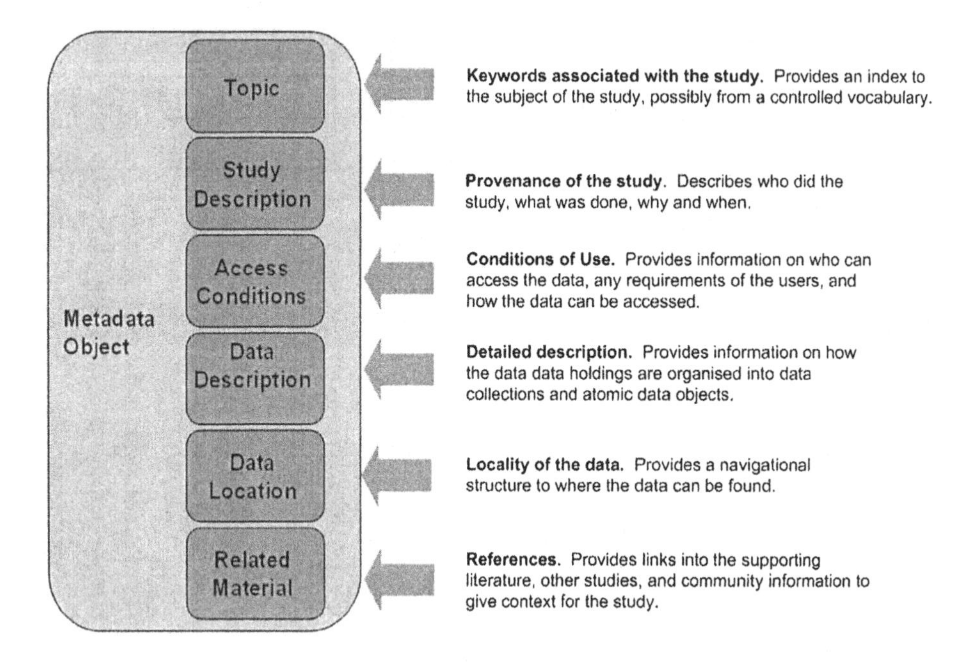

Figure 1. The Top-level Components of the Metadata Model

3. The Metadata Structure

The metadata within the general metadata structure is laid in a series of classes and subclasses. We do not describe the whole model in detail for reasons of space, but rather select some areas of particular interest.

3.1 Modelling Scientific Activity

The data model attempts to capture scientific activities at different levels: the main unit is the Study, which lies in a context of a science research programme, governed by policies. Each study has an Investigator that describes who is undertaking the activity, and the Study Information that captures the details of this particular study. Studies include particular scientific investigations. The general structure of the metadata is given as a UML diagram in Figure 2.

Policy are company or government policies which initiate Programmes of work.

Programmes are related studies that have a common theme which are usually funded and resourced directly or with an intermediary organisation under the rubrick of the programme. The UK e-Science Programme is an example of this.

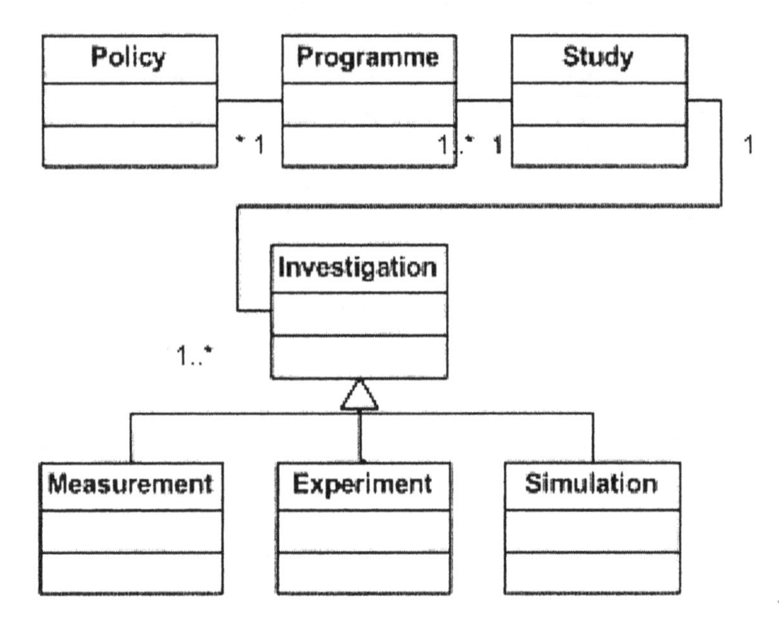

Figure 2. Model of the hierarchy of scientific data holdings

Studies (sometimes referred to as Projects): Studies investigate some aspect of science and have a Principal Investigator and/or institution, co-investigators and are usally funded. e.g. single projects such as EPSRC projects, or application for beam time on ISIS.

Investigations are studies or parts of studies that have links directly to data holdings. More specific types of investigations include experiments, measurements or simulations.

Experiments: investigations into the physical behaviour of the environment usually to test an hypothesis, typically involving an instrument operating under some instrumental settings and environmental conditions, and generating data sets in files. E.g. the subjection of a material to bombardment by X-Rays of known frequency generated by the Synchrotron Radiation Source with the result diffraction pattern recorded.

Measurements: investigations that record the state of some aspect of the environment over a sequence of points in time and space, using some passive detector, e.g. the measurement of temperature at a point on the earth surface taken hourly using a thermometer of known accuracy.

Simulations: investigations that test a model of part of the world, and a computer simulation of the state space of that model. This will typically involve a computer program with some initial parameters, and generate a dataset representing the result of the simulation. E.g. a computer simulation of fluid flow over a body using a specific program, with input parameters the shape of the body, and the velocity and viscosity of the fluid, generating a data set of fluid velocities.

Each investigation has a particular purpose and uses a particular experimental set up of instruments or computer systems. Experiments may be organised within larger studies, which themselves may be organised into programmes of linked studies.

Classes within the model have several fields. For example, investigator has a name, address, status, institution and role within the study. For reasons of space we cannot provide a complete description of all the available classes within the metadata model. For illustration, we consider the Study class. Within a Study, there are several fields, as in Table 1.

Funding	Source of funds of the study, including grant-funding body.
Time	Date, time and duration of study. Can be either a point time and date, or a begin time and end time. We expect it to be in a standard format: dd/mm/yyyy for dates; hh:mm:ss for times.
Purpose	Description of purpose of study, including: ■ Free text abstract of investigation ■ Keywords categorising subject of investigation, preferably selected from a controlled vocabulary. ■ Study type: a field that can be used to indicate the type of study being undertaken.
Status	Status of study, (not-started, in progress, complete).
Resources	Statement of the resources being used, e.g. which facility.

Table 1. Study Description Class Fields

3.2 Modelling scientific data holdings

Investigations have datasets associated with them; similarly, in CSMD, each investigations in associated a set of metadata describing the data holding (DH) associated with that investigation. The metadata format given here is designed for use on general scientific data holdings. Thus, data holdings have three layers: the experiment, the logical data, and the physical files. The overall structure of the model for scientific data holdings is given in Figure 3. Data holdings are considered as hierarchies, with Data Sets, generalised to *Data Collections (DC)*, broken down into individual logical Data Files, generalised in the model as *Atomic Data Objects (ADOs)* as they may not be held in file-store, but in for example databases. At each level of granularity, metadata can be provided giving *representation information* [18] at the appropriate level of the data holding.

An investigation is a study that generates raw data. This raw data can then be processed via a set of tools, forming on the way intermediate data sets, which may or may not be held in the data holding. The final processing step generates the final analysed data set. At each stage of the data process stores data in a set of physical files with a physical location. It is possible that there may be different versions of the data sets in the holding. In a general data portal, all stages of the process should be stored and made available as reviewers of the data holdings may wish to determine the nature of the analysis performed, and other scientist may wish to use the raw data to perform different analyses. Thus type markers ('raw', 'intermediate', 'final') need to be kept with DCs and ADOs and relationships between the DCs of different types recorded.

Thus each data holding takes the form of a hierarchy: one investigation generates a sequence of logical data collection, and each data collection is instantiated via a set of physical objects. The design of the metadata model is tailored to capture such an organisation of data holdings. A single metadata record in this model can provide sufficient metadata to access all the components of the data holding either all together or separately.

This models distinguishes between the logical data holding, describing the data objects and their structural hierarchy, and the data location. The data location provides a mapping between the URIs used in the data definition component of the metadata model, and the actual URLs of the files. This can provide facilities for describing mirror location for the whole structure, and also for individual files.

3.3 Parameters

Parameters can be associated with either Data Holdings, Data Collections, or ADOs. The same metadata item is used to represent either experimental conditions and measured items stored as data points in the data collection, but are rather distinguished via a parameter type qualifier ('fixed' or 'measured'). Each parameter has a set of fields describing its value (if fixed in as an input parameter), the units of measurement used to qualify the data points, the range

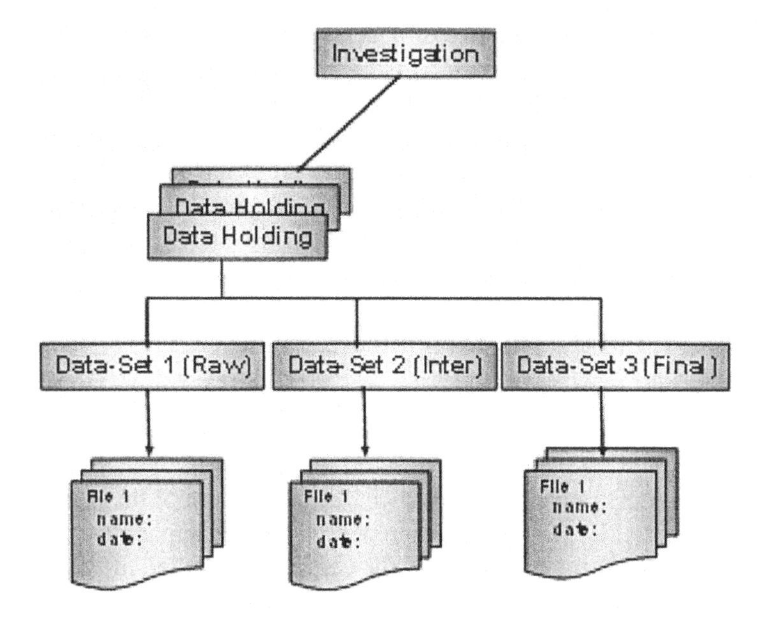

Figure 3. Model of the hierarchy of scientific data holdings

of values over-which a parameter can take and the error margin expected on the value. Additionally, there is support for parameter aggregation.

3.4 Other metadata components

Additionally to the provenance and data holding components of the metadata record in CSMD, there are also components for recording other aspects of the information pertinant to a study. We discuss them here briefly.

Topic. A top-level topic can be associated with an study. This can describe which discipline the study falls under (e.g. Chemistry, Crystallography), and also some more discipline specific keywords, which can be selected from an associated controlled vocabulary; the metadata record will also track which controlled vocabulary is being used. This component in intended for use as a index for searching and browsing through the metadata catalogue.

Access control. Access is controlled by the access entry in the metadata record; how this is actually done is dependent on the data holder. Typically, it will contain a list of users or groups who are allowed access to the metadata and data, or a pointer to an access control system which contains such data for this study. For example, there might be an access type, with settings such as open, on application, restricted, commercial in confidence. This may be given in conjunction with explicit instructions on how to access the data, and who to contact. Access control should be reflected throughout the metadata model allowing different granularity of access control. For example, whilst a study overall maybe public, certain parts of the data holding (perhaps unprocessed files) maybe restricted to the investigators themselves.

Related Materials. One or many links and or textual descriptions of material related to this study e.g. earlier studies or parallel studies. Also, this component would be the appropriate place to link to associated publications derived from the dataset, publications which are cited by the investigation, and supporting material such as glossaries and dictionaries.

4. Metadata Conformance

The full CSMD metadata model is very detailed and using it to its full potential requires a great deal of metadata to be entered. This is a time consuming process, requiring a great deal of effort on the part of the experimentor and/or facility administrator, and in practice, the application of the metadata may not require the full level of detail to support an desired application. Thus we have defined levels of conformance for the CSMD, as detailed in Table 2.

1	Study and Investigation metadata with indexing at the Study level
2	Level 1 + DataHolding metadata (i.e. DataSets and DataObjects)
3	Level 2 + related material, Access condition, indexing to data collection levels
4	Level 3 + indexing to data object level and data object parameter information
5	All metadata components are filled as L4 + funding, resources used, facilities used etc

Table 2. CSMD Conformance Levels

Conformance level 1 provides "search metadata" similar to that typically provided by simple library or publication metadata such as Dublin Core. CSMDs mapping to Dublin Core is discussed in [19]. As the level of conformance is increased, first information about the data holding is included, allowing the data collections to be searched in detail. Then contextual and access control information is added, allowing data collections to be accessed via the portal. Levels 4 and 5 then add further detail to the model for more complex exploration of the data holdings. Currently, the CCLRC Data Portal is conformant to level 2 with additionally more detailed parameter information.

5. An Example

As an example of this scientific metadata model, consider the SXD information from the ISIS Neutron Spallation Source. A study in this case is an application for beam-time, uniquely identified with an RB number, which covers a programme of investigations, and is described by a description of the purpose in the original study application. This programme is in turn broken down into a series of individual investigations, each of which are experiments on the SXD detector. Each investigation may have a sequence of runs, each generating a data set. Each run keeps the major parameters of the experiment the same (e.g. temperature of study), but alter some other parameter (e.g. orientation of the sample in the target). This information needs to be preserved in the metadata model.

For example an investigation with name *Benzene, variable temperature study: 150K*, would have a user, purpose and date and time information associated with it. It should have a unique ID (not necessarily the RB number as that may relate to a programme of investigations), and it will have a set of RAW data files associated with it, for example: files SXD10091, SXD10092, SXD10093, SXD10094, SXD10095. There may also be a set of intermediate SXD files, and also a set of processed final files in standard data formats for specific programs, such as .HKL, .INS and .RES files. The system should keep track of the relationship between files, and record which have been processed. We give a sample of the fields in the metadata. We use *#classname* to represent cross-references between classes. Thus the metadata of the experiment is represent as follows.

	Experiment
StudyID	SXD10091
Study Name	Benzene, variable temperature study: 150K
Investigator	#investigator
Study Information	#study-information
Data holder	#data-holder
Instrument	#instrument
Conditions	#conditions

The Investigator gives details of the people involved in the study.

	Investigator
Name	Anne X. Perimenter
Institution	University of Somewhere
Status	Lecturer
Role	Principal Investigator
Address	Dept of Organic Chemistry, Univ of Somewhere, Somewhere, UK.

Study information gives the information on this study.

	Study Information
Funding Source	EPSRC
Time	1/11/00, 11.45
Purpose	#purpose
Status	Complete
Resources	Beam time on ISIS using the SXD, for 1hr on 1/11/00

The Purpose itself may have several fields.

	Purpose
Abstract	To study the structure of Benzene at a temperature of 150K.
Keywords	Chemistry: organic: benzene: denatured benzene, C6H6, C6D6

The data holder refers to the institution principally responsible for holding the data.

	Data Holder
Institution	ISIS, CCLRC Rutherford Appleton Laboratory

The conditions in this case just record the temperature under which the sample has been studied.

	Conditions
Temperature	150K

This will also have to accommodate different organisations of files, not just the raw/intermediate/final as given in the ISIS model. Files may also be in several different locations, separating out the identity of data sets from the location. Giving filetype/directory pairs does this:

	Data location
Data holding locations	ftp://ftp.isis.rl.ac.uk/SXD/ SXD1009/ http://www.dooc.uos.ac.uk/~perimenter/bezene/
Data set Directories	(RAW, raw/), (Intermediate, SXD/), (HKL, HKL/), (INS, INS/), (RES, RES/).

The data description would break down into a hierarchy of entries. Firstly the top-level entry, which contains references to the data sets of the study.

	Data description
Data Sets	#raw, #intermediate, #processed

Then the raw data set would have references to the metadata for each file (not the file itself):

	Raw
Dataset type	RAW
Files	#SXD10091.RAW, #SXD10092.RAW, #SXD10093.RAW, #SXD10094.RAW, #SXD10095.RAW

Each file would have a metadata entry, giving its URI:

	SXD10091.RAW
URI	SXD10091.RAW

There will also be a dataset entry for intermediate files and processed files, omitted for brevity. The data set can be represented as a XML model, and can be displayed in the CCLRC Data Portal.

6. Conclusions and Future Development

The CCLRC Data Portal has been successfully piloted within the context of the e-Science programme at CCLRC, using sample data from the ISIS and SRS facilities at CCLRC. The CSMD has also been used on a variety of UK e-Science/Grid enabling projects as the premier metadata model, including the NERC e-Minerals [3], EPSRC e-Materials [4], and the EPSRC Integrative Biology [5] projects. Further, it has been used as a template on a variety of other projects in the e-Science field; for example, the EPSRC MyGrid project adopted version 1 and enhanced the provenance information [6]; and the JISC eBank project has developed the format for crystallography data [7]. The model has proven adaptable to a wide variety of situations.

The major current activity is to roll out the data portal onto the ISIS ICAT. This will cover a twenty year back catalogue of experiments on the ISIS Neutron Spallation Source. This projects is using a Relational Schema based on version 2 of the CSMD. Further, the EPSRC CCP1 (Collaborative Computational Project in Quantum Chemistry) is assessing CSMD for metadata needs on their Grid Data Management Middleware. Future work includes using the model and data portal within other facilities at CCLRC, such as the Diamond Light Source, a new x-ray synchrotron, and the Central Laser Facility.

A common metadata format for scientific data also allows the possibility of providing a single point of access to both the major outputs of science: data and publications. By using the common or interoperable features of the generic scientific metadata model, we allow the possibility of combined searches across both domains, or alternatively, using the metadata from one domain (say scientific publications) to search and access appropriate information from the other (say retrieve relevant data sets to test the claims of the publication).

The current work under the JISC funded CLADDIER project [20] seeks to integrate the use of persistent Identifiers across data and publications using existing Publication institutional repository systems, inparticular the CCLRC ePubs system. In order to have a common search mechanism over library and data portals, a base level of simple metadata is required; this can be provided by Dublin Core and as we have seen, CSMD conformance level 1 can provide Dublin Core metadata. The Related Material component of the metadata can record citation of data by publications and conversely the citation of publications by the data, to give context to the study. Common controlled vocabularies can be used to index both data and publications. Further issues arise when we use metadata at different levels of abstraction as in the FRBR model [21] (which appears to have a close relationship to the notions of data holding in CSMD) and versioning of data holdings for citation in a publication.

Future considerations on the use of the CSMD will consider the requirements of Digital Curation (preservation, enrichment and availability) upon the metadata record; metadata population strategies in the scientific process; and re-expression as an ontology. Experience to data has shown that the CSMD covers a wide area of scientific research work in sufficient detail in a robust yet usable fashion. We would anticipate that the model would be suitable as a common core for other more domain specific metadata models; ultimately to allow rich discovery and exploitation of the scientific record into the long-term future.

Acknowledgments

We would like to thank Kerstin Kleese van Dam, and the other members of the CCLRC e-Science Data Management team.

References

[1] S. Sufi, B. Matthews, K. Kleese van Dam. An Interdisciplinary Model for the Representation of Scientific Studies and Associated Data Holdings. *UK e-Science All Hands meeting*, Nottingham, England, 02-04 Sep 2003

[2] S. Sufi, B. Matthews CCLRC Scientific Metadata Model: Version 2. *DL Technical Reports*, DL-TR-2004-001, 2004. http://epubs.cclrc.ac.uk/work-details?w=30324

[3] L. Blanshard, K. Kleese van Dam, M. Dove Environment from the Molecular Level e-Science project and its use of CLRC's Web Services based Data Portal *Proceeding of the 1st. International Conference on Web Services*, 2003.

[4] L. Blanshard, R. Tyler, K. Kleese van Dam. eMaterials: Integrating Grid Computation and Data Management Services. *UK e-Science Programme All Hands Meeting (AHM2004)*, Nottingham, 2004

[5] D. J. Gavaghan, A. C. Simpson, S. Lloyd, D. F. Mac Randal, D. R. S. Boyd. Towards a Grid infrastructure to support integrative approaches to biological research *Phil. Trans. Royal Society Series A 363 1829-1841*, 2005

[6] N. Sharman, N. Alpdemir, J. Ferris, M. Greenwood, P. Li and C. Wroe. The myGrid Information Model. *UK e-Science All Hands Meeting 2004* Nottingham, England, 2004.

[7] S. J. Coles, J. G. Frey, M. B. Hursthouse, M. E. Light, A. J. Milsted, L. A. Carr, D. DeRoure, C. J. Gutteridge, H. R. Mills, K. E. Meacham, M. Surridge, E. Lyon, R. Heery, M. Duke, M. Day. An e-Science environment for service crystallography -from submission to dissemination. *Journal of Chemical Information and Modeling*, Special Issue on eScience, 2006.

[8] J V. Ashby, J. C. Bicarregui, D. R. S. Boyd, K. Kleese van Dam, S. C. Lambert, B. M. Matthews, K. D. O'Neill. The CLRC Data Portal *British National Conference on Databases*, 2001.

[9] J .V. Ashby, J. C. Bicarregui, D. R. S. Boyd, K. Kleese van Dam, S. C. Lambert, B. M. Matthews, K.D. O'Neill. A Multidisciplinary Scientific Data Portal. *HPCN 2001: International Conference on High Performance and Networking Europe,* Amsterdam, 2001.

[10] C. Houstis, S. Lalis. ARION: An Advanced Lightweight Software System Architecture for accessing Scientific Collections, *Cultivate Interactive, no.4*, 2001. http://www.cultivate-int.org/issue4/arion/

[11] J. Ryssevik, S. Musgrave. The Social Science Dream Machine: Resource discovery, analysis and delivery on the Web, *Proceedings of the the IASSIST Conference*, Toronto, 1999. http://www.nesstar.org/papers/iassist_0599.html

[12] The Dublin Core Metadata Initiative. http://www.dublincore.org.

[13] H. Hoeck, H. Thiemann, M. Lautenschlager, I. Jessel, B Marx, M. Reinke. The CERA Metadata Model. *Technical Report No. 9, DKRZ - German Climate Computer Centre,* 1995. http://www.dkrz.de/forschung/reports/report9/CERA.book.html

[14] K. O'Neill, R. Cramer, M. Gutierrez, K. Kleese van Dam, S. Kondapalli, S. Latham, B. Lawrence, R. Lowry, A. Woolf. A specialised metadata approach to discovery and use of data in the NERC DataGrid *Proceedings of the U.K. e-science All Hands Meeting*, 2004.

[15] C. Baru, A. Gupta, V. Chu, B.Ludscher, R. Marciano, Y. Papakonstantinou, P. Velikhov. XML-Based Information Mediation for Digital Libraries *Digital Libraries '99*, 1999. http://www.npaci.edu/DICE/Pubs/dl99-demo.pdf

[16] The Data Documentation Initiative. http://www.icpsr.umich.edu/DDI/

[17] K. G. Jeffery. Metadata. *Information Systems Engineering,* S. Brinkkemper, E. Lindencrona, A. Solvberg (Eds), Lecture Notes in Computer Science, Springer Verlag, 2000.

[18] Reference Model for an Open Archival Information System (OAIS). *CCSDS 650.0-B-1 Blue Book. Issue 1. ISO 14721:2003*, 2002.

[19] B. M. Matthews, M. D. Wilson, K.Kleese van Dam. Accessing the Outputs of Scientific Projects *In Proceedings of CRIS 2002, Current Research Information Systems*, Kassel, Germany, 2002.

[20] CLADDIER http://claddier.badc.ac.uk/

[21] Functional Requirements for Bibliographic Records, *International Federation of Library Associations and Institutions*, UBCIM Publications New Series Vol 19, 1998. http://www.ifla.org/VII/s13/frbr/frbr.pdf

IDEAS FOR THE PROVISION OF ONTOLOGY ACCESS IN GRID ENVIRONMENTS

Miguel Esteban Gutiérrez and Asunción Gómez-Pérez
Ontology Engineering Group
Universidad Politécnica de Madrid
Campus de Montegancedo s/n, 28660, Boadilla del Monte
Madrid, Spain
mesteban@fi.upm.es
asun@fi.upm.es

Abstract Ontologies are the backbone of the Semantic Web. Current grid architectures do not consider their usage, and there are no protocols nor standards in the Grid community for dealing with them. Therefore, the provision of appropriate means for accessing, querying and using ontologies effectively is a key factor if we want to enrich the current grid with semantic technologies and to support progress towards the next generation Grid, that is, the Semantic Grid.

Keywords: ontologies, Semantic Grid, semantic technologies, WS-DAIOnt, WS-DAI, OGSA.

1. Introduction

The increasing use of semantic technologies has reached almost every computer-related field, including the Grid. The next generation Grid should virtualise the notion of distribution in computation, storage, and communication over unlimited resources using well-defined computational semantics, as the Semantic Grid [7] is proposing. A grid node may provide new resources and services and their functional and non functional properties should be explicitly defined by means of *ontologies*, formal and explicit specifications of shared conceptualizations [15]. Therefore, if semantic technologies are to be used, it is fundamental to provide the appropriate means for accessing, querying and using ontologies in the Grid.

In this chapter, we analyse the problem of accessing, querying and using ontologies concerned with the current Grid architecture, taking as starting point the lessons learnt about this topic in the Semantic Web.

The chapter is organised as follows: Section 2 collects some of the most important lessons learnt in the Semantic Web regarding ontology access, query and use. Section 3 comprises an analysis of the ontology access problem in the context of the current Grid. Section 4 presents WS-DAIOnt, a proposed mechanism for ontology access in the current Grid. Finally, Section 5 concludes with the current state of development.

2. Lessons Learnt from the Semantic Web

Recently, the W3C has recommended three languages: RDF [1], RDFS [2] and OWL[3], to represent knowledge in the Semantic Web.

In addition, several ontology development tools (i.e., Protégé[4], WebODE[5], KAON[6]) support the creation of ontologies in such languages. There are also ontology query languages like SPARQL [13], RDQL [14], RQL [12], SeRQL [5] used for retrieving RDF(S) and OWL ontologies, and inference engines like FaCT[7] and RACER [11] that infer knowledge and data that are not explicitly declared in the ontologies. Normally, these querying and inference tools are strongly related to the language in which the ontology is implemented. Such languages differ in their expressiveness (the kind of knowledge that can be represented) and in their inference mechanisms (the kind of reasoning they

[1] http://www.w3.org/RDF/
[2] http://www.w3.org/TR/rdf-schema/
[3] http://www.w3.org/2001/sw/WebOnt/
[4] http://protege.stanford.edu/
[5] http://webode.dia.fi.upm.es/WebODEWeb/
[6] http://sourceforge.net/projects/kaon/
[7] http://www.cs.man.ac.uk/ horrocks/FaCT/

carry out). For a detailed description and comparison of languages and tools we recommend [10].

The diversity of existing ontology languages and tools causes the *translation problem*, which appears when an ontologist decides to reuse an ontology (or part of it) with a tool other than the one used in its development, or in a language other than those in which the ontology is available. On the other hand, several APIs and query languages permit accessing ontologies implemented in a given language and an ontology user (or an application that uses the ontology) should know how to retrieve the ontology content using those APIs. As example, we can say that RDF(S) ontologies can be stored in Sesame[8], 3store[9], Joseki[10], Jena[11], Kowari[12] or even Oracle with its support for RDF(S)[13], and each has its own means for accessing the RDF(S) ontologies.

In this scenario interoperability and portability problems arise since the heterogeneity (different characteristics, properties and capabilities) of the languages and tools used for the development and storage of the ontologies might prevent the reutilization of these ontologies in different infrastructures because of their technological differences, namely, their limitations, restrictions and requirements.

At present, there are some language specific initiatives in the Semantic Web community devoted to solving specific problems, such as the W3C SPARQL query language, created to provide a RDF(S) query language for accessing to RDF(S) stores[14] [13], or the DIG interface, targeted to providing a common API for description logic-based systems interoperability [4].

Despite all these initiatives, the Semantic Web community does not have a standard mechanism or protocol for accessing ontologies implemented regardless of the language and tool used for its development.

3. Possibilities for Providing Ontology Access in the Grid

Up to now, current grid architectures have not taken into consideration ontology use; therefore, no protocols nor standards are available in the grid community to access and use them.

To use ontologies as other resources in the Grid, we must be able to access their contents physically, as we do with any other available resource. Therefore, the first requirement for using ontologies is to have the appropriate means

[8]http://www.openrdf.org/
[9]http://threestore.sourceforge.net/
[10]http://www.joseki.org/
[11]http://jena.sourceforge.net/
[12]http://www.kowari.org/
[13]http://www.oracle.com/technology/tech/semantic_technologies/
[14]Targeted at retrieving data, not creating, deleting or updating data.

for accessing them. Building on these basic capabilities, it will be possible to develop and deploy ontology-based functionalities in the Grid.

In this section we discuss where ontology access fits in the *Open Grid Services Architecture* (OGSA), and how ontology access services can be implemented. By *ontology access* we mean the mechanism or protocol needed for providing physical access to ontologies; by *ontology access services* we refer to the set of services that provide the means for accessing ontologies that are deployed as resources inside an OGSA-based grid.

3.1 Laying Ontology Access Services in OGSA

The Open Grid Services Architecture specification [8] is the blueprint for standard-based service-oriented grid computing. The specification collates the requirements for such an architecture[15] and also identifies the set of capabilities (offered as services) that may be needed in order to satisfy the defined requirements: infrastructure services, job management services, data services, resource management services, security services, self-management services and information services. For a detailed description of both requirements and capabilities, please refer to [8].

Ontologies can be queried as to their content. Content includes the concepts and relationships, as well as intensional information about those concepts, as for example, the definitions that apply to a particular class. Ontology access services should then provide access to all this information and even support queries over this information. Thus, ontology access services can be seen as a particular type of data service, a service that holds some data and provides mechanisms for creating, retrieving, updating and deleting these data. According to this, the most sensible mechanism for providing ontology access services should be based on the existing infrastructure in OGSA for data access.

The following subsection reviews the data access and integration facilities in OGSA, as these must be known to fully understand the rest of the chapter.

3.1.1 The OGSA Data Access and Integration Facilities. The *Global Grid Forum (GGF) Data Access and Integration Working Group* has a number of specifications that support data access on the Grid. The *Web Services Data Access and Integration Core Specification* [1], a.k.a. WS-DAI, and the accompanying realizations [2, 6, 3], provide a general mechanism for defining data services (whose key characteristic is that it offers the possibility of updating and retrieving the data from the data resource with which it interfaces) and specialised mechanisms for accessing specific data resources respectively.

[15]They range from interoperability and support for dynamic and heterogeneous environments and resources to resource sharing across organizations to data access to scalability, availability and extensibility.

The top level WS-DAI specification provides a basic and extensible framework for defining data service interfaces, messages and properties. With such a framework, the set of port types, operations and properties – which are needed to provide access to specific data resources – can be defined in a standard way. However, WS-DAI does not describe the particular interactions it performs with the data resource (in terms of, for example, query languages).

The underlying WS-DAI realizations describe the specific operations needed to interact with specific data resources, i.e., relational databases using SQL, XML sources using XQuery, etc. The upper level specification is irrelevant to the types of query that get passed through — they say nothing about the query language, result formats etc. The interfaces, messages and properties used must be defined in accordance with the WS-DAI framework.

Note that when building an application that interacts with a WS-DAI resource, it should be known beforehand which kind of resource will be used so that the appropriate WS-DAI realization is used. WS-DAI provides the most general properties of the data service as a grid service that the application may need to know about, while the realization provides the specific mechanisms for interacting with the data service.

3.2 Ontology Access through the OGSA Data Access and Integration Facilities

In order to integrate the ontology access services within the WS-DAI framework described in the previous section, several alternative approaches can be adopted according to how the framework is used and where the new services fit.

The approaches range from the mere use of the WS-DAI framework to the extension of this framework to fit our purposes. Here, we also present the idea of *abstract realization*, a realization which is not a plain realization of WS-DAI but a set of guidelines that explain how to use the WS-DAI framework for defining sets of related realizations.

In this section, we analyse each of the possible approaches and give examples that showe possible implementations of each approach; the Semantic Web languages RDF(S) and OWL illustrate these examples.

3.2.1 Several vanilla realizations. The first and most naïve approach consists in providing a specific access mechanism for each ontology language that is to be used; in our case, this means supplying a WS-DAI realization to each possible Semantic Web ontology language.

The specific realizations must adhere to the syntax guidelines given by the WS-DAI framework for defining the access mechanism. The concrete technical aspects needed to access data sources containing ontologies developed with each specific Semantic Web ontology language are defined in its related realization. However, these realizations may have nothing in common, as the semantics of each realization is conditioned by the necessities and requirements of the access mechanism provided for each language, as it happens in the following example.

Here we have two basic realization designs for accessing respirces, one for RDF(S) and other OWL, both developed independently.

The RDF(S) realization may provide access to RDF(S) by relaying on the graph nature of the RDF model: every model is composed of a set of nodes and links between the nodes. The nodes represent specific resources while the links represent properties of the source node resources.

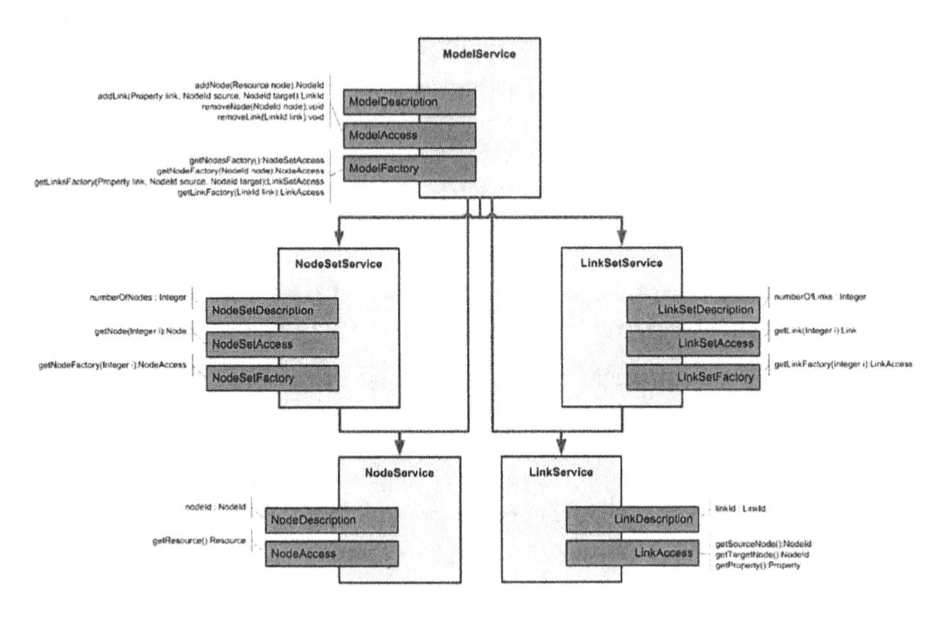

Figure 1. Sample RDF(S) vanilla realization

Following this idea, the realization can provide a set of interfaces that deliver functionalities for dealing with models with data structures that represent nodes (resources) and links (properties). Figure 1 represents a sample set of interfaces (already grouped in services) and the signatures of some of the messages provided by the main interfaces.

The design of the OWL realization can follow other approach, as for instance, an object-oriented one. According to this approach, the realization would provide interfaces which deal with data structures that mimic the conceptual elements defined in the OWL model: classes, properties, individuals, restrictions, etc. Figure 2 represents a sample set of interfaces and the signatures of some of the messages provided by the main interfaces.

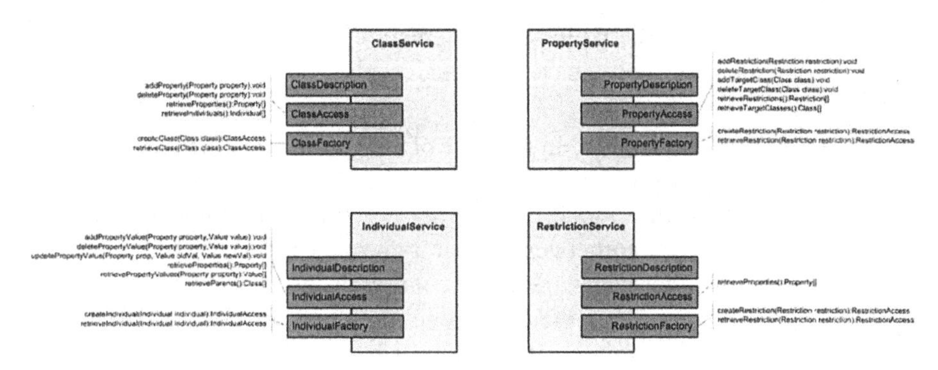

Figure 2. Sample OWL vanilla realization

Even though both realizations offer valid mechanisms for accessing their respective resources, we cannot ensure, according to this design approach, any homogeneity degree between the realizations, as there are no common guidelines that guarantee such homogeneity:

- *Data model structure:* nothing is said about how to structure the data model that is to be used in the messages. In this scenario, the RDF(S) realization uses a graph-based data model, while the OWL realization employs a component-like data model. Therefore, the interaction with the ontology services needs to be adapted to the specific operational model derived from the data model.

- *Naming conventions:* each realization uses its own prefixes and suffixes for denoting the names of the messages; for instance, the RDF(S) realization defines the messages adding the prefixes 'get', 'add' and 'remove' whilst the OWL realization names the messages with similar semantics using the prefixes 'retrieve', 'create' and 'delete'; furthermore, this latter realization defines messages with different semantics using a prefix (add) that clashes with other in the RDF(S) realization. When switching from one realization to other, the user will have to use another data model and to learn which are the concrete semantics of each type of message (being the type defined by the prefix and suffix combination).

- *Access modalities:* the RDF(S) realization provides messages for creating, retrieving and deleting contents, while the OWL realization has an additional functionality for updating the contents. Therefore, if we switch from an ontology developed in OWL to another developed in RDF(S), we have to simulate this extra functionality, as it is not present in the RDF(S) realization. It might happen that missing functionalities cannot be simulated due to the specific design of the other realization;

in that case the patterns of interaction with the ontology in the user's application should have to be reviewed.

- *Access granularity:* in the case of the RDF(S) realization, access to the contents is provided in different granularity degrees: we can interact directly with a model, with a set of components (nodes and links) or with specific components. The richer the messages provided in each level are, the better the interaction with the RDF(S) resource will be. On the other hand, the OWL realization just provides access to specific components of the model. Again, when switching from one realization to other, we will have to reorganize the ontology-based business logic in order to use the services properly.

- *Architectural organization:* messages with similar semantics are defined in different conceptual components. Whilst the creation of components in the RDF(S) realization is carried out in the ModelAccess interface, in the OWL realization this is delegated to the Factory interfaces associated to each component.

According to this scenario, the same interoperability problems that arise in the Semantic Web community appear when following this design approach: we end up having different mechanisms for accessing ontologies represented in RDF(S) and OWL, each one designed according to different criteria, which provide zero interoperability. Therefore, the ontology access service client must know beforehand the language in which the ontology is available, because he/she will have to use one or other realization for modelling the ontology-based business logic of the application. As it follows, switching from one language to other might cause severe changes in the ontology-based business logic, which is the main issue we are trying to solve.

3.2.2 Two-layer realization. The idea here is to separate the common operations from the specific ones, following a two-layer organisation. On the one hand, the upper layer would contain a base WS-DAI realization defining the common specific operations that must be provided by every ontology access mechanism. On the other hand, the lower layer would contain WS-DAI realizations based on the base realization; each realization, which should be related to an ontology language, would define the specific operations for accessing ontologies developed in that particular ontology language.

In terms of operations, the two-layer realization approach introduces the idea of a common *API* that must be followed by each final realization (and so by each implementation). There are several ways of creating this API, here we present two of them:

- *Functional approach.* The API contains the operations that represent functionalities for ontology access and management similar to those offered by ontology resources. According to this approach, the definition of the operations would be driven by the possibilities of the ontology resources.

  Functionalities can be selected in various ways, for instance, according to the desired granularity of the operations (the finer the grain detail is, the more functionalites will have to be provided by the API) or according to the size of the target API: we may want to minimize the number of functionalities provided by the API, so this becomes simple although rigid; or to maximize the number of operations so it becomes more flexible but rather complex.

- *Conceptual approach.* The API contains operations that deal with the conceptual elements available in the knowledge representation formalism of the ontology resources. Following this approach, the definition of the operations is driven by the necessities of the conceptual model, nor by the way the ontology resource deals with it, i.e. managing taxonomies, reasoning over inherited properties, etc.

  The number of operations of the API would depend on the modelling elements chosen (the more elements, the more functionalities needed for dealing with them) and the orthogonality of the operations desired (the more independence between the functionalities and the operands, the more operations to provide).

Thanks to this two-layer organisation, the basic ontology access interfaces can be standardised, thus lowering the risks of interoperability issues in the upper layer, that is, the one that contains the common operations. In Figure 3 we can see that the SchemaAccess interface defines common taxonomical management operations such as retrieving the parents and siblings of a given class, and these operations are common to both underlying realizations.

Unfortunately, no standardisation guidelines are provided for defining the specific operations to be set up in the realizations of the lower layer, nor which kind of operations can be defined in those interfaces. Therefore, interoperability problems might appear in some particular features of concrete languages.

We can see in Figure 3 an example of this case. It shows that the new operations added in the RDF(S) realization just provide extra functionalities for dealing with the elements defined in the base realization following the same naming convention, whereas the OWL realization provides new functionalities for operating over specific elements of the OWL model (restrictions) with its own naming conventions.

Regardless of the approach taken for the development of the API, enforcing the fulfillment of an API poses serious disadvantages. On the one hand,

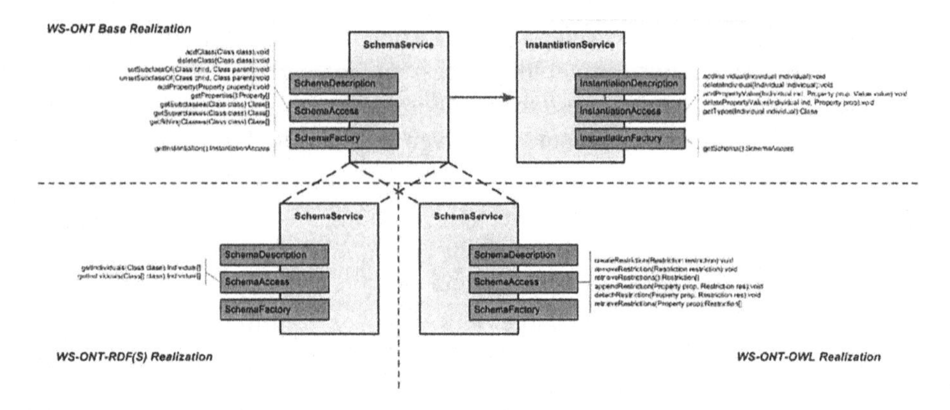

Figure 3. Sample two-layer realizations for RDF(S) and OWL

if the API that is to be fitted defines more operations than those provided by the resources, we may have a set of operations that not usable that will weaken the operational model defined by the API. On the other hand, if the API defines fewer operations than those provided by the resources, the potential of those resources is weakened because many of its capabilities will not be usable through the API.

Despite these disadvantages, we gain a strong advantage when APIs are enforced: the standardisation of the operations that will be used hereafter, which helps to reduce interoperability problems across realizations and implementations.

3.2.3 An extension of WS-DAI. Another approach consists in providing an extension to WS-DAI that, using the WS-DAI framework as basis, defines the specific structural elements needed for defining ontology access mechanisms, which are not defined in the basic WS-DAI framework.

Once the extension is defined, it would be used as the basis for creating specific realizations that would provide ad-hoc access mechanisms to access ontologies developed with concrete knowledge representation formalisms or languages. However, this approach has its pros and cons, as we will see in the following example.

In our sample extension, ontology resources (an specific type of data resources) are composed of *components* which, in their turn, may also be composed of other components. For dealing with these, an extra type of interface will be used. The interface will be named appending the suffix ‘Components’ to the name of the data resource it operates with. The interface will provide

BREAD functionalities [16], named with preffix the type of operation and the suffix 'Component'.

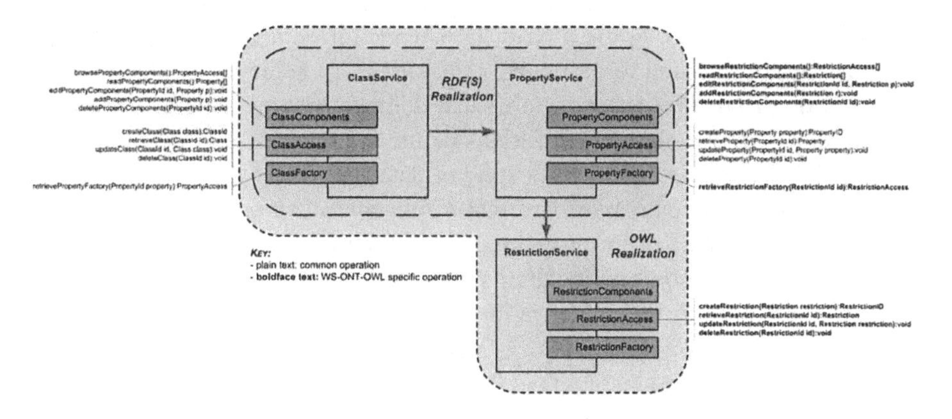

Figure 4. Implementations of the sample extension of WS-DAI

Figure 4 shows implementations of the sample extension for RDF(S) and OWL. Thanks to the extra structural elements defined in the extension, some kind of homogeneity is achieved, i.e. operations share a naming convention, messages with similar semantics are grouped in the same interfaces, etc. Thus, the interoperability problem decreases although unfortunately this effect is limited to these new structural elements.

However, in spite of the homogeneity achieved, the use of extra structural elements makes ontology access services different from plain WS-DAI data access services; therefore, whenever a user needs these services, he/she must know about their specificities to use them properly.

This requirement implies interoperability problems between data services: while a user of ontology access services would be able to understand and exploit plain WS-DAI data services, a user of plain WS-DAI data services would not be able to utilize the ontology access services since he/she has no way of inferring the semantics of the new structural elements used in the declaration of the ontology access services.

3.2.4 An *abstract* realization. This last approach is based on the two previous ones and is targeted at solving the problem of enforcing the fulfillment of a common API, and at creating extra structural elements.

The idea hera is to provide a means for defining the capabilities that might be offered via an ontology access service and the ways in which they are offered, and to provide a mechanism for publishing the specific capabilities im-

[16] Browse, read, edit, add and delete.

plemented by an ontology access service, so a client can discover and exploit them. This can be done by means of an *abstract* realization.

As we reviewed in section 3.1.1, the objective of the base WS-DAI core specification is to define a base framework for defining data access services that can be adapted to particular necessities. To achieve this, the base specification provides a set of patterns that defines messages and properties. With these patterns, concrete realizations define the set of WS-DAI-based elements needed for accessing a specific kind of data resource.

An *abstract* realization is a realization that does not define specific messages nor properties for providing a particular access mechanism; it defines a set of WS-DAI compliant patterns for defining interfaces, messages and properties oriented to the specification of an adaptable set of related data access mechanisms.

In our case, the abstract realization should be created for defining ontology access mechanisms. Later realizations of this abstract realization can choose which capabilities to implement and then define them with the patterns found in the base abstract realization. Let's see in the following example how this could be achieved.

The first step consists in selecting the elements of the data model that is to be supported. In the case of the RDF(S) and OWL languages, these elements are well-known and defined. Therefore, we could say that the ontology access mechanism must be able to operate over the union of both models: classes, properties, restrictions, individuals, etc. Specific realizations will choose which elements to support. In order to shorten the example, we can think that the valid elements are just classes, properties and restrictions, and that classes and restrictions are linked to properties (and viceversa).

Then, we have to select which kind of operations we want to provide in order to operate over the supported data model. In our example we show basic CRUD operations: create, retrieve, update and delete. The create operation provides an *id* for the element created, and that *id* is used in the rest of the operations for referring to that concrete element.

Once we have defined the data model and the way we can operate with it, we have to define the patterns that will drive the definition of the related infrastructure:

- *Interface creation patterns*:

  PATTERN I1: A description interface named *'element'Description* will be created for each element of the model.

  PATTERN I2: An access interface named *'element'Access* will be created for each element of the model.

PATTERN I3: If an element is linked to any other element, a factory interface named *'element'Factory* will be created for that element.

- *Messages creation patterns*:

PATTERN M1: A message named *'operation''element'* will be created in the appropriate access interface for each *'element'* that supports the operation *'operation'*[17].

PATTERN M2: If an element e_i is linked to another element e_j, a message named *retrieve'*e_j*'Factory* will be created in the factory interface of the element e_i.

- *Properties creation patterns*:

PATTERN P1: A property named *'linkedTo'* will be defined in each description interface. If an element e_i is linked to any other element e_j the value of the property will be the list of elements e_j to which e_i is linked. Otherwise, the property will be nil.

PATTERN P2: A property named *'operationsSupported'* will be defined in each description interface. If an element e_i supports an operation op_j, the value of the property will be the list of operations op_j supported by the element e_i.

With all of these patterns we can then produce our RDF(S) and OWL realizations (see Figure 5). As we can see, in the case of classes and properties, the names of the interfaces and messages are shared in both RDF(S) and OWL, so switching from one realization to other (when dealing with classes and properties) would not require changes in the ontology-based business logic.

Following this approach, each realization can choose the capabilities required, and by means of the patterns defined in the abstract realization, the interfaces, messages and properties are defined in an homogeneous and standard way.

3.3 Conclusions

The OGSA specification defines a set of requirements that must be fulfilled by any implementation of the specification; it also defines a set of capabilities (services) that might be offered via implementations to fulfil these requirements.

According to these requirements and capabilities, the data access and integration facilities defined by OGSA constitute the most sensible niche for fitting

[17] op_j is one of 'create', 'retrieve', 'update', 'delete'

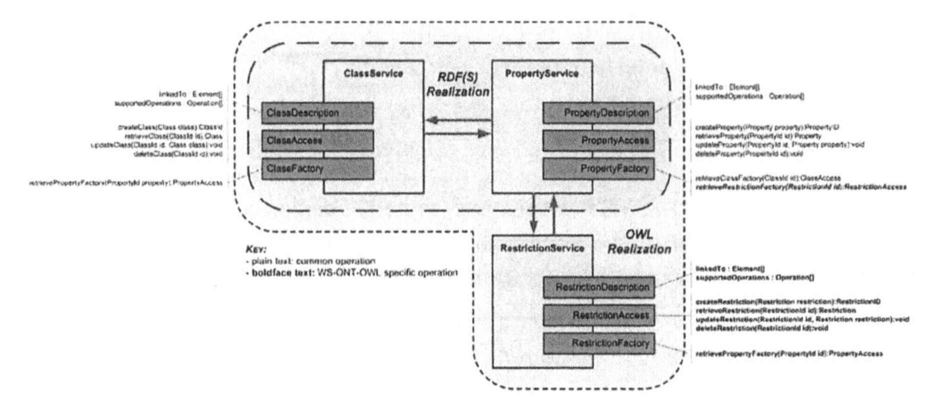

Figure 5. Sample RDF(S) and OWL realizations using the abstract realization approach

the ontology access services inside the OGSA architecture. The data access and integration facilities are governed by the WS-DAI specification, which is still under development inside of the GGF.

In the previous subsections, we have presented several approaches that provide ontology access using the WS-DAI specification as a basis; these approaches range from the realizations to the extensions.

The first approach clearly requires complete new implementations for any additional language introduced, as nothing is reused from other realizations. The second approach, on the contrary, provides some reuse by means of designing a two-layer mechanism that proposes a set of common functionalities. The cost of such reuse is the issue of factoring out a sensible subset of functionalities valid for any possible ontology language, which may end up posing interoperability problems between the services and the ontology resources.

The third approach consists in creating an extension to WS-DAI. This alternative suggests that there are characteristics and properties which distinguish ontology access services from vanilla data access services. Nevertheless, exploiting these differences by means of extra structural features may imply interoperability problems between plain data services and ontology access services.

Finally, the fourth approach suggests that there might be characteristics that distinguish ontology access services from plain data services, but also, that there are subtle differences between ontology resources that must be also taken into consideration. The fourth approach proposes a way for defining operations in a common format (taking into account these differences between ontology resources), so that some kind of standardisation is introduced in the underlying realizations.

Therefore, and bearing in mind the objectives of reducing the amount of different ontology access mechanisms and of facilitating the interoperability between them, the best design approach is the abstract realization one.

4. WS-DAIOnt: a Proposal of an Ontology Access Mechanism in the Grid

The WS-DAIOnt specification [9], which is the short term for "Web Services Data Access and Integration: The Ontology Realization", and the accompanying realizations (WS-DAIOnt-RDF(S), ...) define the data access infrastructure needed for dealing with ontologies in grid environments.

WS-DAIOnt is based on the WS-DAI specification and provides a framework for defining ontology access service interfaces by means of the WS-DAI vocabulary, and for enhacing it with the patterns and properties needed to provide specific ontology access mechanisms. Specific ontology data sources are then addressable according to concrete WS-DAIOnt realizations, i.e. WS-DAIOnt-RDF(S).

In the following subsections, both the foundations of WS-DAIOnt and the components of WS-DAIOnt will be described.

4.1 WS-DAIOnt Foundations

The WS-DAIOnt specification is being designed following the abstract realization approach described in Section 3.2.4. The foundational pillars that drive the design of the specification are the following:

- *Unified basic terminology.* Currently, knowledge representation formalisms use their own terminology for naming the knowledge modelling components (ontology elements) they use. Thus, frames-based formalisms use the name 'class' for referring to what it is named 'concept' in description logics.

  Whereas humans are able to match the names as synonyms and use both of them indistinctly, software agents are not able to do so. Therefore, interoperability problems might appear because of this terminology tangle.

  WS-DAIOnt defines a neutral vocabulary for naming the ontology elements to be used when dealing with ontologies in grid environments, taking into account the specific modeling components of different knowledge representation formalisms (frames, semantic networks, description logics ...)

  This common and standard vocabulary avoids the use of multiple different vocabularies that would hamper the understanding of the provided data components and functionalities.

- *Ontology components relationships patterns.* Each knowledge representation formalism defines a set of modeling elements and the way they are related to each other. For instance, in the frames formalism slots are defined locally (in frames), whereas in description logics properties are defined globally (and can then be restricted to specific classes).

WS-DAIOnt defines how to specify the concrete ways in which ontology components can be related, and which is the expected semantics of these relationships, so clients can deduce how to conceptually use them properly.

- *Ontology components usage patterns.* WS-DAIOnt defines how the interfaces, messages and properties must be specified in terms of WS-DAI patterns, in order to provide functionalities in a standard way. Therefore, clients can deduce how expected functionalities have to be exploited.

- *Ontology access services behaviours.* WS-DAIOnt defines the expected behaviour of the predefined common components and functionalities, so that every concrete implementation must adhere to these behaviours. Therefore, clients may expect some kind of homogeneous behaviour across realizations and implementations.

4.2 WS-DAIOnt Components

The two main components of WS-DAIOnt are the *WS-DAIOnt Data Model* and the *WS-DAIOnt Port Types*.

The WS-DAIOnt Data Model defines how the data managed by the specified interfaces is virtually structured. The data model works as a metamodel from and to which other knowledge representation formalisms may be mapped — by means of these mappings the interfaces provide a common way for accessing heterogeneous ontologies.

The data model defines the unified terminology to be used in WS-DAIOnt regarding the data components and also defines the possible relationships patterns among them.

The organization of the data model has two dimensions:

- *Layered structure.* The components are divided in two layers, the core layer and the extended layer. On the one hand, the core layer contains the common modeling components found in most of the representative knowledge representation formalisms. On the other hand, the extended layer will contain those modeling elements not considered for the core layer because of their specificity or because they are yet to appear.

- *Model and data separation.* The components are also divided with regard to their concerns: those used for the conceptualization are grouped together in the model part, and those used for dealing with individuals are grouped in the data part.

The WS-DAIOnt Port Types proposes a hierarchy of port types (interfaces), providing different granularity levels of access to the data model components for the sake of usability.

The upper levels of the hierarchy are general purpose interfaces that are fixed in the WS-DAIOnt specification and are mandatory for every underlying realization. The lower levels of the hierarchy are realization-dependent. In order to create the port types in a standard way, WS-DAIOnt defines a set of message design and organization criteria based on the components of the WS-DAIOnt data model usage and relationships patterns.

5. Conclusions

Ontology access provisioning is crucial if we want to enrich the Grid with semantic technologies. Furthermore, due to the increasing number of existing ontology languages and tools, an effective mechanism that guarantees interoperability between ontology access mechanisms must be developed. Up to date no protocols nor mechanisms are available in the OGSA architecture for dealing with ontologies in an effective manner.

By extending WS-DAI with WS-DAIOnt and the accompanying realizations, we provide the current grid architecture with a standard way of supplying ontology access and management capabilities, making ontologies available in grid environments like other specialized data resources usable across virtual organizations, thus enabling the future integration of semantic technologies in the grid architecture.

WS-DAIOnt, and the accompanying realizations, are still under development as part of the OntoGrid project.

Acknowledgments

We would like to thank all of those who have helped us anyhow: Sean Bechhofer, Óscar Corcho, Rosario Plaza and Mł del Carmen Suárez de Figueroa.

This work is supported by the OntoGrid project (FP6-511513) and by a U.P.M. pre-doctoral grant.

References

[1] M. Antonioletti, M. Atkinson, A. Krause, S. Malaika, S. Laws, N. W. Paton D. Pearson, and G. Riccardi. Web Services Data Access and Integration – The Core (WS-DAI) Specification, Version 1.0. GWD-R, Global Grid Forum, DAIS Working Group, Jun 2006.

[2] M. Antonioletti, B. Collins, A. Krause, S. Laws, J. Magowan, S. Malaika, and N.W. Paton. Web Services Data Access and Integration - The Relational Realisation (WS-DAIR) Specification, Version 1.0. GWD-R, Global Grid Forum, DAIS Working Group, Jun 2006.

[3] M. Antonioletti, S. Hastings, A. Krause, S. Langella, S. Laws, S. Malaika, and N.W. Paton. Web Services Data Access and Integration – The XML Realization (WS-DAIX)

Specification, Version 1.0. GWD-R, Global Grid Forum, DAIS Working Group, Jun 2006.

[4] S. Bechhofer. The DIG Description Logic Interface: DIG/1.1. Specification, DL Implementation Group (DIG), Feb 2003.

[5] J. Broekstra, A. Kampman, and F. van Harmelen. Sesame: A Generic Architecture for Storing and Querying RDF and RDF Schema. In I. Horrocks and J. Hendler, editors, *The Semantic Web - ISWC 2002: First International Semantic Web Conference*, number 2342 in Lecture Notes in Computer Science, pages 54–68. Springer, May 2002.

[6] B. Collins. Web Services Data Access and Integration - The File Realization (WS-DAIF). Informational recommendation, Global Grid Forum, DAIS Working Group, Oct 2004.

[7] D. De Roure, N. R. Jennings, and N. R. Shadbolt. The Semantic Grid: Past, Present and Future. *Proceedings of the IEEE*, 93(3):669–681, Mar 2005.

[8] I. Foster (Ed), D. Berry, A. Djaoui, A. Grimshaw, H. Kishimoto (Ed) B. Horn, F. Maciel, A. Savva (Ed), F. Siebenlist, R. Subramaniam, J. Treadwell, and J. Von Reich. The Open Grid Services Architecture, Version 1.5. GWD-I, Global Grid Forum, OGSA Working Group, Mar 2006.

[9] M. Esteban Gutiérrez (Ed), S. Bechhofer, O. Corcho, M. Fernndez-Lpez, A. Gómez-Pérez, Z. Kaoudi, I. Kotsiopulos, M. Koubarakis, Mł C. Suárez-Figueroa, and V. Tamma. Specification and Design of Ontology Grid Compliant and Grid Aware Services. Deliverable D3.1, OntoGrid Consortium, Apr 2005.

[10] Asunción Gómez-Pérez, Óscar Corcho, and Mariano Fernández-López. *Ontological Engineering : with examples from the areas of Knowledge Management, e-Commerce and the Semantic Web*. Advanced Information and Knowledge Processing. Springer, first edition, Jul 2004.

[11] V. Haarslev and R. Moeller. Racer: A core inference engine for the Semantic Web. In D. Fensel, K. P. Sycara, and J. Mylopoulos, editors, *The Semantic Web - ISWC 2003, Second International Semantic Web Conference*, number 2870 in Lecture Notes in Computer Science. Springer, Oct 2003.

[12] G. Karvounarakis, S. Alexaki, V. Christophides, D. Plexousakis, and M. Scholl. RQL: A Declarative Query Language for RDF. In *11th International World Wide Web Conference*. ACM, May 2002.

[13] E. Prud'hommeaux and A. Seaborne. SPARQL Query Language for RDF. Working draft, W3C, Feb 2006.

[14] A. Seaborne. RDQL – A Query Language for RDF. Member Submission, W3C, Jan 2004.

[15] Rudi Studer, V. Richard Benjamins, and Dieter Fensel. Knowledge engineering: Principles and methods. *Data & Knowledge Engineering*, 25(1–2):161–197, Mar 1998.

SEMANTIC SUPPORT FOR META-SCHEDULING IN GRIDS

Paolo Missier
School of Computer Science
The University of Manchester
United Kingdom
pmissier@cs.man.ac.uk

Philipp Wieder
Grid Computing and Distributed Systems Group
Research Centre Jülich
52425 Jülich, Germany
ph.wieder@fz-juelich.de

Wolfgang Ziegler
Fraunhofer Institute SCAI
Department of Bioinformatics
53754 Sankt Augustin, Germany
wolfgang.ziegler@scai.fraunhofer.de

Abstract Co-ordinated usage of resources in a Grid environment is a challenging task impeded by the nature of resource usage and provision: Resources reside in different geographic locations, are managed by different organisations, and are by no means accessible via standardised interfaces, protocols or commands. These prerequisites have to be taken into account in order to provide solutions in the area of Grid scheduling and resource management.

In this document we propose the employment of a semantic model for Grid scheduling. The Grid Scheduling Ontology describes the capabilities and state of a scheduler, providing a machine-processable and interoperable model for the integration of local schedulers into Grid resource management. Along with the model we present a meta-scheduling architecture based on the VIOLA Meta-Scheduling Service that uses ontology modelling and reasoning capabilities of OWL to provide semantic support for meta-scheduling in Grids.

Keywords: resource management, advance reservation, meta-scheduling, semantic model, Grid Scheduling Ontology.

1. Introduction

The resources needed to execute workflows in a Grid environment are commonly highly distributed, heterogeneous, and managed by different organisations. One of the main challenges in the development of Grid infrastructure services is the effective management of those resources in such a way that much of the heterogeneity is hidden from the end-user. This requires the ability to orchestrate the use of various resources of different types. In this work we focus on the co-allocation of resources to assemble a virtual machine that enables the execution of distributed workflows consisting of many parallel tasks.

1.1 Previous Work

Recent research [19] has shown how a meta-scheduler can be employed to schedule workflows by co-allocating resources on multiple Grid nodes. A meta-scheduler is a Grid service that interfaces with multiple local schedulers or other meta-schedulers to negotiate with them advance reservation of resources based on user requirements such as time or QoS constraints. The goal of this negotiation is to determine feasible time slots in which all required resources are available for the requested start time to execute the distributed workflow.

In order to be able to participate in negotiation, local schedulers should be capable and willing to accommodate specific meta-scheduler requests:

- Advance reservation of resources by offering job execution start and stop times.

- At least partial access to local schedules, e.g. by providing information about available time slots.

- Some control over existing reservations, e.g. to cancel or extend a reservation.

Currently only a few local scheduling systems such as CCS [9], PBS Professional [14], or LSF [11] offer these capabilities; however, more are expected to appear as it is in the interest of resource owners to advertise their resources with guarantees for QoS to the Grid.

The main functions of a meta-scheduler include (i) allocation of a single resource for a single application for a fixed period of time, (ii) co-allocation of multiple resources for the same fixed period of time for single or multiple applications, (iii) allocation of multiple resources for multiple applications for different fixed periods of time, and (iv) allocation of dedicated resources for either of the cases above.

The prototype *Meta-Scheduling Service* described in [19] currently realizes functions (i) and (ii). The scheduling algorithm is based on a multi-step negotiation process, involving the pre-selection of suitable local schedulers, the acquisition of feasible start times from them, selecting resources, and a confirmation of the available start times from each of the schedulers involved.

The Meta-Scheduling Service interfaces with local schedulers through dedicated adapters (as depicted in Figure 1) that hide the heterogeneity of the schedulers' native interfaces. These adapters offer a uniform set of abstract operations to the meta-scheduler which include requesting available start time slots for jobs, submitting scheduling requests for a specific time slot, and requesting the state of the current reservation. Meta-scheduling requests are communicated by client applications using WS-Agreement [1] while the adapters forward local requests using proprietary commands. This architecture allows an easy integration of meta-scheduling capabilities into existing Grid environments.

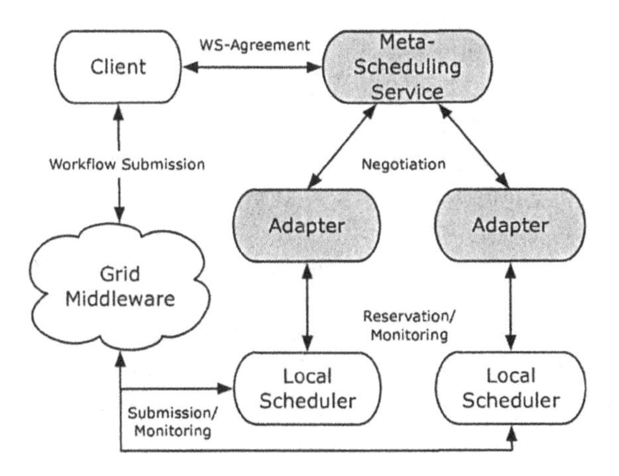

Figure 1. High-level meta-scheduling architecture

1.2 Motivation to Employ Semantic Models

One shortcoming of the current architecture is that, while the adapters provide uniform operations, no shared data model is available to describe a scheduler's set of capabilities and current schedule state. For example, there is no explicit and shared definition of scheduling concepts like *time slot* or *schedule queue*, or of capabilities like *time slot reservation change*. Instead, these concepts are left implicit in the implementation of the adapters, which expose a set of generic scheduling operations.

Although the adapter in its current form fulfils the initial use case requirements as presented in Section 1.1, this approach still holds potential to increase the flexibility of the meta-scheduler. Assuming that a modified version of the scheduling algorithm is needed to query the schedulers' ability to modify the time slot allocation after the initial reservation (a feature that was previously not needed). At present, the only option available would be to accommodate the new feature to upgrade the adapters (all of them) in order to support the new query.

In this paper we introduce a novel approach to extensible meta-scheduling, based on the definition of a shared, explicit and extensible vocabulary to describe a scheduler state as well as its capabilities. We show how such a shared information model for scheduling concepts supports the negotiation process in a more flexible and adaptable way than it is currently possible.

Our approach is inspired by a number of recent initiatives towards the design of *semantic models* for describing Grid resources [15], mainly for interoperability purposes [4, 3, 5]. Common to all these efforts is the explicit representation of knowledge regarding available resources, encoded in such a way as to make it machine-processable.

Following the same principles, but on a more limited scope, we have developed a lightweight semantic model, called the Grid Scheduling Ontology (GSO), to describe the capabilities and state of Grid schedulers. The ontology definition process has recently been described in [20] and is based partially on the Grid Scheduling Dictionary of Terms and Keywords [16].

Along with the model we also present an enhanced meta-scheduling architecture and show how it can improve support for meta-scheduling algorithms and negotiation processes. The ontology modelling and reasoning framework offered by the OWL semantic modelling language [12] provides the necessary functions. Specifically the GSO includes a collection of scheduler classes, where each class is defined in terms of a set of underlying capabilities, for instance the ability to expose the current schedule, to accommodate changes in a reservation, and so forth.

Using a *OWL DL reasoner* [2], individual schedulers whose capabilities can be expressed using the terms in the ontology can then be automatically classified as belonging to one or more of the scheduler classes. This classification is then exploited by the meta-scheduler, as described in detail in Section 3.

1.3 Organisation of the Paper

The remainder of the paper is organised as follows. In Section 2 we present the requirements and use cases that provide basis for the knowledge modelling activity. The semantic model itself is described in Section 3, followed by the proposed implementation in Section 4. An overview of further developments for this work concludes the paper.

2. Requirements for the Scheduling Domain Knowledge Model

The introductory section already listed three general requirements that define the meta-scheduling environment our work is based on. The fulfilment of these requirements is currently realised through adapters which provide an abstraction level between local schedulers and the Meta-Scheduling Service. With respect to the flexibility of this approach we discovered a certain potential for improvement, as reported in Section 1.2, and, to achieve this, we suggest the definition of a scheduling domain vocabulary. Since such a vocabulary makes a thorough knowledge acquisition process necessary, we re-visit and examine the original meta-scheduling use cases in this section.

2.1 The Resource Pre-selection Use Case

Many Grid resource management and scheduling scenarios include a resource pre-selection phase where resources are selected as candidates for the actual scheduling process based on static properties [17]. "Static" in this case refers to properties which do not change from the time the resource request is submitted until the work is finished. Such properties are e.g. the operating system of a compute resource or the maximum bandwidth of a network connection, but also the capability of a resource management system to support meta-scheduling.

According to [19] a local scheduler/resource manager has to provide the following two functions to support meta-scheduling:

1 Schedule a reservation at a fixed date and time for a well-defined period of time (*Advance reservation*).

2 Provide an aggregated overview of the usage of the managed resource between now and a well-defined date and time in future (*Usage preview*).

The first functionality is a prerequisite: a local scheduler that cannot perform advance reservation will not be able to participate in the meta-scheduler process. The second functionality is not as essential, but it has implications on the scheduling algorithm: ideally the meta-scheduler receives all information from the local schedulers it needs to execute a co-ordinated schedule for all resources involved. But even if a local scheduler does not provide any information about the future usage of the managed resource, the meta-scheduler (or the entity that pre-selects resources) may decide to include it into the scheduling process given that first requirement is fulfilled.

The vocabulary should therefore provide answers to the following questions:

- Does the local scheduler support advance reservation?

- Does the information provided by the local scheduler with respect to the future usage of the resource fulfils the second requirement?

2.2 The Schedule Enquiry Use Case

This use case extends the second requirement of the previous use case.

Once the resource pre-selection is finished the local schedulers involved in the meta-scheduling process are queried for a resource usage preview (provided that they deliver this kind of information). With the current adapter in place it is no problem for the meta-scheduler to retrieve the usage preview in the required format since the adapter converts the preview information into the format needed by the meta-scheduler. Assuming that we want to make the design of the adapter generic and independent of the local scheduler, it is necessary to provide metadata to convert the local scheduler's parameters to the format consumed by the meta-scheduler. One of the local schedulers that have already been integrated into the meta-scheduling environment presented earlier is the EASY scheduler [18]. It provides commands to, inter alia, return the current queue (`pq`), reserve e.g. 10 nodes for 5 minutes for an interactive job (`psubmit -n 10 -i -t 5`), show an estimation when the jobs in the current queue will be executed (`pwhen`), or give a preview of the free nodes (`prevlist`).

The vocabulary representing the scheduling domain should therefore help to answer questions like:

- What is the total estimated run time of all jobs under the control of the local scheduler?
- What is the status of a certain queue?
- What is the first possible date and time a certain job can be scheduled on the managed resource?

2.3 Alter Reservation Use Case

A third and final use case involves altering an existing reservation, i.e., extending its lifetime or cancelling it. Our semantic model does support this use case by including the description of the possible reservation states, while the current implementation of the adapter already allows for the cancellation of an existing workflow. Full support for this use case, however, is beyond the scope of our current work and will be undertaken in a later stage.

3. A Semantic Model for Grid Scheduling

As outlined in the introduction, a meta-scheduler is able to negotiate resource allocation with local schedulers that are capable of providing advance reservation of resources (requirement 1), and that optionally allow at least partial access to the local schedules (requirement 2), and allow some control over existing reservations (requirement 3). In this section we describe the semantic model called Grid Scheduling Ontology which we use in our new meta-scheduling architecture to fully support the first two functionalities and to lay the foundations to support the third.

The negotiation process relies on a registry of available local schedulers, in which each scheduler is described according to the common semantic model. The meta-scheduler uses the registry to pre-select schedulers, as well as to query their state throughout the reservation and resource allocation process.

The model is defined using the semantic web language OWL DL [12]. OWL DL allows the definition of classes, relationships among the classes (called *object properties*) as well as individuals.[1] Classes can be organised into hierarchies, and a class can have any number of parents. Individuals may be instances of multiple classes. We write $x \in C$ to indicate that individual x is a member of class C.

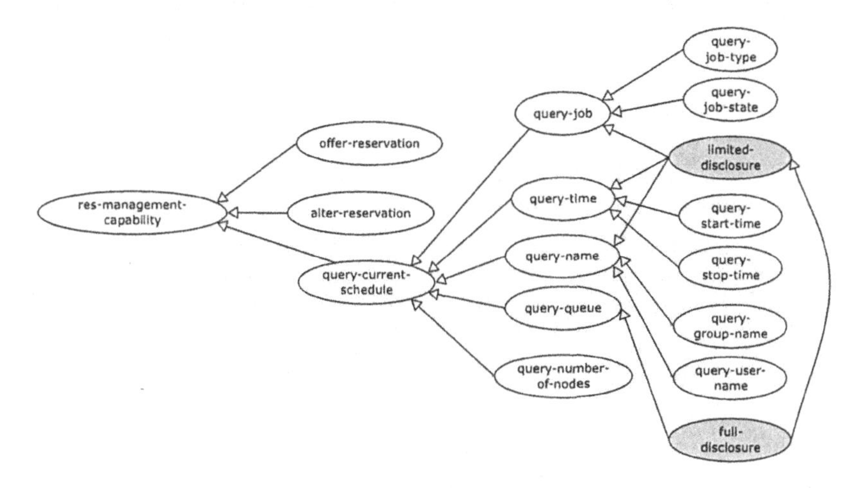

Figure 2. Fragment of the capability hierarchy (some nodes are not expanded)

At first we introduce a hierarchy of classes to model *resource management capabilities*, as shown in Figure 2. The capability `offerReservation` corresponds to the first of our requirements: a scheduler not providing it cannot take part in the advance reservation negotiation. Additionally, we model the ability to query the current scheduler as a tree with multiple levels of precision, and the ability to alter reservations that have already been made (this node is not expanded in Figure 2). Other branches of the hierarchy, which describe for in-

[1] Additional features of the language will be introduced when needed as part of this description.

stance the access control mechanisms enforced by schedulers, are not shown. Note that some of the classes are defined in terms of other classes using OWL class construction operators. For example, `limited-disclosure` is defined by composition, as the capability to request the job names, the job types and the submission times from a schedule.

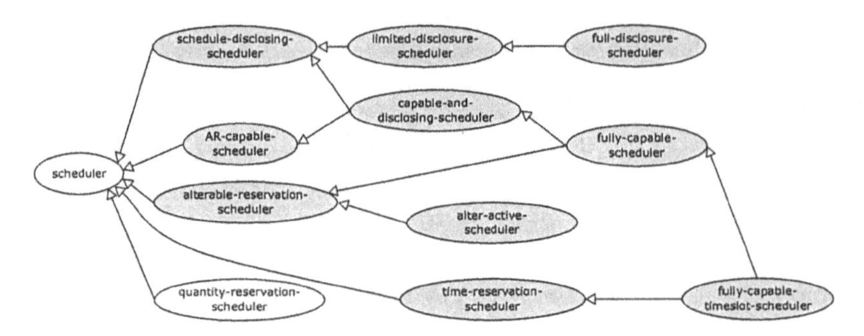

Figure 3. A classification of schedulers

As a next step we introduce a classification for local schedulers, rooted at the top-level `scheduler` class. The property `scheduler-has-capability` allows us to define various subclasses of schedulers in terms of capability sets.

Consider the schedulers classification hierarchy shown in Figure 3. Each of the classes in this hierarchy is defined in terms of other classes and properties in the ontology, using OWL DL's class definition operators. For instance, `schedule-disclosing-scheduler` is the class of all schedulers whose set of capabilities includes at least the ability to query the current schedule. Note that the type of query that is allowed (i.e., queryJob, queryTime) is not specified. Therefore, any scheduler whose capability includes at least the generic `query-current-scheduler` class, is a `schedule-disclosing-scheduler`. Using these operators, it is easy to define classes that correspond exactly to the set of schedulers which are eligible for negotiation in the context of meta-scheduling.

In general, OWL DL allows classes to be defined as a set of necessary and sufficient conditions, as in the example above.[2] An `AR-capable-scheduler`, for example, is any scheduler that, among other capabilities, offers advance reservation, and for this reason satisfies our requirement 1 property.

The next example of a scheduler class highlights an important feature offered by the OWL DL language. The `capable-and-disclosing-scheduler` class represents all schedulers whose capabilities include *both* `offerReservation` and `query-current-schedule`. In Figure 3 this

[2]Formal notation is avoided in this paper for the sake of readability.

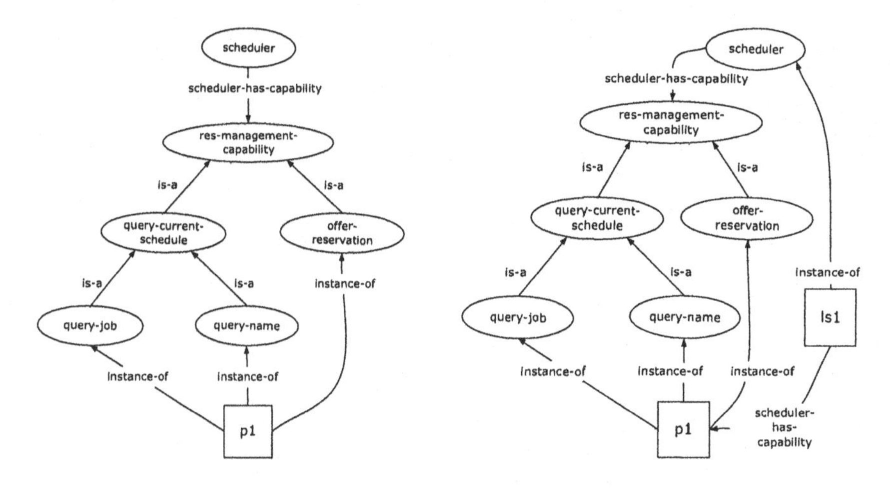

Figure 4. A scheduler profile

Figure 5. A scheduler with a profile

class appears as a subclass of both `AR-capable-scheduler` and `schedule-disclosing-scheduler`, although these *is-a* relationships are not part of the definition. The OWL DL operators are defined in such a way that it is possible to perform specific types of reasoning on the definitions of classes and individuals. In particular, an OWL DL reasoner [2] computes the set of most specific *is-a* relationships for a collection of classes defined using necessary and sufficient conditions as shown above. Thus, the hierarchy shown in Figure 3 is an example of *inferred* classification that has been computed from the class definitions just given.

Let us now return to the definition of scheduler classes for meta-scheduling. A *scheduler profile* is any individual p_1, which is an instance of one or more capability classes, for instance `offerReservation`, `queryJob`, or `queryName` (see Figure 4). If we introduce an instance ls_1 of `scheduler`, and assert that ls_1 has capability profile $p1$ (Figure 5), we can leverage the OWL DL reasoning capabilities again, this time to infer the *most specific classes* of which the individuals of the ontology are instances. In other words, can we say that ls_1 must be a member of some specific subclass of `scheduler`, given that it has capabilities $p1$, and that `scheduler`'s subclasses are indeed defined in terms of sets of capabilities? In this case, the reasoner is indeed able to infer that $ls_1 \in$ `capable-and-disclosing-scheduler`, because p_1 includes both `offerReservation` (necessary for any `AR-capable-scheduler`) as well as two schedule querying capabilities that are more specific than the required generic resource management capability `query-current-scheduler` (Figure 6).

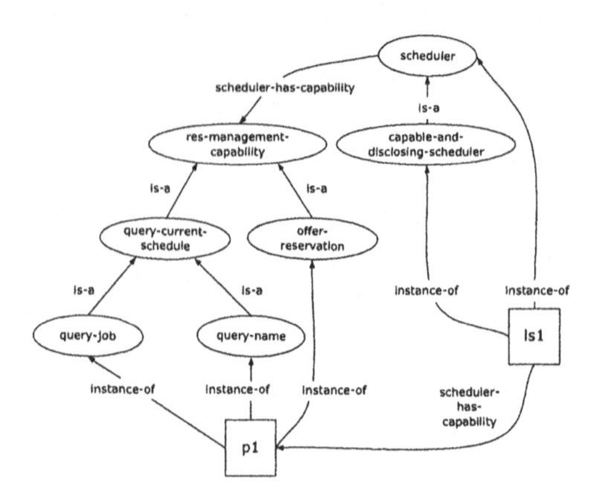

Figure 6. Classified scheduler

In practice, using this model and the associated reasoning features, we are able to obtain a classification of schedulers on the grounds of capability profiles. This automatic classification enables a meta-scheduler to retrieve all the schedulers of interest with minimal effort, simply by querying the model for all instances of one or more specific classes. As a more complete example, consider the following assertions for a set of capabilities and schedulers:

- $p_1 \in$ `offerReservation` $\sqcap$ `queryJob` $\sqcap$ `queryName`
- $p_2 \in$ `queryTime` $\sqcap$ `alter-from-booked` $\sqsubseteq$ `alterReservation`
- $p_3 \in$ `offerReservation`
- ls_1 has capabilities p_1;
- ls_2 has capabilities p_2;
- ls_3 has capabilities p_3;
- ls_4 has capabilities p_2 and p_3.

With these definitions, the reasoner computes the schedulers' classification shown in Figure 7. A query for all AR-capable schedulers would now return $\{ls_3, ls_1, ls_4\}$, while the alterable-reservation schedulers are $\{ls_2, ls_4\}$.

4. Environment for Semantic Exploitation

An architecture for providing Web and Grid services with a semantic description in order to facilitate their semantic discovery, called S-OGSA, has been proposed recently [6]. S-OGSA identifies key Grid services that enable the collection and exploitation of semantics within a Grid architecture, and prescribes patterns of interaction among these services. The realisation of the environment described here follows the S-OGSA architectural patterns.

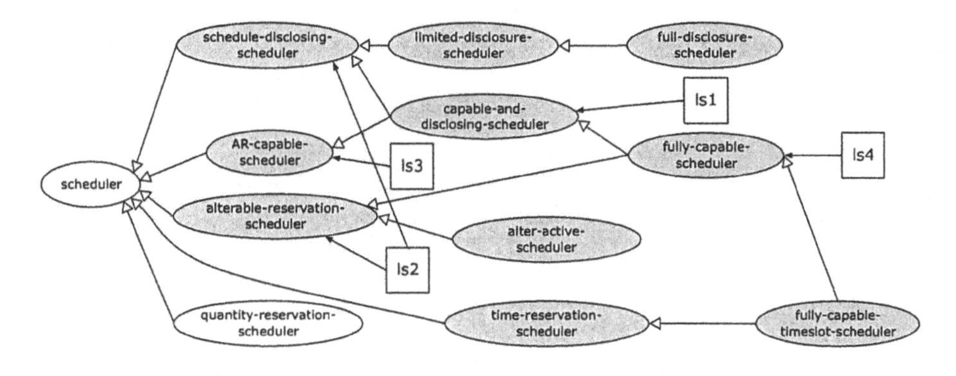

Figure 7. An automatic classification of schedulers

4.1 S-OGSA-based Architecture

An instantiation of an S-OGSA architecture for the meta-scheduling usage scenario is presented, at a high level, in Figure 8.

Two types of knowledge characterise local schedulers:

- Their capabilities with respect to reservation management, as discussed earlier. This knowledge is expected to be fairly stable in time, and independent of the current scheduling activity.

- A representation of the current scheduling activity which includes the current advance reservations that have been accepted and their states. The meta-scheduler must consider that such dynamic information may not be available, as not all schedulers will be configured to provide it. If available, however, it allows a meta-scheduler to pre-select resources based for example on the current scheduler workload.

All this knowledge is encoded using the RDF format [10], a W3C standard for describing semantic annotations, and stored in a *Metadata Service*. The meta-scheduler may query the metadata service using an S-OGSA-compliant Web Service interface, in order to obtain the capability profiles and current state of registered schedulers. An *Ontology Management Service* can be used to obtain the latest version of the Grid Scheduling Ontology in a location-transparent way. At this point, the meta-scheduler holds both the individuals (in RDF format) and the class definitions (in OWL) required to carry out the inferencing process described in Section 3, using a separate *Reasoning Service* as shown in Figure 8.

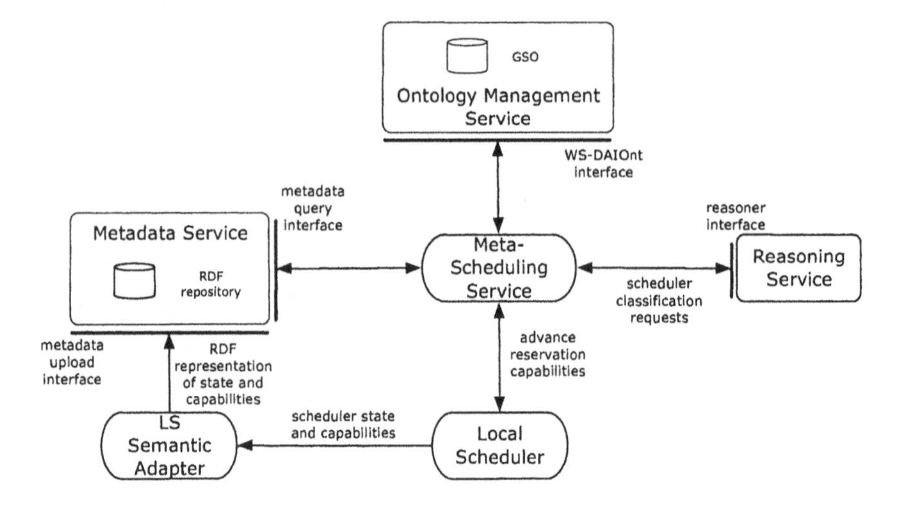

Figure 8. Architecture for exploitation of semantics by the Meta-Scheduling Service

4.2 Evolution of the current Architecture

The transition from the current VIOLA meta-scheduling architecture, presented in Section 1.1 (shown in Figure 1), to an architecture which integrates the semantic model (as shown in Figure 8) can be done in several steps without breaking the overall architecture. To achieve this, four components have to be added:

1 The Metadata Service (MS) with a query interface for the Meta-Scheduling Service (MSS) and a metadata upload interface for the Local Scheduler' Semantic Adapter (LSSA). The MS also implements the RDF repository that contains the RDF representation of state and capabilities of the different local schedulers.

2 The LSSA which converts the scheduler state and capabilities, transforms them into an RDF representation and uploads them to the RDF repository. The LSSA is needed for those local schedulers - currently all - which are not able to provide the metadata. Future schedulers may have this capability and will then be able to upload their metadata directly to the RDF repository.

3 The Ontology Management Service (OMS) based on WS-DAIOnt [8] as defined by the OntoGrid project [13]. The OMS stores the GSO and provides a WS-DAIOnt interface towards the MSS for accessing the GSO.

4 The Reasoning Service (RS) with an interface to the MSS allowing to receive scheduler classification requests and to submit the classifications needed for the pre-selection back to the MSS

Once these new components are available the transition to the new architecture can be performed by adding the following to the MSS:

- The metadata query interface between MSS and MS,
- the WS-DAIOnt interface to access the GSO,
- the interface to the RS, and
- logic that allows to pre-select appropriate local schedulers based on their capabilities and actual state, and to use the metadata to negotiate the advance reservation with the pre-selected local schedulers.

Finally the current adapters may be removed as they are obsolete in the new MSS framework.

5. Future Perspectives

Once implemented we will evaluate the GSO-based architecture and compare it to the solution presented in Section 1.1. Since the current implementation of the VIOLA Meta-Scheduling Service is already used to co-allocate MPI workflows it seems feasible to set up a testbed combining "semantically-enriched" and "classical" adapters. It will then be possible to compare the functional range of both solutions. It is envisaged that this evaluation will lead to another iteration of the ontology building process.

In this context it will also be necessary to review the model by means of usage scenarios that include arbitrary resource types. Although the use cases described in Section 2 reflect mostly general Grid scheduling requirements, the `query-current-schedule` capability is modelled according to the requirements of queue-based local resource managers. The integration of network resource managers into the VIOLA meta-scheduling environment will allow us to do this review.

In addition we will examine the `alter-reservation` resource management capability and negotiation-related issues linked to the negotiation protocol activities of the GRAAP Working Group at GGF [7].

Acknowledgments

This paper includes work carried out jointly within the CoreGRID Network of Excellence founded by the European Commission's IST programme under grant #004265. This paper also includes work funded by the German Federal Ministry of Education and Research through the VIOLA project under grant #01AK605F.

References

[1] A. Andrieux, K. Czajkowski, A. Dan, K. Keahey, H. Ludwig, T. Nakata, J. Pruyne, J. Rofrano, S. Tuecke, and M. Xu. Web Services Agreement Specification (WS-Agreement) Version 2005/09, September 2005. 12 Mar. 2006 <https://forge.gridforum.org/projects/graap-wg/document/WS-AgreementSpecificationDraft.doc/en/24>.

[2] F. Baader, D. Calvanese, D. L. McGuinness, D. Nardi, and P. F. Patel-Schneider, editors. *The Description Logic Handbook: Theory, Implementation, and Applications*. Cambridge University Press, 2003.

[3] J. Brooke, D. Fellows, K. Garwood, and C. Goble. Semantic matching of Grid Resource Descriptions. In *Proc. of the 2nd European Across Grids Conference*, Nicosia, Cyprus, January 28–30, 2004.

[4] J. Brooke, D. Fellows, and J. MacLaren. Interoperability of Resource Description Across Grid Domain Boundaries. In *Proc. of the European Congress on Computational Methods in Applied Science and Engineering (ECCOMAS 2004)*, Jyväskylä, Finland, July 24–28, 2004.

[5] J. Brooke, K. Garwood, and C. Goble. Interoperability of Grid Resource Descriptions: A Semantic Approach. In *Proc. of the 1st GGF Semantic Grid Workshop in conjunction with GGF 9*, Chicago, USA, October 5, 2003.

[6] O. Corcho, P. Alper, I. Kotsiopoulos, P. Missier, S. Bechhofer, D. Kuo, and C. Goble. An Overview of S-OGSA: A Reference Semantic Grid Architecture. *Journal of Web Semantics*, n.d. To appear.

[7] Grid Resource Allocation Agreement Protocol (GRAAP-WG), 2006. 13 Mar. 2006 <https://forge.gridforum.org/projects/graap-wg/>.

[8] M. E. Gutirrez, A. Gmez-Prez, O. M. Garca, and B. V. Terrazas. Ontology Access in Grids with WS-DAIOnt and the RDF(S) Realization. In *Proc. of the 3rd GGF Semantic Grid Workshop in conjunction with GGF 16*, Athens, Greece, February 15, 2006. 12 Mar. 2006 <http://www.semanticgrid.org/GGF/ggf16/papers/OntoGrid-GGF16-SemGrid-Wrkshp.pdf>.

[9] A. Keller and A. Reinefeld. Anatomy of a Resource Management System for HPC Clusters. In Y. C. Kwong, editor, *Annual Review of Scalable Computing*, volume 3 of *Series on Scalable Computing*, pages 1–31. Singapore University Press and World Scientific Publishing, 2001.

[10] G. Klyne and J. J. Carroll. Resource Description Framework (RDF): Concepts and Abstract Syntax. W3C Recommendation, World Wide Web Consortium (W3C), February 10, 2004. 12 Mar. 2006 <http://www.w3.org/TR/rdf-concepts/>.

[11] Platform LSF, 2006. 12 Mar. 2006 <http://www.platform.com/Products/Platform.LSF.-Family/Platform.LSF/>.

[12] D. L. McGuinness and F. v. Harmelen. OWL Web Ontology Language Overview. W3C Recommendation, World Wide Web Consortium (W3C), February 10, 2004. 12 Mar. 2006 <http://www.w3.org/TR/owl-features/>.

[13] OntoGrid Project, 2006. 12 Mar. 2006 <http://www.ontogrid.net/ontogrid/home.jsp>.

[14] PBS Professional, 2006. 12 Mar. 2006 <http://www.altair.com/software/pbspro.htm>.

[15] S. Quirolgico, P. Assis, A. Westerinen, M. Baskey, and E. Stokes. Toward a Formal Common Information Model Ontology. In *International Workshop on Intelligent Networked*

and Mobile Systems, Web Information Systems Engineering (WISE 2004), volume 3307 of *Lecture Notes in Computer Science*, pages 11–21. Springer, 2004.

[16] M. Roehrig, W. Ziegler, and Ph. Wieder. Grid Scheduling Dictionary of Terms and Keywords. Grid Forum Document GFD.11, Global Grid Forum, 2003.

[17] J. Schopf. Ten Actions When Grid Scheduling – The User as a Grid Scheduler. In J. Nabrzyski, J. Schopf, and J. Weglarz, editors, *Grid Resource Management – State of the Art and Future Trends*, pages 15–23. Kluwer Academic Publishers, 2004.

[18] J. Skovira, W. Chan, H. Zhou, and D. Lifka. The EASY — LoadLeveler API Project. In D. G. Feitelson and L. Rudolph, editors, *Proc. of 2nd Workshop on Job Scheduling Strategies for Parallel Processing*, volume 1162 of *Lecture Notes in Computer Science*, pages 41–47. Springer, 1996.

[19] O. Wäldrich, Ph.Wieder, and W. Ziegler. A Meta-scheduling Service for Co-allocating Arbitrary Types of Resources. In *Proc. of the Second Grid Resource Management Workshop (GRMWS'05) in conjunction with the Sixth International Conference on Parallel Processing and Applied Mathematics (PPAM 2005)*, Poznan, Poland, September 11–14, 2006. To appear.

[20] Ph. Wieder and W. Ziegler. Bringing Knowledge to Middleware – Grid Scheduling Ontology. In V. Getov, D. Laforenza, and A. Reinefeld, editors, *Future Generation Grids, Proceedings of the Workshop on Future Generation Grids*, pages 47–59, Dagstuhl, Germany, November 1–5, 2004. Springer. ISBN: 0-387-27935-0.

SEMANTIC GRID RESOURCE DISCOVERY IN ATLAS*

Zoi Kaoudi, Iris Miliaraki, Matoula Magiridou
Dept. of Informatics and Telecommunications
National and Kapodistrian University of Athens, Greece
{zoi, iris, matoula}@di.uoa.gr

Erietta Liarou
Dept. of Electronic and Computer Engineering
Technical University of Crete, Greece
erietta@intelligence.tuc.gr

Stratos Idreos
CWI
Amsterdam, The Netherlands
S.Idreos@cwi.nl

Manolis Koubarakis
Dept. of Informatics and Telecommunications
National and Kapodistrian University of Athens, Greece
koubarak@di.uoa.gr

Abstract We study the problem of resource discovery in the Semantic Grid. We show how to solve this problem by utilizing *Atlas*, a P2P system for the distributed storage and retrieval of RDF(S) data. Atlas is currently under development in project OntoGrid funded by FP6. Atlas is built on top of the distributed hash table Bamboo and supports pull and push querying scenarios. It inherits all the nice features of Bamboo (openness, scalability, fault-tolerance, resistance to high churn rates) and extends Bamboo's protocols for storing and querying RDF(S) data. Atlas is being used currently to realize the metadata service of S-OGSA in a fully distributed and scalable way. In this paper, we concentrate on the main features of Atlas and demonstrate its use for Semantic Grid resource discovery in an OntoGrid use case scenario.

Keywords: peer-to-peer networks, DHT, RDF, query processing, Semantic Web.

---

*This work is partially funded by FP6/IST project OntoGrid.

1. Introduction

For the Semantic Grid vision [15] to become a reality, *high quality of service* must be offered to users and applications at all levels of the Grid fabric. In this paper, we concentrate on high quality of service in the provision of *resource discovery* services in Semantic Grids. Resource discovery is an important problem in Grids in general, and Semantic Grids in particular. We discuss how to achieve *high-performance, scalability, resilience to failures, robustness* and *adaptivity* in the provision of resource discovery services in Semantic Grids, and especially in OntoKit, the Semantic Grid toolkit currently under development in project OntoGrid [24].

OntoGrid (`http://www.ontogrid.net`) is a Semantic Grid project funded by the Grid Technologies unit of the European Commission under the strategic objective "Grid-based systems for Complex Problem Solving" of the Information Society Technologies programme of FP6.

Our basic assumption in this paper is that Semantic Grid resources (e.g., machines, services or ontologies) will be annotated by RDF(S) metadata. Metadata pervades the Semantic Grid and is used to describe Grid resources, the environment, provenance and trust information etc. [15]. The Resource Description Framework (RDF) and RDF Schema (RDFS) are frameworks for representing information about Web resources. RDF(S) consists of W3C recommendations that enable the encoding, exchange and reuse of structured metadata, providing the means for publishing both human-readable and machine-processable information and vocabularies for semantically describing things on the Web. Although RDF(S) was originally proposed in the context of the Semantic Web, it is also a very natural framework for representing information about Grid resources. As a result, it is used heavily in various Semantic Grid projects e.g., ^{my}Grid (`http://www.mygrid.org.uk`) or OntoGrid.

We propose to view resource discovery in Semantic Grids as *distributed RDF query answering* on top of a P2P network of Grid resource *providers* and *requesters*. Our proposal complements well-known Grid information services such as MDS4 of GT4 in two ways:

- We offer service providers and service requesters expressive *semantics-based* data models and query languages (i.e., RDF(S) and RQL instead of XML and XPath).

- We implement resource discovery using techniques from P2P systems. This allows us to achieve *full distribution, high-performance, scalability, resilience to failures, robustness* and *adaptivity*. Related experimental work is presented in [26, 28, 27].

In the context of OntoGrid, our proposal is realized with the implementation of *Atlas*, a P2P system for the distributed storage and querying of RDF(S) metadata describing Semantic Grid resources.

The rest of the paper is organized as follows. Section 6 briefly discusses related work at the crossroads of Grid and P2P computing research. Section 3 gives a short description of the various components and protocols of Atlas. Section 4 shows how to use Atlas for service discovery in OntoKit. Finally, Section 5 concludes the paper.

2. Related Work

Our research can be understood to lie at the intersection of P2P and Grid computing. Although these computing paradigms have different origins and have been developed largely independently, there has been a lot of interesting work lately at the crossroads of these paradigms [13, 34, 11].

Previous papers that explore connections among Grids and P2P networks can be distinguished in the following categories:

1 General papers that discuss the similarities and differences of P2P and Grid systems pointing out important areas where more work is needed [13, 34, 11].

2 Papers where ideas from P2P computing are used in Grid systems. Here, we can further differentiate as follows:

   (a) Works where Grid computing problems are given as a primary motivation, but the contributions are essentially in the P2P domain and can also be applied elsewhere. For example, [4, 23, 7] consider attribute-value data models that can be used to describe Grid resources (e.g., by specifying the CPU power, disk space capacity, operating system and location of a computer) and show how to evaluate queries in these models on top of DHTs (e.g., I am looking for an idle PC that runs Linux and has CPU $\geq$ 3GHz).

   (b) Works where P2P techniques are used to improve functionality in existing Grid systems e.g., resource discovery [20, 18, 19] and replica location management in Globus [8] or flocking in Condor [6].

   (c) Service-oriented application development frameworks that enhance existing frameworks for Web or Grid service computing [1, 16] with P2P protocols.

3 Papers where ideas from Grid computing are used in P2P systems. For example, [10] shows how to implement a P2P data integration framework using OGSA-DAI [2].

Our work should be classified in categories 2(b) and 2(c) above. Work with goals similar to ours that uses description logics instead of RDF(S) is reported in [17].

3. The P2P System Atlas

In Atlas, we use state of the art *distributed hash table (DHT)* technology [5] to implement a distributed system that will be able to scale to hundreds of thousands of nodes and to large amounts of RDF(S) data and queries. Nodes in an Atlas network are organized under the Bamboo DHT protocol [31]. Bamboo is a DHT based on Pastry [32] from where it takes the circular identifier space and the routing algorithms. Bamboo improves on Pastry by being able to withstand very dynamic changes in network membership i.e., it is resilient to churn [31]. Like most implementations of DHTs, Bamboo offers a very simple interface consisting of two operations: `put(ID, item)` and `get(ID)`. The `put` operation inserts an item with key `ID` and value `item` in the DHT. The `get` operation returns a pointer to the DHT node responsible for key `ID`. Our operations for storing data and querying Atlas, described below, are based on these simple operations offered by Bamboo.

Atlas nodes can enter RDF(S) data into the network and pose RQL queries. Two kinds of querying functionality are supported by Atlas: *one-time* querying and *publish/subscribe*. Each time a node poses a one-time query, the network nodes cooperate to find RDF(S) data that form the answer to the query. In the publish/subscribe scenario, a node can *subscribe* with a *continuous* query. A continuous query is indexed somewhere in the network and each time matching RDF(S) data is published, nodes cooperate to *notify* the subscriber.

The current implementation of Atlas (Atlas v0.6) supports a subset of the query language RQL [22] as we explain in Section 3.4 below. The query processing algorithm we use for one-time queries is an extension of the algorithm proposed in [9] for a smaller class of queries based on triple patterns [9]. Publish/subscribe scenarios in Atlas are handled using the algorithms in [28, 27] that are briefly discussed in Section 3.3 below but have not been fully implemented in Atlas v0.6. In the future, Atlas will also support the recently proposed RDF update language RUL for inserting, deleting and updating RDF metadata [30].

Atlas is used in OntoKit for realizing a fully distributed *metadata service*. A high level view of Atlas and the metadata service of OntoKit is shown in Figure 1.

3.1 RDF Documents and Queries in Atlas

Atlas nodes provide their data in the form of RDF documents [25]. These documents are decomposed into RDF triples that are indexed in various nodes

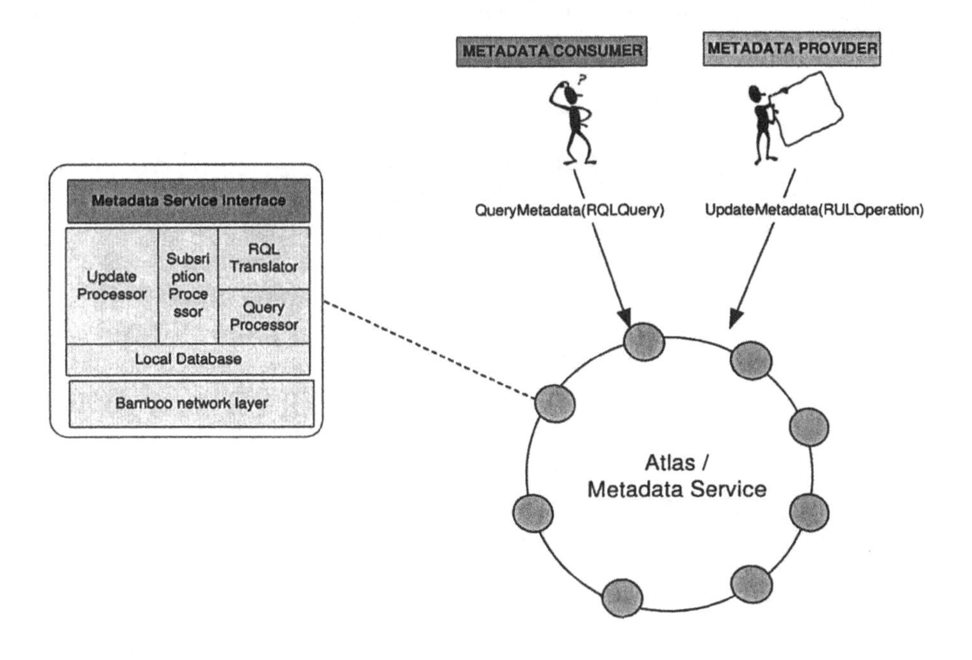

Figure 1. Atlas and the metadata service

of the network. A *triple* represents a statement about a domain and has the form $(subject, predicate, object)$ where $subject$ and $predicate$ are URIs and $object$ is a URI or a literal. We adopt the triple indexing algorithm presented in [9], where each triple is indexed on the DHT *three times*, once for its subject, once for its predicate and once for its object. For each of these storage operations we make use of the `put` operation provided by the Bamboo DHT using as key the subject, predicate or object value respectively. The key is hashed to create the identifier that leads to the appropriate node where the triple is stored.

Atlas supports internally the query language TPQL (*triple-pattern query language*) which allows the expression of *positive* (i.e., without negation) *conjunctive queries* where each conjunct is a *triple pattern*.

A *conjunctive query* q is a formula of the form

$$?x_1, \ldots, ?x_k : (s_1, p_1, o_1) \wedge (s_2, p_2, o_2) \wedge \cdots \wedge (s_m, p_m, o_m)$$

where $s_1, \ldots, s_m, p_1, \ldots, p_m$ are variables or URIs, $o_1, \ldots, o_m$ are variables, URIs or literals, $?x_1, \ldots, ?x_k$ are variables and $\{?x_1, \ldots, ?x_k\} \subseteq \{s_1, \ldots, s_m, p_1, \ldots, p_m, o_1, \ldots, o_m\}$. Variables will always start with the '?' character. The triple patterns $(s_1, p_1, o_1), \ldots, (s_m, p_m, o_m)$ are the *subqueries* of q. A query will be called *atomic* if it consists of a single conjunct.

The class of conjunctive queries can be used to express many interesting requests in P2P applications using RDF. For example, assume that a service requester wants to discover a Web service for arranging the repair of a car. This request can be expressed as a conjunctive query as follows:

$$?x, ?y : (?x, hasServiceKeyword, \text{"}Cars\text{"}) \wedge$$

$$(?x, hasServiceKeyword, \text{"}Repair\text{"}) \wedge (?x, hasLocationURI, ?y)$$

3.2 One-Time Query Processing in Atlas

In this section, we describe the algorithm for one-time query processing in Atlas using terminology from relational databases. Each triple can be understood to be a tuple in a relation $TRIPLE(S, P, O)$ with attributes S for subject, P for predicate and O for object. Then, conjunctive queries are *select-project-join* queries over the database that consists simply of the relation $TRIPLE$. The exact query processing algorithm of Atlas is as follows.

Let n_1 be a node that wants to pose a conjunctive query q of the form introduced in Section 3.1. Node n_1 creates a message

$$queryRequest(id, triplePattern, restTriplePatterns,$$

$$partialResult, variables, returnAddress)$$

and sends it to the node with identifier id using the underlying Bamboo infrastructure. In this message, $triplePattern$ is the triple pattern of q which node n_1 chooses to be evaluated first[1], id is the identifier obtained by hashing one of the constants in triple pattern $triplePattern$, $restTriplePatterns$ is the list of remaining triple patterns of q, $partialResult$ is a relation for partial results (see below) which is initially empty, $variables$ is the list of answer variables of q, and $returnAddress$ is the IP address of node n_1.

When another node n_2 receives the above message $queryRequest$, it does the following. It first computes the bindings of the variables included in the given triple pattern by finding the triples in its local database that match $triplePattern$. These bindings form a new relation R with attributes the variables in question. If $partialResult$ is empty, then node n_2 assigns R to $partialResult$. Otherwise, n_2 computes the natural join of R and $partialResult$ (i.e., $partialResult \bowtie R$) and assigns it to $partialResult'$. Then, n_2 creates a new message

$$queryRequest(id', triplePattern', restTriplePatterns',$$

$$partialResult', variables, returnAddress)$$

[1]This choice is crucial depending on the metric one wants to optimize; in Atlas v0.6, we simply pick the first triple pattern/conjunct.

When this message is received by another node n_3, the same procedure is followed. These nodes join the relation R of the bindings they retrieve locally with the relation $partialResult$ and send a message to the next node. This procedure terminates in two possible ways. Either, the list $restTriplePatterns$ becomes empty or the relation $partialResult$ becomes empty. The latter means that the current triple pattern does not match with any triples stored locally, and thus relation R becomes empty and the join operation results in an empty relation. In both cases, a response with the results should be returned to node n_1 which issued the query. The field $returnAddress$ is used for this purpose; it remains unchanged throughout the whole procedure and refers to the IP address of node n_1.

The node n_m that determines that the query evaluation procedure is finished computes the bindings of the answer variables $?x_1, \ldots, ?x_k$. In order to do that, n_m computes the projection of relation $partialResult$ on the variables included in the list $variables$ and inserts the results in the relation $variableBindings$ i.e.,

$$variableBindings = \pi_{variables}(partialResult).$$

Then, n_m sends a response message $queryResponse(variableBindings)$ to node n_1, where $variableBindings$ is a relation with the answer to the query.

The key idea in the algorithm we described above is that we split a conjunctive query to the triple patterns that is consists of and evaluate each one at a different node of the network. In this way, we try to distribute the responsibility of answering a query to several nodes. Intermediate results flow through these nodes and finally the last one delivers the results back to the node that submitted the query. Notice that in order to determine which node will evaluate a triple pattern the algorithm uses *one* of the constants contained in it. Finally, the distributed query plan is created once, i.e., at the time that the query is submitted.

In [26], we propose an improved algorithm for the evaluation of conjunctive RDF queries on top of DHTs. In this algorithm, the distributed query plan is created *dynamically* by exploiting the values of matching triples found while processing the query incrementally. This time we use combination of constants in a triple pattern to determine which will be the node to evaluate it. By enriching the triple patterns with new values we have more combinations to use. In this way, this algorithm distributes the responsibility of evaluating a query to more nodes than the previous one. Our initial experiments show a significant improvement on load distribution but, on the other hand, there is an overhead in network traffic.

3.3 Publish/Subscribe in Atlas

In [28, 27], we propose two distributed algorithms for publish/subscribe on top of DHTs when publications are RDF triples and subscriptions are conjunctive multi-predicate queries.

In our algorithms, when a continuous query is submitted, it is *indexed* somewhere in the network and waits for triples to satisfy it. Each time a new triple is inserted, the network nodes cooperate to determine what queries are satisfied, compute their answers and create notifications for the subscribers. The case of conjunctive queries is an interesting one, since a single triple may *satisfy* a query q only *partially* by satisfying a subquery of q. In other words, more than one triples may be needed to answer a query. Moreover, since the appropriate triples do not necessarily arrive in the network at the same time, the network should "remember" the queries that have been partially satisfied in the past (e.g., by keeping intermediate results) and create notifications only when all subqueries of a given query are satisfied.

We could index queries to a globally known node or set of nodes, but this would eventually overload these nodes. In a P2P environment, we want as many nodes as possible to contribute some of their resources (storage, cpu, bandwidth, etc.) for achieving the overall network functionality. The resource contribution of each node will obviously depend on its capabilities, its gains from participating in the network, etc. In our work, we make the simplifying assumption that all nodes are altruistic, with equivalent capabilities, and, thus, can contribute to query evaluation in identical ways.

Let us now discuss the issues involved in publish/subscribe with conjunctive queries. We first consider an atomic query $q = (?s_1, p_1, ?o_1)$. We can simply assign q to the successor node x of $Hash(p_1)$ by using the constant part p_1 of the query. Triples that have predicate value equal to p_1 will be indexed to x too, where they will meet q. Assume now the atomic query $q' = (?s_2, p_2, o_2)$. We can index q' either to node $x_1 = Successor(Hash(p_2))$ or to node $x_2 = Successor(Hash(o_2))$. We prefer the second option since intuitively there will be more object values than predicate values in an instance of a given schema, which will allow us to distribute queries to a greater number of nodes. Another solution is to index q' to the node $x_3 = Successor(Hash(p_2 + o_2))$. We use the operator $+$ to denote the *concatenation* of string values. This is the best option because the possible combinations of predicate and object values will be greater than the number of object values alone, so this will lead to an even better distribution of queries.

The difficulty with arbitrary conjunctive queries is that they demand more than one conditions to be satisfied before the whole query can be satisfied. As an example, consider the query $q = q_1 \wedge q_2 \wedge q_3$. Our approach is to *split* the query to the subqueries that it consists of, and to index each subquery *separately*. Then, three usually different nodes will be responsible for query processing regarding q. Each one will be responsible for a single subquery of q, e.g., nodes r_1, r_2 and r_3 will be responsible for q_1, q_2 and q_3 respectively. These nodes will form the *query chain* of q, denoted by $chain(q)$. Each one of these nodes will monitor the satisfaction of only the subquery that it is responsible for. To determine the satisfaction of q, we have to allow some kind of communication between these three nodes. In this way, as triples arrive and satisfy a subquery e.g., in node r_1, r_1 will forward *partial results* of q to r_2. Node r_2 will forward partial results that also satisfy the second subquery to r_3 and r_3 will realize that the whole query is satisfied and create a notification.

The first algorithm that we present in [28] creates a *single query chain* for each conjunctive query while the second one creates *multiple query chains* for a single query to achieve a better query processing load distribution. The first algorithm of [28] is essentially identical to the one-time query processing algorithm discussed in Section 3.2 except that, in the publish/subscribe case, it is executed in a reactive manner as matching triples arrive in the network. In [28], the two algorithms presented are experimentally evaluated for conjunctive *multi-predicate* queries (i.e., queries where the subject of all the triple patterns is the same variable $?s$ and predicates $p_1, \ldots, p_m$ are all constant). However, the general idea of these algorithms is easily extensible to support the full class of conjuctive queries as we show in the forthcoming paper [27].

3.4 The RQL-to-TPQL Translator

Atlas offers to users the ability to write queries in TPQL or in the well-known RDF query language RQL. RQL [22], which stands for RDF Query Language, is a declarative language which relies on a formal graph model that captures the RDF modelling primitives. The novelty of RQL lies in its ability to combine schema and data querying smoothly while exploiting the taxonomies of labels and multiple classification of resources. The syntax of RQL includes a set of basic queries (e.g. `Resource, SubClassOf()` etc.) as well as SQL-like `select-from-where` queries to iterate over RDF collections and introduce variables[2].

Consider the schema of Figure 2 which describes information about Web services in RDFS. This example is part of the core services data model used in project ^{my}Grid[3]. Suppose we want to find a Web service for arranging the repair of the car. What follows is an appropriate RQL query:

```
SELECT X
FROM {X}ns:hasServiceDescription{Y}
```

[2] RQL is implemented in ICS-FORTH's Suite `http://139.91.183.30:9090/RDF/`

[3] http://www.mygrid.org.uk

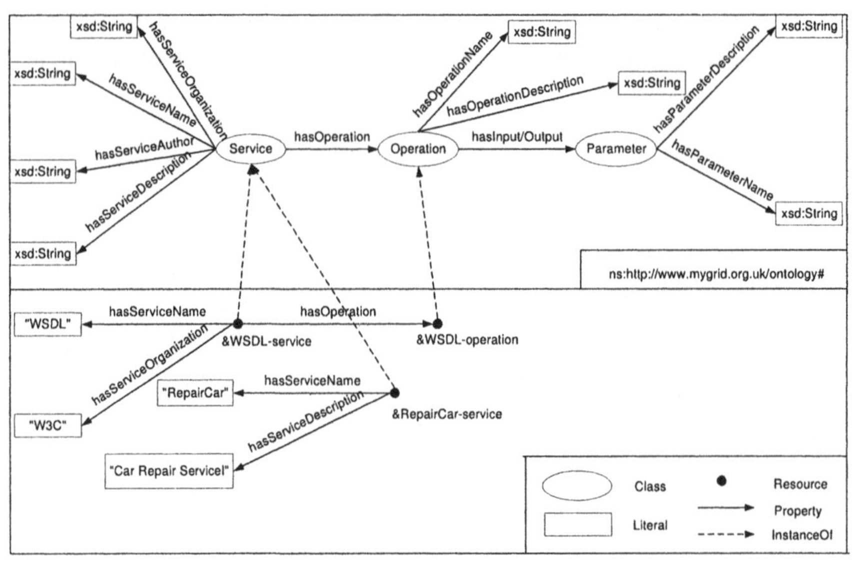

Figure 2. RDFS schema for Web Services

```
WHERE Y like "*car*"
USING NAMESPACE ns=&http://www.mygrid.org.uk/#ontology
```

In order to support RQL queries in Atlas, we have introduced a module responsible for mapping a query expressed in RQL to a query in TPQL, which is the query language supported internally by Atlas and described in Section 3.1. In Atlas v0.6, we do not support the full functionality of RQL but only *data queries with filtering conditions.*

Recall the RQL query presented earlier, about the discovery of service for arranging the repair of the car. The equivalent conjunctive query is the following:

$$?x : (?x,\ http://www.mygrid.org.uk/ontology\#hasServiceDescription,\ ?y)$$

$$\wedge\ ?y\ like\ ``*car*"$$

To design the RQL-to-TPQL translator we have followed the RQL Interpreter architecture developed by ICS-FORTH [14] (see Figure 3). Our implementation has been done in Java using the Java Compiler Compiler (JavaCC) [3] parser generator.

The *syntax analyser* module receives as input a string, representing an RQL query, and returns the corresponding CNF syntax tree (if the query is valid). The syntax tree is passed to the *graph constructor* module, which creates a graph corresponding to the semantic representation of the query. These two modules are based on the code of RQL Interpreter. The *translator* module takes as input the syntax tree and graph of an RQL query and returns the

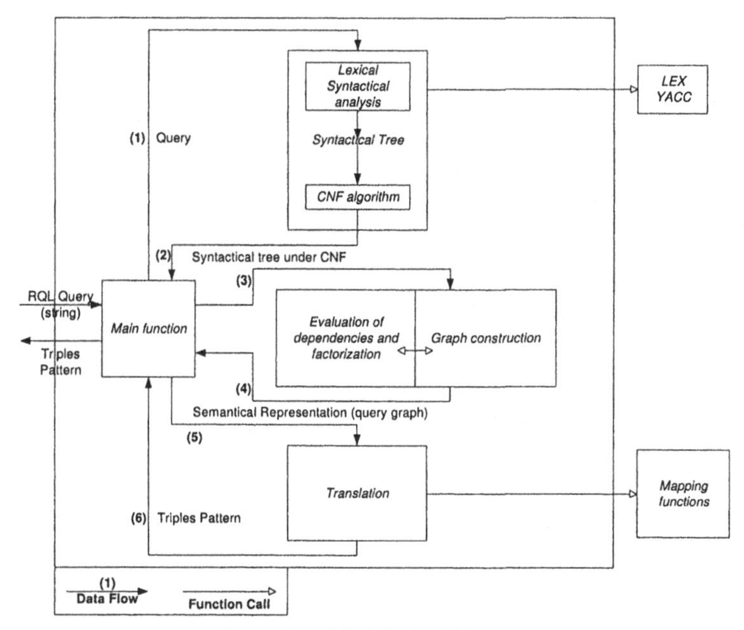

Figure 3. Module Architecture

equivalent expression in TPQL, as a list of triple patterns and constraints. It consists of a list of *mapping* functions, which implement the mapping rules between RQL and TPQL presented in [21]. The *main* module contains either a *JNI-client* and a standalone application for the management of the RQL query translator or directly creates the triple patterns data structures to be passed to the rest of the Atlas modules for query processing.

4. Atlas in Operation: Service Discovery in OntoKit

In this section, we show how Atlas can be used in OntoKit during service annotation and discovery [24]. The whole scenario is depicted in Figure 4.

OntoGrid is developing annotation technology for Grid services [33]; this technology is deployed as the *annotation service* of OntoKit. For the purposes of this section, it is also important to mention another service of OntoKit, the *ontology service* [12]. The current version of the ontology service provides a Grid interface to an RDFS store where RDFS ontologies are stored (e.g., *service ontologies* or *domain ontologies* etc.).

An ontology for services and various domain ontologies are needed in order to create a service annotation. Let us suppose that the annotation service chooses to search for an ontology about cars in order to annotate a car-repair service (the example comes from a car insurance use case studied in OntoGrid). The annotation service can pose an RQL query to the metadata service and get

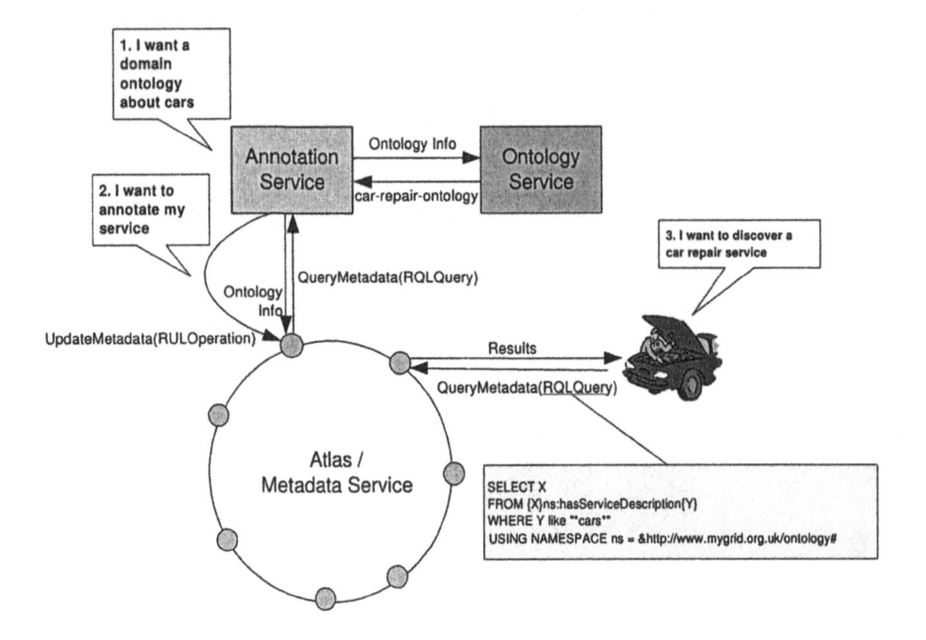

Figure 4. Using Atlas for Service Annotation and Discovery

information about such ontologies e.g., the location and description of a particular ontology – let us call it `car-repair-ontology`. After discovering information about `car-repair-ontology`, the annotation service can retrieve it from the ontology service.

If the annotation service does not know the ontology for annotating services, it has to search for such an ontology as well. An example ontology describing services that could be found in this case is the ^{my}Grid service ontology [29]. We should mention here that this step may be unnecessary if a specific service ontology has been selected for annotating services in OntoKit.

Using these ontologies, the annotation service can complete the service annotation process. The result of the annotation process will be stored in Atlas by calling the `UpdateMetadata` operation (see Figure 4). The ontology used for describing the service should have been stored previously in Atlas by calling the `StoreOntology` operation.

Let us suppose now that an OntoKit user wants to discover a service for repairing cars. This is accomplished by submitting RQL queries using appropriate service and domain ontologies (see Figure 4).

Finally, notice that after an annotation is stored, it might be necessary to be able to update it. An appropriate update operation can be expressed in RUL and executed in Atlas.

5. Conclusions

We have argued that resource discovery services for Semantic Grids can be made scalable, fault-tolerant, robust and adaptive, by exploiting distributed RDF query processing algorithms implemented on top of DHTs. We have discussed the implementation of our ideas in the system Atlas and its role in the Semantic Grid toolkit OntoKit. The implementation of Atlas was started at the Technical University of Crete and is currently continued at the National and Kapodistrian University of Athens. More information on the current version of Atlas is available in [21]. Although we have stressed performance issues, we have not provided any measurements or experimental results in this paper. Experimental results based on simulations can be found in [28] and more experimentation is underway [27, 26]. Finally, we expect to be able to analyse the performance of Atlas soon on real-world wide-area networks using the PlanetLab infrastructure.

References

[1] jxta. http://www.sun.com/software/jxta/.

[2] Open Grid Services Architecture Data Integration (OGSA-DAI). http://www.ogsadai.org.uk/.

[3] Java Compiler Compiler(JavaCC). https://javacc.dev.java.net/, 2004.

[4] A. Andrzejak and Z. Xu. Scalable, Efficient Range Queries for Grid Information Services. In *the second IEEE International Conference on Peer-to-Peer Computing (P2P2002)*, Linkoping, Sweden, 5-7 September 2002.

[5] H. Balakrishnan, M. Frans Kaashoek, D. R. Karger, R. Morris, and I. Stoica. Looking up data in P2P systems. *Communications of the ACM*, 46(2):43–48, 2003.

[6] A. Raza Butt, R. Zhang, and Y. Charlie Hu. A Self-Organizing Flock of Condors. In *Proceedings of Supercomputing Conference (SC)*, Phoenix, Arizona, November 2003.

[7] M. Cai, M. Frank, and P. Szekely. MAAN: A Multi-Attribute Addressable Network for Grid Information Services. In *Proceedings of the 4th International Workshop on Grid Computing (Grid2003)*, 2003.

[8] M. Cai, A. Chervenak, and M. Frank. A Peer-to-Peer Replica Location Service Based on A Distributed Hash Table. In *the 2004 ACM/IEEE Conference on Supercomputing (SC2004)*, Pittsburgh, November 2004.

[9] M. Cai, M. R. Frank, B. Yan, and R. M. MacGregor. A Subscribable Peer-to-Peer RDF Repository for Distributed Metadata Management. *Journal of Web Semantics: Science, Services and Agents on the World Wide Web*, 2(2):109–130, December 2004.

[10] D. Calvanese, G. De Giacomo, M. Lenzerini, R. Rosati, and G. Vetere. Hyper: A Framework for Peer-to-Peer Data Integration on Grids. In *Proceedings of the International Conference on Semantics of a Networked World: Semantics for Grid Databases (ICSNW 2004)*, pages 144–157, 2004.

[11] J. Crowcroft, T. Moreton, I. Pratt, and A. Twigg. *The GRID2: Blueprint for a New Computing Infrastructure*, chapter Peer-to-Peer Technologies. 2004.

[12] M. Esteban Gutirez (ed), S. Bechhofer, O. Corcho, M. Ferndez-Lez, A. Gez-Perez, Z. Kaoudi, I. Kotsiopoulos, M. Koubarakis, M C. Suez-Figueroa, and V. Tamma. Specification and Design of Ontology Grid Compliant and Grid Aware Services. Deliverable 3.1 OntoGrid project.

[13] I. Foster and A. Iamnitchi. On Death, Taxes, and the Convergence of Peer-to-Peer and Grid Computing. In *2nd International Workshop on Peer-to-Peer Systems (IPTPS'03)*, Berkeley, CA, February 2003.

[14] G. Karvounarakis. RQL. http://139.91.183.30:9090/RDF/RQL/, 2003.

[15] C. A. Goble and D. De Roure. The Semantic Grid: Myth Busting and Bridge Building. In *Proceedings of ECAI*, pages 1129–1135, 2004.

[16] A. Harrison and I. Taylor. Dynamic Web Service Deployment Using WSPeer. In *Proceedings of 13th Annual Mardi Gras Conference - Frontiers of Grid Applications and Technologies*, pages 11–16. Louisiana State University, February 2005.

[17] F. Heine, M. Hovestadt, and O. Kao. Towards Ontology-Driven P2P Grid Resource Discovery. In *5th International Workshop on Grid Computing (GRID 2004)*, pages 76–83, Pittsburgh, PA, USA, November 2004.

[18] A. Iamnitchi, I. Foster, and D. C. Nurmi. A Peer-to-Peer Approach to Resource Location in Grid Environments. In *Proceedings of the 11th Symposium on High Performance Distributed Computing*, Edinburgh, UK, August 2002.

[19] A. Iamnitchi, I. Foster, and D.C. Nurmi. A Peer-to-Peer Approach to Resource Discovery in Grid Environments. Technical Report TR-2002-06, University of Chicago, 2002.

[20] A. Iamnitchi and I. Foster. On Fully Decentralized Resource Discovery in Grid Environments. In *International Workshop on Grid Computing*, Denver, Colorado, 2001. IEEE.

[21] Z. Kaoudi, I. Miliaraki, M. Magiridou, A. Papadakis-Pesaresi, E. Liarou, S. Idreos, S. Skiadopoulos, and M. Koubarakis. Deployment of Ontology Services and Semantic Grid Services on top of Self-organized P2P Networks. Deliverable D4.2, Ontogrid project, February 2006.

[22] G. Karvounarakis, S. Alexaki, V. Christophides, D. Plexousakis, and M. Scholl. RQL: A Declarative Query Language for RDF. In *Proceedings of the 11th International World Wide Web Conference*, May 2002.

[23] A. Kothari, D. Agrawal, A. Gupta, and S. Suri. Range Addressable Network: A P2P Cache Architecture for Data Ranges. In *Proceedins of the 3rd International Conference on Peer-to-Peer Computing (P2P'03)*, Linkoping, Sweden, 2003.

[24] I. Kotsiopoulos, S. Bechhofer, P. Alper, P. Missier, O. Corcho, D. Kuo, and C. Goble. Specification of a Semantic Grid Architecture. Deliverable 1.2, OntoGrid project.

[25] O. Lassila and R. R. Swick. Resource Description Framework (RDF) Model and Syntax Specification. Technical report, W3C Recommendation, 1999.

[26] E. Liarou, S. Idreos, and M. Koubarakis. Evaluating Conjunctive Triple Pattern Queries over Large Structured Overlay Networks. Submitted.

[27] E. Liarou, S. Idreos, and M. Koubarakis. Evaluating Continuous Conjunctive RDF Queries over Large Structured Overlay Networks. Manuscript in preparation.

[28] E. Liarou, S. Idreos, and M. Koubarakis. Publish-Subscribe with RDF Data over Large Structured Overlay Networks. In *Proceedings of the 3rd International Workshop on Databases, Information Systems and Peer-to-Peer Computing (DBISP2P 2005)*, Trondheim, Norway, 28-29 August.

[29] P. Lord, P. Alper, C. Wroe, and C. Goble. Feta: A light-weight architecture for user oriented semantic service discovery. In *Proceedings of the 2nd European Semantic Web Conference (ESWC 2005)*, Heraklion, Crete.

[30] M. Magiridou, S. Sahtouris, V. Christophides, and M. Koubarakis. RUL: A Declarative Update Language for RDF. In *Proceedings of the 4rth International Semantic Web Conferece (ISWC2005)*, 2005.

[31] S. Rhea, D. Geels, T. Roscoe, and J. Kubiatowicz. Handling Churn in a DHT. In *USENIX Annual Technical Conference*, 2004.

[32] A. Rowstron and P. Druschel. Pastry: Scalable, Distributed Object Location and Routing for Large-Scale- Peer-to-Peer Storage Utility. In *Proceedings of the 18th IFIP/ACM International Conference on Distributed Systems Paltforms (Middleware 2001)*, November 2001.

[33] J. O. Segura, R. Benjamins, J. M. Gómez Pérez, J. Contreras, R. Salla, O. Corcho, R. González, G. Aguado de Cea, I. Álvarez de Mon y Rego, A. Pareja Lora, and R. Plaza Arteche. Specification and Design of Annotation Services. Deliverable D5.1, Ontogrid project, March 2005.

[34] D. Talia and P. Trunfio. Toward a Synergy Between P2P and Grids. *IEEE Internet Computing*, 7(4):94–96, 2003.

IV

DISTRIBUTED DATA MINING

WSRF-BASED SERVICES FOR DISTRIBUTED DATA MINING

Antonio Congiusta, Domenico Talia, and Paolo Trunfio
DEIS, University of Calabria
Via P. Bucci 41C, 87036 Rende (CS)
Italy
acongiusta@deis.unical.it
talia@deis.unical.it
trunfio@deis.unical.it

Abstract Computational Grids can be effectively used as an infrastructure for distributed data mining and knowledge discovery in large data sets. To utilize Grids for high-performance knowledge discovery, software tools and mechanisms are needed. To this purpose we designed a system called Knowledge Grid and we are implementing its services as WSRF-compliant Grid Services. This chapter describes the composition of distributed knowledge discovery services, according to the service oriented architecture model, by using the Knowledge Grid environment. We discuss Grid Services for searching Grid resources, composing software and data elements, and executing the resulting data mining application on the Knowledge Grid. The chapter focuses in particular on the application modeling. Applications are designed using a UML model, which is translated into a BPEL representation, in turn processed by the Knowledge Grid services for its execution.

Keywords: distributed data mining, Knowledge Grid, WSRF, UML, BPEL.

1. Introduction

Today huge amounts of data are produced, stored, and moved within Grid systems as a result of data acquisitions from remote instruments, or scientific experiments, simulations, and so forth. Handling and mining large volumes of data is still the most critical issue currently affecting scientists and companies attempting to make a profitable use of their data. One of the most important challenges of the Grid is thus making the production and ownership of such data competitive and useful by allowing effective and efficient extraction of valuable knowledge from it. To this end, knowledge discovery and data mining services are needed to analyze the very large amount of data that today is distributed over computational Grids.

The Knowledge Grid [1] is a framework for implementing distributed knowledge discovery tasks and applications in Grids. The Knowledge Grid offers to the users a set of services by which it is possible to integrate Grid resources to support all the phases of the knowledge discovery process, as well as single tasks such as data management, data mining, and knowledge representation. Previous research activities on the Knowledge Grid have been focused on the development of a system prototype by using early Grid middleware, as well as the design and evaluation of distributed knowledge discovery applications [2–4].

Currently, the *Open Grid Services Architecture* (*OGSA*) paradigm and the emerging *Web Services Resource Framework* (*WSRF*) family of standards are being adopted for re-implementing the Knowledge Grid services [5]. These services will permit the design and orchestration of distributed data mining applications running on large-scale, OGSA-based Grids composed of data and compute services available all over the world.

This chapter describes the development of the Knowledge Grid services by using OGSA and WSRF. After discussing design aspects and execution mechanisms, the chapter focuses on application modeling. It discusses how the application models are represented and supported by the different Grid services for their execution over the Knowledge Grid. Applications are modeled through UML and translated in BPEL, then they are processed by the Knowledge Grid services for their execution on the Grid.

The remainder of the chapter is organized as follows. Section 2 discusses the service-oriented approach and its relationships with Grid computing. Section 3 describes the implementation of the Knowledge Grid in terms of the OGSA and WSRF models. Section 4 discusses application modeling and execution plan representation. Section 5 gives some performance data about WSRF service execution. Section 6 briefly discusses related work. Finally, Section 7 concludes the chapter.

2. SOA and the WS-Resource Framework

The *Service Oriented Architecture* (*SOA*) is a programming model for building flexible, modular, and interoperable software applications. Concepts behind SOA are mostly derived from component-based software and the object-oriented programming. SOA enables the assembly of applications through parts regardless of their implementation details, deployment location, and initial objective of their development.

A *service* is a software building block capable of fulfilling a given task or business function. It does so by adhering to a well defined interface that defines required parameters and the nature of the result. Once defined and deployed, services operate independently of the state of any other service defined within the system, that is they are like "black boxes." Nonetheless, services independence does not prohibit to have services cooperating with each other to achieve a common goal. In fact, the final objective of SOA is to provide for an application architecture within which all functions are defined as independent services with well-defined interfaces, which can be called in defined sequences to form business processes [6].

The most important implementation of SOA is represented by *Web Services*. The popularity of Web Services is mainly due to the adoption of universally accepted technologies such as XML, SOAP, and HTTP. The Web is not the only area that has been attracted by the SOA paradigm. Also the Grid can provide a framework whereby a great number of services can be dynamically located, balanced, and managed, so that applications are always guaranteed to be securely executed, according to the principles of on-demand computing. The trend of the latest years proved that not only the Grid is a fruitful environment for developing SOA-based applications, but also that the challenges and requirement posed by the Grid environment can contribute to further developments and improvements of the SOA model.

The Grid community has adopted the *Open Grid Services Architecture* (*OGSA*) as an implementation of the SOA model within the Grid context. In OGSA every resource is represented as a Web Service that conforms to a set of conventions and supports standard interfaces. OGSA provides a well-defined set of Web Service interfaces for the development of interoperable Grid systems and applications [7]. Recently the *WS-Resource Framework* (*WSRF*) has been adopted as an evolution of early OGSA implementations [8]. WSRF defines a family of technical specifications for accessing and managing *stateful resources* using Web Services. The composition of a Web Service and a stateful resource is called *WS-Resource*.

The possibility to define a "state" associated to a service is the most important difference between WSRF-compliant Web Services, and pre-WSRF ones. This is a key feature in designing Grid applications, since WS-Resources provide a way to represent, advertise, and access properties related to both computational resources and applications. Besides, the *WS-Notification* specification [9] defines a *publish-subscribe* notification model for Web Services, which is exploited to notify interested clients and/or services about changes that occur to the status of a WS-Resource.

The combination of stateful resources and the notification pattern can be exploited to build distributed, long-lived Grid applications in which the computation status is managed across multiple nodes, and services cooperate in a highly-decentralized way.

3. WSRF-based Data Mining Services

The design of the WSRF-based version of the Knowledge Grid benefitted from the service-oriented approach used in the original design of the system [1]. That design approach conceived the Knowledge Grid architecture and functionality as a set of basic and high-level services that did not pose any constraints on the implementation strategy. This choice facilitated re-designing the system and implementing the new WSRF-version by maintaining the same architecture and exposing the same functionalities as Web Services.

Figure 1 shows the Knowledge Grid architecture, in which each Knowledge Grid service (*K-Grid service*) is exposed as a Web Service that exports one or more operations, by using WSRF conventions and mechanisms.

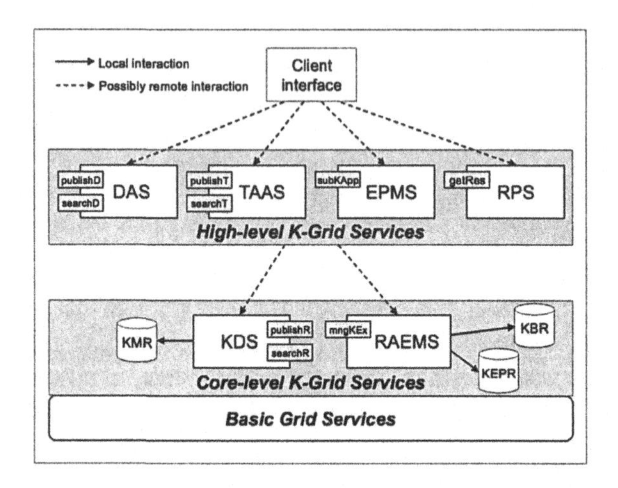

Figure 1. The Knowledge Grid architecture.

The Knowledge Grid services are organized in two hierarchical levels: the *Core K-Grid layer* and the *High-level K-Grid layer*. The High-level K-Grid layer includes services to compose, validate, and execute a distributed knowledge discovery computation. The main services of the High-level K-Grid layer are:

- The *Data Access Service* (*DAS*) manages the publication and search of data to be mined (data sources), as well as the search of inferred models (mining results). This service exports two operations: `publishData`, invoked for publishing a newly available dataset, and `searchData`, invoked for locating data to be used in a data mining computation.

- The *Tools and Algorithms Access Service* (*TAAS*) is responsible for publishing and searching extraction tools, data mining tools, and visualization tools. It exports two operations: `publishTools` and `searchTools`. The first operation is used to publish metadata about a data mining tool. As a result of the publishing, a new data mining service is made available for utilization in data mining computations. The second operation is similar to the DAS `searchData` operation except that it is targeted to data mining tools.

- The *Execution Plan Management Service* (*EPMS*). An *execution plan* is represented by a workflow describing interactions and data flows between data sources, extraction tools, data mining tools, and visualization tools. The EPMS allows for defining the structure of an application by building the corresponding execution plan and adding a set of constraints about resources. The execution plan generated by this service is referred to as *abstract execution plan*, because it may include both well identified resources and *abstract resources*, i.e., resources that are defined through constraints about their features, but are not known a priori. The EPMS exports its functionality through the `submitKApplication` operation, which receives a conceptual model of the application to be executed and generates the corresponding abstract execution plan, which is in turn submitted to the RAEMS service (see below) for its execution.

- The *Results Presentation Service* (*RPS*) offers facilities for presenting and visualizing the extracted knowledge models (e.g., association rules, clustering models, classifications). It exports the `getResults` operation, which retrieves results of a performed data mining computation and presents them to the user.

The Core K-Grid layer offers basic services for the management of metadata describing features of hosts, data sources, data mining tools, and visualization tools. This layer also coordinates the application execution by attempting to fulfill the application requirements with respect to available Grid resources. The Core K-Grid layer comprises two main services:

- The *Knowledge Directory Service* (*KDS*) handles metadata describing Knowledge Grid resources. Such resources include hosts, data repositories, tools and algorithms used to extract, analyze, and manipulate data, distributed knowledge discovery execution plans, and knowledge models obtained as result of mining processes. The metadata information is represented by XML documents stored in a *Knowledge Metadata Repository* (*KMR*). The KDS exports two operations: `publishResource`, invoked by the DAS or TAAS services for publishing data or tools in the KMR, and `searchResource`, which is the core-level operation for searching data or tools.

- The *Resource Allocation and Execution Management Service* (*RAEMS*) is used to find a suitable mapping between an abstract execution plan and available resources, with the goal of satisfying the constraints (e.g., CPU, storage, memory, database, and network bandwidth requirements) imposed by the execution plan. The output of this process is an *instantiated execution plan*, which defines the resource requests for each data mining process. Generated execution plans are stored in the *Knowledge Execution Plan Repository* (*KEPR*). After the execution plan activation, this service manages the application execution and the storing of results in the *Knowledge Base Repository* (*KBR*). This service exports the `manageKExecution` operation, which receives the abstract execution plan of an application. The RAEMS generates an instantiated execution plan and manages its execution.

The operations exported by High-level K-Grid services (DAS, TAAS, EPMS, and RPS) are designed to be invoked by user-level applications, whereas operations provided by Core K-Grid services (KDS and RAEMS) are thought to be invoked both by High-level and Core K-Grid services.

As shown in Figure 1, users can access the Knowledge Grid functionalities by using a *client interface* located on their machine. The client interface is an integrated visual environment that allows for performing basic tasks (e.g., searching of data and software, data transfers, simple job executions), as well as defining distributed data mining applications described by arbitrarily complex execution plans. The client interface performs its tasks by invoking the appropriate operations provided by the different High-level K-Grid services. Those services may be generally executed on a different Grid node; therefore the interactions between the client interface and High-level K-Grid services are possibly remote.

Besides their specific operations (described above), all K-Grid services export three mandatory operations: `createResource`, `subscribe` and `destroy`. The `createResource` operation is used to create a stateful resource, which is then used to maintain the state (e.g., results) of the computations performed by the service-specific operations. The `subscribe` operation is used to subscribe for notifications about computation results. The `destroy` operation removes a resource.

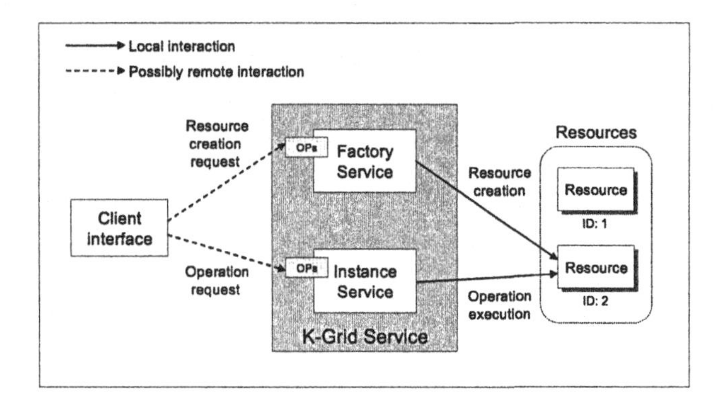

Figure 2. K-Grid service design

The implementation of a K-Grid service follows the *WS-Resource factory pattern* (see Figure 2). In this pattern, a *factory service* is in charge of creating the resources and an *instance service* is used to operate on them. Thus the `createResource` mandatory operation introduced above is provided by the factory service, while the other operations are exported by the instance service. To create a resource the client contacts the factory service, which creates a new resource and assigns to it a unique key. The factory service will return an *endpoint reference* that includes the *resource id* and is used to directly access the resource through the instance service.

3.1 Execution Management

Figure 3 describes the interactions that occur when an invocation of the EPMS service is performed. In particular, the figure outlines the sequence of invocations to others services, and the interchanges with them when a KDD application is submitted for allocation and execution. To this purpose, the EPMS exposes the `submitKApplication` operation, through which it receives a conceptual model of the application to be executed (step 1). The conceptual model is a high-level description of the KDD application more targeted to distributed knowledge discovery aspects rather than to Grid-related issues.

The basic role of the EPMS is to transform the conceptual model into an abstract execution plan for subsequent processing by the RAEMS. It is worth recalling here that an abstract execution plan is a more formal representation of the structure of the application. Generally, it does not contain information on the physical Grid resources to be used, but rather constraints and other criteria about them.

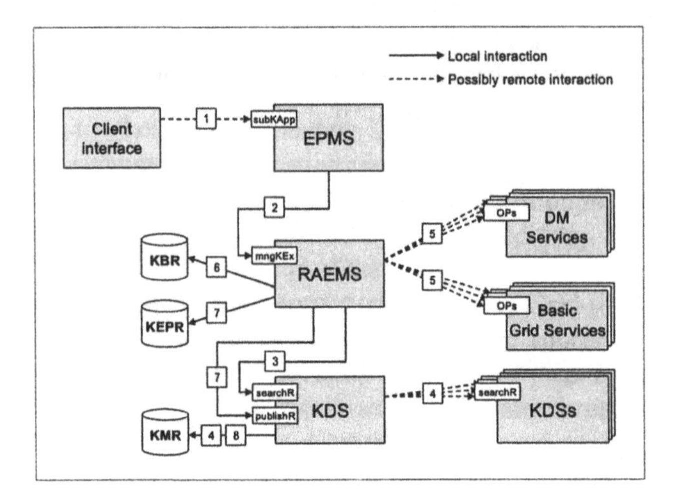

Figure 3. EPMS interactions.

The RAEMS exports the `manageKExecution` operation, which is invoked by the EPMS and receives the abstract execution plan (step 2). First of all, the RAEMS queries the local KDS (through the `searchResource` operation) to obtain information about the resources needed to instantiate the abstract execution plan (step 3). Note that the KDS performs the searching both accessing the local KMR and querying remote KDSs (step 4).

After the instantiated execution plan is obtained, the RAEMS coordinates the actual execution of the overall computation. To this purpose, the RAEMS invokes the appropriate data mining services (DM Services) and basic Grid services (e.g., file transfer services), as specified by the instantiated execution plan (step 5). The results of the computation are stored by the RAEMS into the KBR (step 6), while the execution plan is stored into the KEPR (step 7). To make available the results stored in the KBR, it is necessary to publish results metadata into the KMR. To this end, the RAEMS invokes the `publishResource` operation of the local KDS (steps 7 and 8).

3.2 Data and Tools Access

DAS and TAAS services are concerned with the publishing and searching of datasets and tools to be used in a KDD application. They possess the same basic structure and perform their main tasks by interacting with a local instance of the KDS that in turn may invoke one or more other remote KDS instances.

Figure 4 describes the interactions that occur when the DAS service is invoked; similar interactions apply also to TAAS invocations. The `publishData` operation is invoked to publish information about a dataset (step 1). The DAS passes the corresponding metadata to the local KDS, by in-

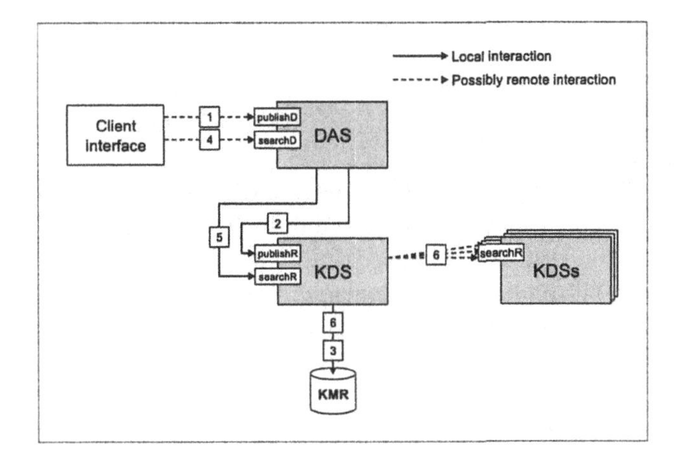

Figure 4. DAS interactions.

voking the `publishResource` operation (step 2). The KDS, in turn, stores that metadata into the local KMR (step 3).

The `searchData` operation is invoked by a client interface that needs to locate a dataset on the basis of a given set of criteria (step 4). The DAS submits its request to the local KDS, by invoking the corresponding `searchResource` operation (step 5). As mentioned before, the KDS performs the searching both accessing the local KMR, and querying remote KDSs (step 6). This is a general rule enforced in all the interactions between a high-level service and the KDS when a searching is requested. The local KDS is thus responsible for dispatching the query to remote KDSs and for generating the final answer.

The search for a dataset is performed through the `searchData` operation starting from a search string passed by the client. It contains the searching criteria expressed as attribute-value pairs regarding key properties through which datasets are categorized within the system by using metadata.

The outcome of the searching is a set of URLs pointing to the metadata of the datasets corresponding to that searching criteria. These kinds of URLs are specifically targeted at the KDS service: it implements, in fact, a custom protocol for locating metadata descriptions of Grid resources.

A KDS URL has the form:

```
kds://<hostname>/<metadataLocator>
```

and uniquely identifies a metadata file in the Knowledge Grid.

4. Application Modeling and Representation

Designing and executing a distributed KDD application over the Knowledge Grid is a multi-step task that involves interactions and information flows between services at the different levels of the architecture. A key aspect in the Knowledge Grid is how applications are modeled, and how the application models are represented and processed through the different services.

As mentioned in the previous section, applications are described at a high level using a *conceptual model*, generated by the user through the design facilities provided by the client interface. In the current approach we use UML to represent the conceptual model of an application. The conceptual model is then passed to the EPMS, which is in charge of transforming it into an *abstract execution plan* for subsequent processing by the RAEMS. The execution plan is expressed through a BPEL document. The RAEMS is in turn responsible for producing an *instantiated execution plan* and coordinating the actual execution of the overall application.

This section describes the process through which the conceptual model is transformed into the instantiated execution plan and how it is then executed on the Grid. To describe how the EPMS and RAEMS components enforce such a process and interact each other in order to manage a distributed data mining application, a sample mining task is introduced and analyzed during the whole design and execution phases within the Knowledge Grid environment.

The application we consider to such purpose is inspired to a real classification task that has been tested over the pre-WSRF implementation of the Knowledge Grid, as detailed in [3]. The goal of the classification task is to generate an intrusion detection model based on the analysis of a dataset containing network monitoring data.

While the original dataset is maintained on a single node, the computation is distributed across a suitable number of Grid nodes. To this end, a number of independent classifiers are first computed by applying in parallel the same learning algorithm over a set of distributed training sets, generated through a random partitioning of the original data set. Afterwards, the best classifier is chosen by means of a voting operation taking into account evaluation criteria like computation time, error rate, confusion matrix, etc.

4.1 Conceptual Model Representation

The application model must specify, at some level of abstraction, the tasks that compose the process, as well as the logic ruling their integration. Many formalisms have been traditionally used for modelling application workflows, such as directed acyclic graphs (DAGs), Petri Nets, and UML activity diagrams. Many Grid workflow systems adopt standard coordination languages such as BPEL [10] and WSCI [11], or XML-based ad-hoc solutions.

Within the Knowledge Grid, the UML activity diagram formalism is used to represent the conceptual model of the application, while BPEL is used for representing execution plans. The activity diagram represents the high-level flow of service invocations that constitute the application logic, whereas BPEL expresses how the various services are actually coordinated and invoked.

Figure 5 shows the activity diagram for the example described above. The *sampling* activity specifies number and sizes of the testing sets that are extracted from the original dataset. The *mining process* is invoked in parallel on three different nodes. Before that, each testing set is transferred to the related node. The resulting models are then moved to the node on which the *voting* activity will take place.

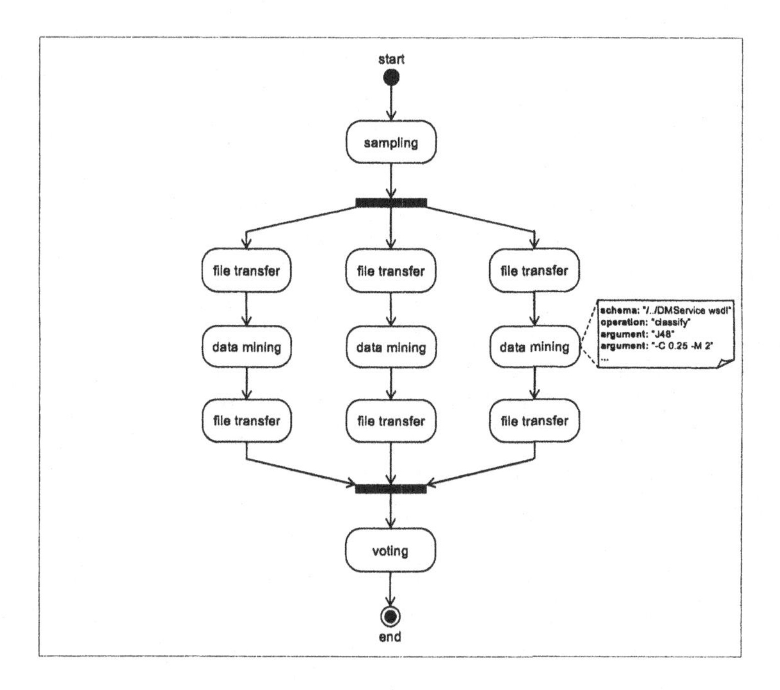

Figure 5. Conceptual model for the example application.

Notice that the *sampling* activity is followed by a *fork* operator, which specifies that the subsequent activity sequences are to be performed in parallel. The *fork* operator is used in combination with a *join* operator, which prescribes that the execution flow can proceed only when all of the incoming branches have been performed. Therefore, the *voting* activity is executed only when all the classification model have been computed and transferred on the same node.

Many details of the application (such as the data mining algorithm, invocation parameters, and so on), are hidden behind the visual notation, but they are specified by the designer as properties of the activities. For example, Figure 5 shows some properties for a data mining activity. They represent basic characteristics of the computations and are stored within the application model as activity attributes. This approach for modeling a data mining application abstracts from details of the Grid infrastructure used to execute the application.

4.2 Execution Plan Representation

As mentioned in Section 3, "abstract" and "instantiated" execution plans are distinguished. At the abstract level, the execution plan may not refer to specific implementations of services, application components, and input data. All these entities may be referred through logical names and, in some cases, by means of a set of constraints about some of their properties, possibly expressing quality of service requirements. For example, requirements on processor speed, amount of main memory or disk space can be used to single out Grid nodes, while requirements on Grid software may concern input data or target platforms.

Prior of the application execution, all of the resource constraints need to be evaluated and resolved on a set of available Grid resources, in order to choose the more appropriate ones w.r.t. the current status of the Grid environment. Of course, due to the dynamic nature of the Grid, an abstract execution plan can be instantiated into different execution plans at different times. Instantiated execution plans include real names and locations of services, data files, etc. According to this approach the workflow definition is decoupled from the underlying Grid configuration. This brings many advantages, such as reusability of application models in time and space, easiness of design, etc.

A *Business Process Execution Language* (*BPEL*) document is used to express the business logic of the application being modelled. This constitutes a fundamental part of both abstract execution plans and instantiated execution plans. The main difference among them is that in the BPEL document of the abstract execution plan the WSDL of services are used without specifying the service locations. On the other hand, in the instantiated execution plan the service locations are included. In both documents services are referred through the `partnerLinkType` element provided by BPEL. This element is able to link the BPEL workflow with the WSDL description of each service included in it.

As mentioned before, the translation of the conceptual model (represented by the UML formalism) into the abstract execution plan (represented by a BPEL document) is performed by the EPMS. To this end, the EPMS incorporates an engine which is able to map the UML operators into corresponding BPEL notations. The BPEL notation is explicitly targeted to service invocations and thus more rich with respect to the UML one. It includes several constructs for interacting with services at different levels, as well as other BPEL processes, and manipulating and accessing services input messages and responses (both through explicit variable manipulation operators and XPath expressions). One important feature about service invocation is the availability of patterns reflecting the typical invocation mechanisms supported by services (one-way, two-way, synchronous or asynchronous). Such basic patterns are particularly useful and adaptable to the WSRF context, in which in addition to typical Web services invocation mechanisms, the factory pattern is the main way for WS-Resources creation, and response messages can originate not only from the services to which the requests have been sent.

Figure 6 shows the structure of the BPEL document corresponding to the UML diagram shown in Figure 5. The overall workflow is defined within a `process` tag. `partnerLinks` defines the services involved in the application. Variables used as input and output in service invocations, as well as for other purposes (e.g., faults and internal variables) are declared within the `variables` section. The `sequence` tag specifies the main structure of the application, including a sampling phase, a set of parallel activities, and the final voting. The parallel activities are specified using a `flow` operator, which in turn includes three sequences. Each `sequence` is composed by a set of invocations that perform transfer and mining tasks.

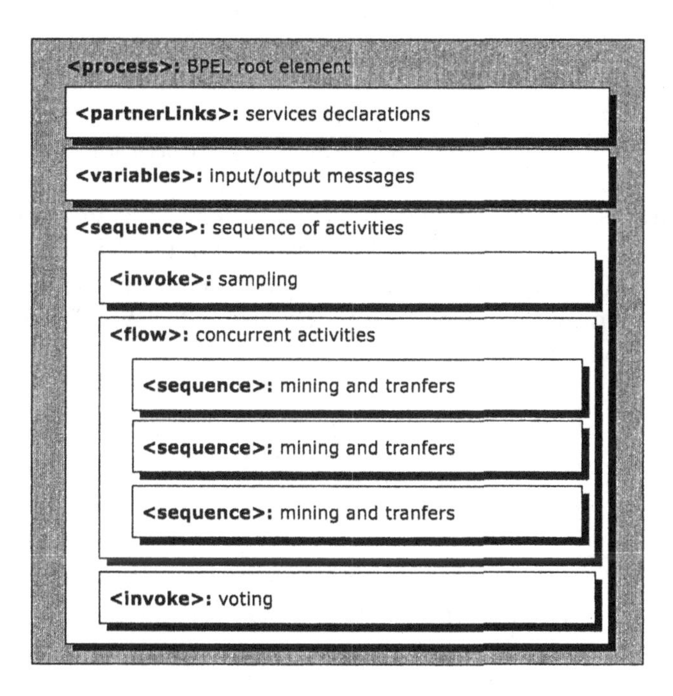

Figure 6. Structure of the BPEL document.

Figure 7 shows an extract of the BPEL document reporting one of the data mining service invocations. Notice that the classification task is invoked after the service instance creation and the results notification subscription, following the general pattern described in Section 3.

```
<invoke name="DM service creation"
        partnerLink="DMFactoryService"
        portType="DMFactoryPortType"
        operation="createResource"
        inputvariable="DMCreationRequest"
        outputvariable="DMCreationResponse">
</invoke>
...
<invoke name="DM service subscription"
        partnerLink="DMServiceInstance"
        portType="DMServicePortType"
        operation="subscribe"
        inputvariable="SubscribeInputMessage"
        outputvariable="SubscribeOutputMessage">
</invoke>
...
<invoke name="DM service classification"
        partnerLink="DMServiceInstance"
        portType="DMServicePortType"
        operation="classify"
        inputvariable="ClassificationInputMessage">
</invoke>
...
<receive name="DM service notification"
        partnerLink="DMServiceInstance"
        portType="tns:ProcessPortType"
        operation="deliver"
        variable="NotificationMessage">
</receive>
```

Figure 7. An excerpt of the BPEL document.

Figure 8 shows the definition of the `partnerLinkType` for the data mining factory. This definition has to be included in the WSDL definition of the data mining factory service in order to allow its invocation within the BPEL process. Similar definitions are also included in the WSDL documents of the other services.

```
<partnerLinkType name="DMFactoryService">
    <role name="DMFactoryServiceProvider">
        <portType name="DMFactoryPortType"/>
    </role>
</partnerLinkType>
```

Figure 8. Example of `partnerLinkType` definition.

The BPEL and all the associated WSDL documents are passed to the RAEMS for the instantiation process. It is important to note that the WSDL documents received by the RAEMS may not include the actual location of the service to be invoked, reflecting the fact that this has not been specified by the user during the conceptual model definition. Therefore, the RAEMS attempts to locate suitable service instances that match the service requirements specified as WSDL definitions. Whenever an instantiated execution plan is obtained, the RAEMS is in charge of submitting it to the workflow engine which coordinates its execution.

5. WSRF Service Execution Performance

In the previous sections we discussed the design of the Knowledge Grid using WSRF-compliant services and data mining application modeling in the Knowledge Grid based on UML and BPEL. This activity has been preceded by a performance evaluation phase in which we analyzed the execution times of the WSRF Grid services for estimating the overhead introduced in the remote execution of data mining tasks on a Grid.

To evaluate the efficiency of the WSRF mechanisms discussed throughout the previous sections, we developed an experiment in which single WSRF-compliant K-Grid services executed the different steps described above for invoking the service, creating the resource, and accessing it. The deployed K-Grid service exported a service-specific operation named `clustering`, as well as the mandatory operations `createResource`, `subscribe` and `destroy`. In particular, the `clustering` operation was used to perform a data clustering analysis on a local data set using the expectation maximization (EM) algorithm. The K-Grid service and the client program have been developed using the WSRF Java library provided by Globus Toolkit 3.9.2. The data set on which to apply the mining process contained 17000 instances (with a size of 5 MBytes) extracted from the *census* data set provided by the UCI repository [12].

After performing 20 independent experiments the execution times of the single steps have been measured. The experiments have been executed both within a local area Grid scenario and within a wide area Grid. The measurements showed that the data mining phase represents the 99.5% of the total execution time if client and service reside on a local Grid, whereas the execution time on the wide area Grid took about 88.3% of total time; the latter case included also the data-set download phase which accounted for about 10% of the total time. In both cases, the overhead due to specific WSRF mechanisms (resource creation, notification subscription, task submission, results notification) was very low with respect to the overall execution time; it accounted for an amount of time of about 0.5% and about 1.5% respectively.

In general, we can conclude that the overhead introduced by the WSRF mechanisms is marginal when the duration of the service-specific operations is long enough, as in typical data mining algorithms working on large data sets. Therefore, the WS-Resource Framework is suitable to be exploited for developing high-level services and distributed knowledge discovery applications on Grids.

6. Related work

Several Grid-based data mining systems have been proposed (see [3] for a quick survey). Among those, two systems that exploit a service-oriented approach for providing Grid-based KDD services are *Discovery Net* [13] and *Grid Miner* [14].

Discovery Net allows users to integrate data analysis software and data sources made available by third parties. The building blocks are the so-called *Knowledge Discovery Services*, distinguished in *Computation Services* and *Data Services*. Discovery Net provides services, mechanisms and tools for specifying knowledge discovery processes.

The functionalities of Discovery Net can be accessed through an interface exposed as an OGSA-compliant Grid service. However, Discovery Net currently uses an early implementation of OGSA - namely, the *Open Grid Services Infrastructure* (*OGSI*) - which has been replaced by WSRF for lack of compatibility with standard Web Services technologies.

GridMiner aims at covering the main aspects of knowledge discovery on Grids. Key components in GridMiner are *Mediation Service*, *Information Service*, *Resource Broker*, and *OLAP Cube Management*. These are the so called GridMiner Base services, because they provide basic services to GridMiner Core services. GridMiner Core services include services for data integration, process management, data mining, and OLAP. The services themselves do not communicate with each other. No service is aware of any other existing service. Hence each of them is able to run completely independently. To support the individual steps of KDD processes, the output of each service can be used as input for the subsequent service. Like Discovery Net, also Grid Miner has been implemented on OGSI.

It can be observed that the Discovery Net approach is similar in many aspects to the approach followed in the Knowledge Grid to provide a service-based middleware for distributed data mining. On the contrary, the Grid Miner system provides single services implementing the main steps of a KDD process and a service composition engine to execute a multi-step data mining application.

To the best of our knowledge, none of the existing systems makes use of WSRF as basic technology. Therefore, the Knowledge Grid is the first system leveraging WSRF for building a comprehensive high-level framework for distributed knowledge discovery in Grid environments, supporting also the integration of data mining algorithms exposed through a Web Service interface.

7. Conclusions

In this chapter we addressed the definition and composition of Grid services for implementing distributed knowledge discovery applications on WSRF-compliant Grids. We presented Grid services for searching Grid resources, composing software and data elements, and managing the execution of data mining applications on Grids. The chapter discussed the definition of data mining Grid services in the context of the Knowledge Grid architecture. The services and operations presented in this paper allow for data and tools publishing and searching, execution submission and resource management, and retrieving of the produced results.

After discussing design aspects and low-level execution mechanisms, the chapter focused on the application modeling problem; that is, how the application models are represented and processed through the different services for their execution over the Knowledge Grid. This work demonstrated that the use of high-level standard formalisms that abstract from Grid architecture details, such as UML and BPEL, in cooperation with emerging technologies such as the WS-Resource Framework, can be effectively exploited for designing and composing distributed data mining applications on computational Grids. Using the service-based Knowledge Grid, the data sets and data mining components used in knowledge discovery applications can be offered by different providers distributed all over the world.

Acknowledgments

This research work is carried out under the FP6 Network of Excellence CoreGRID funded by the European Commission (Contract IST-2002-004265). This work has been also supported by the Italian MIUR FIRB Grid.it project RBNE01KNFP on High Performance Grid Platforms and Tools.

References

[1] M. Cannataro and D. Talia. The Knowledge Grid. *CACM.* 46(1):89-93, 2003.

[2] M. Cannataro, A. Congiusta, D. Talia and P. Trunfio. A Data Mining Toolset for Distributed High-Performance Platforms. Int. Conference Data Mining 2002, WIT Press, pp. 41-50, 2002.

[3] M. Cannataro, A. Congiusta, A. Pugliese, D. Talia and P. Trunfio. Distributed Data Mining on Grids: Services, Tools, and Applications. *IEEE Transactions on Systems, Man, and Cybernetics, Part B.* 34(6):2451-2465, 2004.

[4] G. Bueti, A. Congiusta and D. Talia. Developing Distributed Data Mining Applications in the KNOWLEDGE GRID Framework. VECPAR'04, LNCS 3402, pp. 156-169, 2005.

[5] A. Congiusta, D. Talia, P. Trunfio. On Designing and Composing Grid Services for Distributed Data Mining. In: V. Getov, D. Laforenza, A. Reinefeld (Eds.), Future Generation Grids, pp. 113-132, Springer-Verlag, 2006.

[6] K. Channabasavaiah, K. Holley and E. M. Tuggle. Migrating to a service-oriented architecture. 2003. http://www-106.ibm.com/developerworks/library/ws-migratesoa.

[7] I. Foster, C. Kesselman, J. Nick and S. Tuecke. The Physiology of the Grid. In: Grid Computing: Making the Global Infrastructure a Reality, Wiley, pp. 217-249, 2003.

[8] K. Czajkowski et al. The WS-Resource Framework Version 1.0. 2004. http://www-106.ibm.com/developerworks/library/ws-resource/ws-wsrf.pdf.

[9] Web Services Notification. http://www-128.ibm.com/developerworks/library/specification/ws-notification.

[10] BPEL for Web Services version 1.1. http://www-128.ibm.com/developerworks/library/specification/ws-bpel.

[11] Web Service Choreography Interface (WSCI) 1.0. http://www.w3.org/TR/wsci.

[12] The UCI Repository. http://www.ics.uci.edu/~mlearn/MLRepository.html.

[13] S. Al Sairafi et al. The Design of Discovery Net: Towards Open Grid Services for Knowledge Discovery. *Int. Journal of High Performance Computing Applications.* **17**(3):297-315, 2003.

[14] P. Brezany, J. Hofer, A. M. Tjoa and A. Woehrer. GridMiner: An Infrastructure for Data Mining on Computational Grids. APAC'03, 2003.

MINING FREQUENT CLOSED ITEMSETS FROM DISTRIBUTED REPOSITORIES

Claudio Lucchese, Salvatore Orlando
Dept. of Computer Science
Ca' Foscari University of Venice, Italy
{clucches, orlando}@dsi.unive.it

Raffaele Perego
HPC Laboratory
ISTI-CNR of Pisa, Italy
perego@isti.cnr.it

Claudio Silvestri
Dept. of Computer Science
Ca' Foscari University of Venice, Italy
silvestri@dsi.unive.it

Abstract In this paper we address the problem of mining frequent closed itemsets in a highly distributed setting like a Grid. The extraction of frequent (closed) itemsets is a very expensive phase needed to extract from a transactional database a reduced set of meaningful association rules. We figure out an environment where different datasets are stored in different sites. We assume that, due to the huge size of datasets and privacy concerns, dataset partitions cannot be moved to a centralized site where to materialize the whole dataset and perform the mining task. Thus it becomes mandatory to perform separate mining at each site, and then merge local results for deriving global knowledge.

This paper shows how frequent closed itemsets, mined independently at each site, can be merged in order to derive globally frequent closed itemsets. Unfortunately, such merging might produce a superset of all the frequent closed itemsets, while the associated supports could be smaller than the exact ones because some globally frequent closed itemsets might be not locally frequent in some partitions. To avoid an expensive post-processing phase, needed to compute exact global results, we use a method to approximate the supports of closed itemsets. The approximation is only needed for those globally (closed) frequent itemsets which are locally infrequent on some dataset partitions, and thus are not returned at all from the corresponding sites.

Keywords: frequent itemsets, closed itemsets, Knowledge Grid, distributed data mining.

1. Introduction.

Data Mining is the process of extracting knowledge hidden in huge amounts of data. The kind of knowledge we are interested in, together with the organization of input data and the criteria used to discriminate among useful and useless information, contributes to characterize a specific data mining problem and its possible algorithmic solutions. Common data mining tasks are the classification of new objects according to a scheme learned from examples, the partitioning of a set of objects into homogeneous subsets, the extraction of rules from a database. Association Rule Mining (ARM) is one of the most popular Data Mining topic, and consists in the discovery of rules concerning the co-occurrence of items in a collection of set of items. The result of this task is a set of rules similar to *"a set containing item B and item D will also contain item G with a 60% probability"*. ARM has been successfully exploited in several fields. A widely known application is the analysis of customer behavior. In this case the items are objects sold in a shop, the input sets represents objects sold in the same transactions and the expected result is a set of rules about items frequently bought in the same transaction. Analyst can use such rules for direct marketing, or to reorganize the shop shelves and help the customer in the search of commonly associated items, e.g., by placing the barbecue spices close to the refrigerator containing meat.

In this paper we are interested in the most computationally expensive phase of ARM, i.e the Frequent Itemset Mining (FIM) one, during which the set of all the frequent itemsets are extracted from a transactional database. Informally, the FIM problem can be stated as follows: given a *transactional database*, where each transaction is a set of *items*, extract all the set of items that occur frequently in the database. The FIM problem has been extensively studied in the last years. The first proposed algorithm is Apriori [2], but many different approaches have been investigated such as DIC [3], FP-GROWTH [5], ECLAT [24] and many others [1, 15, 20, 7, 10]. One of the main issues emerging from these studies regards the size of the collection of frequent itemsets $\mathcal{F}$. This makes the task of the analyst hard, since he has to extract useful knowledge from a huge amount of patterns. Consider that the size of $\mathcal{F}$ may be comparable with the size of the dataset, when using very low minimum support thresholds.

Closed itemsets are a solution to this problem. For any given collection of frequent itemsets $\mathcal{F}$, there exist a collection of closed itemsets $\mathcal{C}$, which is a concise and lossless representation of $\mathcal{F}$. It is concise because $|\mathcal{C}|$ may be orders of magnitude smaller than $|\mathcal{F}|$. This allows to extract additional potentially interesting patterns by using lower minimum support thresholds, which are intractable when extracting all the frequent itemsets. It is lossless, because from $\mathcal{C}$ it is possible to derive the identity and the support of every frequent itemset in $\mathcal{F}$. Moreover, the extraction of association rules directly from closed itemsets has been shown to be more meaningful for analysts [21, 23], since $\mathcal{C}$ does not include many redundancies that are present in $\mathcal{F}$. Many efficient Frequent Closed Itemsets Mining (FCIM) algorithms have been recently proposed, such as A-CLOSE [14], CHARM [25], CLOSET+ [16] and DCI_CLOSED [8].

In this paper we address the problem of mining frequent closed itemsets in a highly distributed settings [12, 6], such as a Data Grid. While many papers address the problem of parallel/distributed FIM (e.g. PARTITION [17]), to our best knowledge, no proposal for distributed closed itemset mining exists. We figure out a distributed framework where there are many data sources of interest, and where we want to extract knowledge from a virtual transactional dataset made by joining all those data sources together. We assume that, due to the huge size of every single datasets and due to privacy concerns, the original datasets cannot be moved to a centralized site where to materialize the whole dataset and perform the mining task. Thus it becomes mandatory to apply a loosely coupled distributed mining approach, according to which we perform separate mining on each site, and then merge the local results to derive the global knowledge.

The main contributions of this paper are the theoretical basis for the distributed computation of closed itemsets based on a collect and merge approach. In particular, the theorems we have introduced allow to extend previous algorithms for frequent itemsets (Partition [17] and AP [18]) to the closed itemsets case.

The rest of the paper is organized as follows. Section 2 presents the FIM problem and the concept of closed itemsets. Section 3 discusses the issues for realizing a loosely-coupled distributed algorithm, inspired by Partition, for extracting all the frequent itemset from an horizontally partitioned transactional dataset. Section 4 analyzes the additional challenges that a frequent closed itemset mining algorithm has to face, and proposes methods for coping with them. These methods are the building blocks of the AP_{Closed} algorithm we propose. Finally, Section 5 draw our conclusions.

2. Frequent and Closed Itemsets

The problem of mining all frequent itemsets from a transactional dataset can be stated as follows. Let $\mathcal{I} = \{a_1, ..., a_M\}$ be a finite set of *items* or *singletons*, and let $\mathcal{D} = \{t_1, ..., t_N\}$ be a dataset containing a finite set of *transactions*, where each transaction t is a subset of $\mathcal{I}$. We call k-itemset a set of k items $I = \{i_1, ..., i_k \mid i_j \in \mathcal{I}\}$. Given a k-itemset I, let $\sigma(I)$ be its *support*, defined as the number of transactions in $\mathcal{D}$ that include I. Mining all the frequent itemsets from $\mathcal{D}$ requires to discover all the itemsets having support at least

$\overline{\sigma} = minsupp \cdot |\mathcal{D}|$, where $0 < minsupp \leq 1$ is a given minimum support threshold. We denote with $\mathcal{F}$ the collection of frequent itemsets, which is indeed a subset of the huge search space given by the power set of $\mathcal{I}$.

As we discussed before, we are going to focus on a significant subset of $\mathcal{F}$, composed of only those frequent itemsets that are also *closed.* To define the property of an itemset of being closed, we first introduce two auxiliary functions. Given T and I, with $T \subseteq \mathcal{D}$ and $I \subseteq \mathcal{I}$, we define the two following functions f and g:

$$f(T) = \bigcap_{t \in T} t$$

$$g(I) = \{t \in \mathcal{D} \mid I \subseteq t\}.$$

Function f returns the set of items appearing in all the transactions of T, while function g returns the set of transactions supporting a given itemset I.

DEFINITION 1 *An itemset I is said to be* closed *if and only if*

$$c(I) = f(g(I)) = f \circ g(I) = I$$

where the composite function $c = f \circ g$ *is called* Galois operator *or* closure operator.

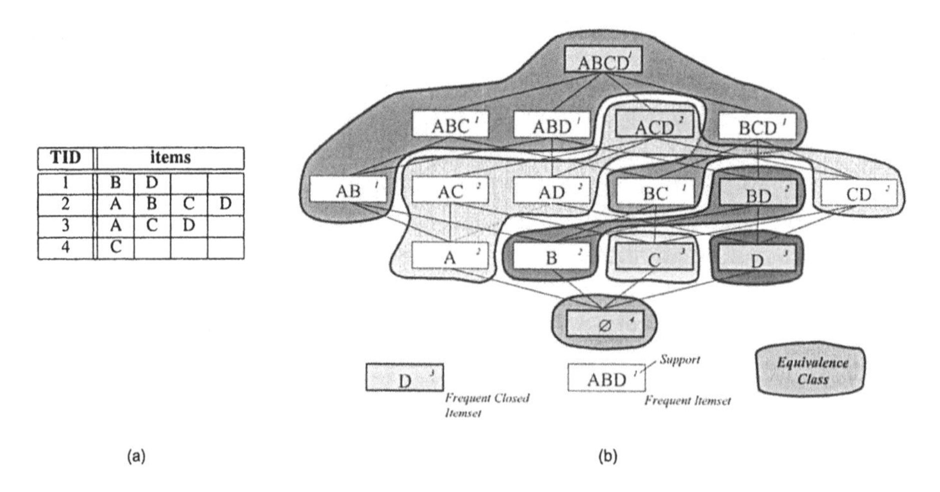

TID	items			
1	B	D		
2	A	B	C	D
3	A	C	D	
4	C			

Figure 1. (a) The input transactional dataset, represented in its horizontal form. (b) Lattice of all the frequent itemsets ($\overline{\sigma} = 1$), with closed itemsets and equivalence classes.

The closure operator defines a set of equivalence classes over the lattice of frequent itemsets: two itemsets belong to the same equivalence class *iff* they have the same closure, i.e. they are supported by the same set of transactions.

We can also show that an itemset I is closed *iff* no supersets of I with the same support exist. Therefore mining the *maximal* elements of all the equivalence classes corresponds to the extraction of all the closed itemsets.

Fig. 1(b) shows the lattice of frequent itemsets derived from the simple dataset reported in Fig. 1(a), mined with $\overline{\sigma} = 1$. We can see that all the itemsets with the same closure are grouped in the same equivalence class. Each equivalence class contains elements sharing the same supporting transactions, and closed itemsets are their maximal elements. Note that closed itemsets (six) are remarkably less than frequent itemsets (sixteen). For example, only the closed itemset $\{ACD\}$ is returned, among the 5 frequent itemsets that are supported by the same set of transactions.

Note that, given the above definition, it is clear that the property of an itemset of being closed does depend on the whole dataset. This is because we need to apply the closure operator $c = f \circ g$ to understand whether an itemset is closed or not.

In the following we introduce two important lemmas that are going to be useful in the next sections.

LEMMA 2 *Given an itemset X and an item $i \in \mathcal{I}$, $g(X) \subseteq g(i) \Leftrightarrow i \in c(X)$.*

PROOF 2.1 Proof.
($g(X) \subseteq g(i) \Rightarrow i \in c(X)$):

> *Since $g(X \cup i) = g(X) \cap g(i)$, $g(X) \subseteq g(i) \Rightarrow g(X \cup i) = g(X)$. Therefore, if $g(X \cup i) = g(X)$ then $f(g(X \cup i)) = f(g(X)) \Rightarrow c(X \cup i) = c(X) \Rightarrow i \in c(X)$.*

($i \in c(X) \Rightarrow g(X) \subseteq g(i)$):

> *If $i \in c(X)$, then $g(X) = g(X \cup i)$. Since $g(X \cup i) = g(X) \cap g(i)$, $g(X) \cap g(i) = g(X)$ holds too. Thus, we can deduce that $g(X) \subseteq g(i)$.*

LEMMA 3 *If Y is a closed itemset, and $X \subset Y$, then $c(X) \subseteq Y$.*

PROOF 3.1 *Note that $g(Y) \subseteq g(X)$ because $X \subseteq Y$. Moreover, Lemma 2 states that if $j \in c(X)$, then $g(X) \subseteq g(j)$. Thus, since $g(Y) \subseteq g(X)$, then $g(Y) \subseteq g(j)$ holds too, and from Lemma 2 it also follows that $j \in c(Y)$. So, if $j \notin Y$ held, Y would not be a closed itemset because $j \in c(Y)$, and this is in contradiction with the hypothesis.*

3. Distributed Frequent Itemsets

In a distributed setting, the data are partitioned among several nodes, connected by networks which possibly have limited bandwidth and high latency. In such a context, gathering all data to a central node, in order to apply an high performance algorithm, is often impossible, due to either the amount of data or privacy reasons. Hence, Distributed Data Mining algorithms typically work by producing a local model per site. Unfortunately, even if local models are coherent and accurate with respect to local site repository, inferring a global model by aggregating the local models may be very complex.

In the distributed frequent itemsets case, we have several data sources $\mathcal{D}_j$, and our goal is to extract the frequent itemsets in the *virtual dataset* $\mathcal{D} = \bigcup \mathcal{D}_j$. We denote with $\mathcal{F}_j$ the collection of frequent itemsets extracted from $\mathcal{D}_j$, i.e. having a local support σ_j at least $minsupp \cdot |\mathcal{D}_j|$.

It is easy to show that the union of locally frequent itemsets contains the global solution. In fact, if $\mathcal{D}_j$ is mined using the same relative support threshold $minsupp$, each *globally* frequent pattern I ($\sigma(I) \geq minsupp \cdot |\mathcal{D}|$) must be *locally* frequent in at least one partition ($\sigma_i(I) \geq minsupp \cdot |\mathcal{D}_j|$. However, an itemset in $\bigcup \mathcal{F}_j$ may be infrequent in one or more $\mathcal{D}_j$, so that its local support σ_j is unknown. If this is the case, we cannot decide whether the itemset is globally frequent or not, since we cannot calculate its support $\sum \sigma_j$.

A trivial solution to this problem is to mine every locally occurring pattern, but clearly this would cause a combinatorial explosion. A more viable alternative consists in a two phase computation, as proposed by the Partition algorithm [17], which can be easily implemented in distributed settings using a master/slave paradigm [9], where each slave is responsible for managing and mining a distinct $\mathcal{D}_i$. After collecting and merging the local solutions, the master gathers from the slaves the support count of each global candidate itemset $I \in \bigcup_j \mathcal{F}_j$ where I resulted infrequent. We call this straightforward distributed version of the algorithm Distributed Partition.

While the Distributed Partition algorithm is able to return the exact support values, it has pros and cons with respect to other distributed algorithms. The *pros* are related to the number of communications and synchronizations. Other methods as count-distribution [4, 22] require much more communications and synchronizations, while the Distributed Partition algorithm only requires two communications from the slaves to the master, and a single one from the master to the slaves. The *cons* are the volume of messages exchanged, and the additional computation performed by the slaves during the first phase. Consider that, when low absolute minimum supports are used, it is likely to produce a lot of candidate itemsets, i.e. locally frequent itemsets, due to data skew present in the various dataset partitions [13]. This has a large impact on the cost of the second phase of the algorithm too: most of the slaves will participate in counting the local supports of these candidates, thus wasting a lot of time. A way to work around this problem consists in stopping Distributed Partition after the first-pass. We name this naive algorithm Distributed One-pass Partition. So in Distributed One-pass Partition each slave independently computes locally frequent patterns and sends them to the master which sum-reduces the support for each pattern and returns only patterns having the sum of the known supports greater than (or equal to) $\overline{\sigma}$.

Distributed One-pass Partition has obvious performance advantages vs Distributed Partition. On the other hand it yields an approximate result. Since σ_j maybe unknown from some data source, the global support σ can be underestimated. This not only introduces an approximation in the itemsets support, but it may produce a support below $\overline{\sigma}$ also for globally frequent itemsets.

In [18–19] we have tried to overcome some of the problems encountered by Distributed One-pass Partition and Distributed Partition. We have proposed the AP_{Interp} (Approximate Partition) algorithm that exploits an interpolation method to infer the unknown support counts, and does not require the additional communication and computation cost of a second scan of each $\mathcal{D}_j$ as in Distributed Partition.

When AP_{Interp} needs to know the support $\sigma_i(x)$ of a pattern x in $\mathcal{D}_i$, the master of our distributed algorithm infers an approximate value $\sigma_i(x)^{interp}$ by reasoning on the knowledge of:

- the exact support of each *single item* in all $\mathcal{D}_j$, and
- an *interpolation factors* $r(x)$, used to infer the unknown support counts $\sigma_i(x)$. $r(x)$ is computed on the basis of the exact knowledge of $\sigma_j(x)$ for all $\mathcal{D}_j$ where x has been recognized as a frequent pattern.

For example, given two itemsets x and x', $x' \subset x$, if the exact value of $\sigma_j(x)$ is known, while $\sigma_i(x)$ is unknown, the interpolated value $\sigma_i^{interp}(x)$ is approximated on the basis of the following proportion:

$$\sigma_j(x) \ : \ \sigma_j(x') \ = \ \sigma_i^{interp}(x) \ : \ \sigma_i(x')$$

so that

$$\sigma_i^{interp}(x) \ = \ \sigma_j(x) \ \cdot r(x)$$

where $r(x) = \frac{\sigma_i(x')}{\sigma_j(x')}$. Note that also $\sigma_j(x')$ might be an approximate value previously interpolated. Indeed, the actual interpolation factor $r(x)$ must be computed by considering all the known $\sigma_j(x)$, for all $\mathcal{D}_j$ from which x has been returned as a frequent pattern.

Table 1 resumes the characteristics of the above algorithms, in particular their phases and the approximation of the result.

4. Distributed Frequent Closed Itemsets

In this section we discuss how we can exploit the same approach shown in Section 3, in order to mine frequent closed itemsets in a distributed setting.

We need to show that it is possible to perform independent computations on each data source $\mathcal{D}_j$, and then join the local result by using an appropriate merging operator $\oplus$ in order to obtain the global results. From each partition we will first mine collections of *locally* frequent and *locally* closed itemsets,

Table 1. Comparison of the algorithms for Distributed Frequent Itemset Mining presented in subsection 3

Algorithm	*Phases*	*Results*
Distributed Partition	First phase: compute local solutions. Second phase: merge local solutions to build the global candidates. Third phase: check the global support of candidates.	Exact.
Distributed One-pass Partition	First phase: compute local solutions. Second phase: merge local solutions to build the global solution. The support of a pattern is the sum of local known support values.	Approximate: support values are underestimated.
AP	First phase: compute local solutions. Second phase: merge local solutions to build the global solution. The support of a pattern is interpolated from the known support values.	Approximate: support values obtained using interpolation. Results similar to the exact ones [18].

and then we will use such information in order to identify *globally* closed and *globally* frequent itemsets.

Hereinafter, we will use the following notation to discriminate between the virtual global dataset and local datasets. We define the closure operator over a single partition j as the composite function $c_j(I) = f \circ g_j(I)$, where

$$g_j(I) = \{t \in \mathcal{D}_j \mid I \subseteq t\}.$$

Finally, we denote with $\mathcal{C}_j$ the set of closed itemsets in $\mathcal{D}_j$ and with $\mathcal{C}$ the closed itemsets in $\mathcal{D}$.

For the sake of simplicity, we limit the following discussion to a setting with only two data sources $\mathcal{D}_1$ and $\mathcal{D}_2$. However, it is trivial to generalize our results to an arbitrary number of partitions.

In the following we will deal separately with the two tasks of the $\oplus$ operator, i.e. reconstructing identities of global closed itemsets and reconstructing supports of global closed itemsets.

4.1 Identities of frequent closed itemsets.

In this section, since we are only dealing with identities of frequent itemsets and not with their supports, we will refer to $\mathcal{C}_j$ and $\mathcal{C}$ to indicate the result of a mining task with a minimum support threshold of $\overline{\sigma} = 1$. We denote with Γ_1 the mining function which returns the collection of frequent closed itemsets having support at least 1, i.e. appearing at least once in $\mathcal{D}$.

In order to define $\oplus$ we will first solve the simpler problem of having only two datasets, where one of them only contains a single transaction.

THEOREM 4 *Given a datasets $\mathcal{D}_1$, and another dataset $\mathcal{D}_2$ that contains a single transaction t, it holds that:*

$$\Gamma_1(\mathcal{D}_1 \cup \mathcal{D}_2) = \Gamma_1(\mathcal{D}_1 \cup \{t\}) = \Gamma_1(\mathcal{D}_1) \cup t \cup \left(\bigcup_{I \in \Gamma_1(\mathcal{D}_1)} I \cap t \right) \quad (1)$$

PROOF 4.1 *First we prove that $\Gamma_1(\mathcal{D}_1 \cup \{t\}) \subseteq \Gamma_1(\mathcal{D}_1) \cup t \cup \left(\bigcup_{I \in \Gamma_1(\mathcal{D}_1)} I \cap t\right)$. Let $X \in \Gamma_1(\mathcal{D}_1 \cup \{t\})$ be a closed itemset. If $X = t$ then the theorem trivially holds. If X is not a subset of t then $t \notin g(X)$, and therefore $X = f(g(X)) = f(g_1(X)) = c_1(X)$, which means that $X \in \Gamma_1(\mathcal{D}_1)$. If $X \subset t$, then $X = f(g(X)) = f(g_1(X) \cup t) = f(g_1(X)) \cap t = c_1(X) \cap t = I \cap t$, where $I \in \Gamma_1(\mathcal{D}_1)$.*

Last we prove that $\Gamma_1(\mathcal{D}_1 \cup \{t\}) \supseteq \Gamma_1(\mathcal{D}_1) \cup t \cup \left(\bigcup_{I \in \Gamma_1(\mathcal{D}_1)} I \cap t\right)$. Note that an itemset I is closed if and only if there is no item $i \notin I$ such that $g(I) = g(I \cup i)$, otherwise we would have that $I \neq f(g(I))$.

t is trivially closed, since no other item can be added to t without decreasing $g(t)$.

Similarly, each closed itemset in $I \in \mathcal{D}_1$ is closed in $\{\mathcal{D}_1 \cup t\}$, since by definition $g_1(I \cup i) \neq g_1(I)$, and therefore $g(I \cup i) \neq g(I)$.

Lastly, given $I \cap t$ where I is a closed itemset in $\mathcal{D}_1$, we must consider two cases too see whether there exists an item $i \notin \{I \cap t\}$ such that $i \in c(I \cap t)$. The first is when $i \notin t$, which means that $g(I \cap t) \neq g(I \cap t \cup i)$ and $I \cap t$ must be closed. The second is when $i \in t$ ($i \notin I$), in which case, if $I \cap t$ was not closed we would have that $g_1(I \cap t) = g_1(I \cap t \cup i)$ which, by Lemma 3 implies that $i \in c_1(I)$, i.e. $i \in I$ which is a contradiction.

Let us introduce a new operator $\overline{\bigcap}$, named *power-set-intersection*:

$$\overline{\bigcap} S = \bigcup_{S' \in (\mathcal{P}(S) \setminus \{\emptyset\})} \bigcap_{s \in S'} s$$

where $\mathcal{P}(S)$ is the power set of S, i.e. the set of all possible subsets of S. The power-set-intersection $\overline{\bigcap} S$ corresponds to the union of all the intersections among the elements of every possible subset of S but the empty set. For example, let $S = \{s_1, s_2, s_3\}$, we have that $\overline{\bigcap} S = \{\{s_1\}, \{s_2\}, \{s_3\}, \{s_1 \cap s_2\}, \{s_1 \cap s_3\}, \{s_2 \cap s_3\}, \{s_1 \cap s_2 \cap s_3\}\}$.

Now, we can show another theorem giving a new and interesting insight in the problem of frequent closed itemset mining.

THEOREM 5 *Mining all the frequent closed itemsets from $\mathcal{D}$ when $\overline{\sigma} = 1$ is equivalent to applying the power-set-intersection operator to $\mathcal{D}$:*

$$\Gamma_1(\mathcal{D}) = \overline{\bigcap} \mathcal{D}$$

PROOF 5.1 *We prove the theorem by induction on the number of transactions n of $\mathcal{D}$.*

Case $n = 1$. It is obvious that when the minimum support threshold is 1, the only closed itemset in a dataset with a single transaction is the transaction itself. Thus:

$$\Gamma_1(\mathcal{D} = \{t\}) \ = t \ = \overline{\bigcap} \mathcal{D}$$

Case $n = 2$. It is clear that the only closed itemsets are the two transactions themselves along with their intersection. Thus:

$$\Gamma_1(\mathcal{D} = \{t_1, t_2\}) \ = \ t_1 \cup t_2 \cup (t_1 \cap t_2) \ = \ \overline{\bigcap} \mathcal{D}$$

Inductive step. Let us assume that the hypothesis holds for all datasets with a number of transaction $\leq N$. Given a dataset $\mathcal{D}$ with $N + 1$ transactions, let $\mathcal{D} = \mathcal{D}^* \cup t^*$, we prove the inductive step:

$$\begin{aligned}
\Gamma_1(\mathcal{D}) &= \Gamma_1(\mathcal{D}^* \cup t^*) \\
&= \Gamma_1(\mathcal{D}^*) \cup t^* \cup \left(\bigcup_{I \in \Gamma_1(\mathcal{D}^*)} I \cap t^* \right) \qquad \text{(from Theorem 4)} \\
&= \overline{\bigcap} \mathcal{D}^* \cup t^* \cup \left(\bigcup_{I \in \Gamma_1(\mathcal{D}^*)} I \cap t^* \right) \\
&= \overline{\bigcap} \{\mathcal{D}^* \cup t^*\} \\
&= \overline{\bigcap} \mathcal{D}
\end{aligned}$$

Theorem 5 formally states the equivalence of two different exploration techniques of the search space. The first one is known as *item enumeration*, where the exploration traverses every possible combination of items, i.e. $\mathcal{P}(\mathcal{I})$. The second one, which is suggested by the equivalence of Γ_1 and $\overline{\bigcap}$, is known as *row enumeration*, where the exploration takes place by traversing every possible intersection of rows of the dataset, i.e. intersections of elements in $\mathcal{P}(\mathcal{D})$. The first is the most commonly used, since the number of transactions is usually orders of magnitude larger then the number of items. Nonetheless, in some biomedical dataset we find the opposite setting and, additionally, the only useful minimum support threshold is 1, and therefore the second approach has been shown to be the only feasible [11].

Theorems 4 and 5 allow us to come back to the problem of mining frequent closed itemsets in a distributed setting.

THEOREM 6 *Given two datasets $\mathcal{D}_1$ and $\mathcal{D}_2$, the closed itemsets $\mathcal{C}$ in $\mathcal{D} = \{\mathcal{D}_1 \cup \mathcal{D}_2\}$ can be extracted using only the closed itemsets $\mathcal{C}_1$ and $\mathcal{C}_2$ that have been independently mined from the two datasets, by applying an appropriate merging operator $\oplus$:*

$$\mathcal{C} = \mathcal{C}_1 \oplus \mathcal{C}_2 = \Gamma_1(\mathcal{C}_1 \cup \mathcal{C}_2)$$

PROOF 6.1

$$\begin{aligned}
\mathcal{C} &= \Gamma_1(\mathcal{C}_1 \cup \mathcal{C}_2) \\
&= \Gamma_1(\Gamma_1(\mathcal{D}_1) \cup \Gamma_1(\mathcal{D}_2)) \\
&= \Gamma_1\left(\overline{\bigcap} \mathcal{D}_1 \cup \overline{\bigcap} \mathcal{D}_2\right) \\
&= \Gamma_1\left(\bigcup_{T \in \{\mathcal{P}(\mathcal{D}_1) \setminus \{\emptyset\}\}} \bigcap_{t \in T} t \cup \bigcup_{T \in \{\mathcal{P}(\mathcal{D}_2) \setminus \{\emptyset\}\}} \bigcap_{t \in T} t\right) \\
&= \overline{\bigcap}\left(\bigcup_{T \in \{\mathcal{P}(\mathcal{D}_1) \setminus \{\emptyset\}\}} \bigcap_{t \in T} t \cup \bigcup_{T \in \{\mathcal{P}(\mathcal{D}_2) \setminus \{\emptyset\}\}} \bigcap_{t \in T} t\right) \\
&= \bigcup_{T \in \{\mathcal{P}(\mathcal{D}_1 \cup \mathcal{D}_2) \setminus \{\emptyset\}\}} \bigcap_{t \in T} t \\
&= \overline{\bigcap} \{\mathcal{D}_1 \cup \mathcal{D}_2\} \\
&= \Gamma_1(\mathcal{D}_1 \cup \mathcal{D}_2)
\end{aligned}$$

Theorem 6 gives us a way for mining all the frequent closed itemsets in a distributed setting, i.e., for extracting $\Gamma_1(\mathcal{D}_1 \cup \mathcal{D}_2)$. First we can mine separately the closed itemsets $\mathcal{C}_1$ and $\mathcal{C}_2$ from the two partitions. Then we can merge these local results by performing an additional mining on the collection of locally closed itemsets, and this could be done by applying the power-set-intersection operator.

It is really interesting that we can apply the mining operator Γ_1 to a collection of closed itemsets, or that, in other words, by mining our previous knowledge we can obtain further knowledge. This result can be generalized to the case of P partitions of $\mathcal{D}$ by the following Theorem, which can be easily shown by induction.

THEOREM 7 *Given the sets of closed itemsets $\mathcal{C}_1, \ldots, \mathcal{C}_P$ mined respectively from P different data sources $\mathcal{D}_1, \ldots, \mathcal{D}_P$, we have that:*

$$\mathcal{C} = (\ldots((\mathcal{C}_1 \oplus \mathcal{C}_2) \oplus \ldots) \oplus \mathcal{C}_P) \ldots)$$

4.2 Support of frequent closed itemsets

Unfortunately this merging function, when used to combine all locally frequent closed itemsets extracted from local repositories, i.e., $\mathcal{C}_1, \ldots, \mathcal{C}_m$, may generate similar problems as those discussed in Section 3 for frequent itemsets. A possible solution is to adopt an expensive method like the one suggested by the Distributed Partition algorithm, which requires a second global scan of each $\mathcal{D}_i$ to check whether locally frequent itemsets (or closed ones) are also globally frequent. In order to avoid this second scan, similarly to AP_{Interp}, we propose reconstructing the unknown support counts by using an interpolation based on known counts. We call this distributed algorithm to extract closed itemsets AP_{Closed}.

A further issue that AP_{Closed} has to deal with is the final result of the merge operator $\oplus$, which can identify further closed itemsets besides the ones included in $\mathcal{C}_1 \cup \mathcal{C}_2 \cup \ldots \cup \mathcal{C}_P$. For example, let x be one of these new closed itemset x, such that $x \notin \mathcal{C}_i$. However, if there exists y, where $y \in \mathcal{C}_i$ and $x \subset y$, we can conclude that x is surely frequent on $\mathcal{D}_i$. Unfortunately, in order to know $\sigma_i(x)$, we have to to infer it from the known support counts of their supersets in $\mathcal{D}_i$. In particular, it is easy to show that $\sigma_i(x)$ is the same as the support count of the smallest superset of x belonging to $\mathcal{C}_i$.

5. Conclusion

We have addressed the problem of mining frequent closed itemsets in a distributed environment. In the distributed mining of frequent itemsets, a three steps algorithm is sufficient in order to get exact results. First, independent mining tasks are performed on each partition, then the results are merged to form a big candidate set, and, finally, an additional check is needed for each candidate to retrieve its actual support in the partitions where it was found to be infrequent.

In this paper we investigate the merging step in the case of closed itemset mining. We have shown that in this case the merging step is completely different and surely more complex. The theorems that we have introduced, however, show how to extend the collect and merge approach to the distributed discovery of closed itemsets.

References

[1] *Proc. of the 1st Workshop on Frequent Itemset Mining Implementations (FIMI'03)*. 2003.

[2] R. Agrawal and R. Srikant. Fast algorithms for mining association rules. In *Proc. VLDB '94*, pages 487–499, September 1994.

[3] Sergey Brin, Rajeev Motwani, Jeffrey D. Ullman, and Shalom Tsur. Dynamic itemset counting and implication rules for market basket data. In Joan Peckham, editor, *SIGMOD 1997, Proceedings ACM SIGMOD International Conference on Management of Data, May 13-15, 1997, Tucson, Arizona, USA*, pages 255–264. ACM Press, 05 1997.

[4] E-H. S. Han, G.Karypis, and V.Kumar. Scalable parallel data mining for association rules. In *IEEE Transaction on Knowledge and Data Engineering*, 2000.

[5] Jiawei Han, Jian Pei, and Yiwen Yin. Mining frequent patterns without candidate generation. In *Proc. SIGMOD '00*, pages 1–12, 2000.

[6] H. Kargupta and P. Chan (Eds.). *Advances in Distributed and Parallel Knowledge Discovery*. AAAI Press/The MIT Press, 2004.

[7] J. Liu, Y. Pan, K. Wang, and J. Han. Mining Frequent Item Sets by Opportunistic Projection. In *Proc. 2002 Int. Conf. on Knowledge Discovery in Databases (KDD'02), Edmonton, Canada*, 2002.

[8] Claudio Lucchese, Salvatore Orlando, and Raffaele Perego. Fast and memory efficient mining of frequent closed itemsets. *IEEE Transactions on Knowledge and Data Engineering*, 18(1):21–36, January 2006.

[9] A. Mueller. Fast sequential and parallel algorithms for association rules mining: A comparison. Technical Report CS-TR-3515, Univ. of Maryland, 1995.

[10] S. Orlando, P. Palmerini, R. Perego, and F. Silvestri. Adaptive and resource-aware mining of frequent sets. In *Proc. The 2002 IEEE International Conference on Data Mining (ICDM '02)*, pages 338–345, 2002.

[11] Feng Pan, Gao Cong, Anthony K. H. Tung, Jiong Yang, and Mohammed Javeed Zaki. Carpenter: finding closed patterns in long biological datasets. In *KDD*, pages 637–642, 2003.

[12] B. Park and H. Kargupta. Distributed Data Mining: Algorithms, Systems, and Applications. In *Data Mining Handbook*, pages 341–358. IEA, 2002.

[13] Srinivasan Parthasarathy. Efficient progressive sampling for association rules. In *Proceedings of the 2002 IEEE International Conference on Data Mining (ICDM'02)*, page 354. IEEE Computer Society, 2002.

[14] Nicolas Pasquier, Yves Bastide, Rafik Taouil, and Lotfi Lakhal. Efficient mining of association rules using closed itemset lattices. *Information Systems*, 24(1):25–46, 1999.

[15] J. Pei, J. Han, H. Lu, S. Nishio, and D. Tang, S. amd Yang. H-Mine: Hyper-Structure Mining of Frequent Patterns in Large Databases. In *Proc. The 2001 IEEE International Conference on Data Mining (ICDM'01)*, San Jose, CA, USA, 2000.

[16] Jian Pei, Jiawei Han, and Jianyong Wang. Closet+: Searching for the best strategies for mining frequent closed itemsets. In *SIGKDD '03*, August 2003.

[17] Ashoka Savasere, Edward Omiecinski, and Shamkant B. Navathe. An efficient algorithm for mining association rules in large databases. In *VLDB'95, Proceedings of 21th International Conference on Very Large Data Bases*, pages 432–444. Morgan Kaufmann, September 1995.

[18] C. Silvestri and S. Orlando. Distributed Approximate Mining of Frequent Patterns. In *Proc. of the 2005 ACM Symposium on Applied Computing, SAC 2005, special track on Data Mining*, pages 529–536, 2005.

[19] C. Silvestri and S. Orlando. Approximate mining of frequent patterns on streams. *Intelligent Data Analysis*, 2006. To appear.

[20] Rafik Taouil, Nicolas Pasquier, Yves Bastide, Lotfi Lajhal, and Gerd Stumme. Mining freqent patterns with counting inference. *SIGKDD Explorations*, 2(2):66–75, December 2000.

[21] Rafik Taouil, Nicolas Pasquier, Yves Bastide, and Lotfi Lakhal. Mining bases for association rules using closed sets. In *ICDE*, 2000.

[22] M. J. Zaki. Scalable algorithms for association mining. *IEEE Transactions on Knowledge and Data Engineering*, 12:372–390, May/June 2000.

[23] Mohammed J. Zaki. Mining non-redundant association rules. *Data Min. Knowl. Discov.*, 9(3):223–248, 2004.

[24] Mohammed J. Zaki and Karam Gouda. Fast vertical mining using diffsets. In *Proceedings of the ninth ACM SIGKDD international conference on Knowledge discovery and data mining*, pages 326–335. ACM Press, 2003.

[25] Mohammed J. Zaki and Ching-Jui Hsiao. Charm: An efficient algorithm for closed itemsets mining. In *2nd SIAM International Conference on Data Mining*, April 2002.

DISTRIBUTED DATA MINING AND KNOWLEDGE MANAGEMENT WITH NETWORKS OF SENSOR ARRAYS

Maurice Dixon
Computing, Communications Technology and Mathematics,
London Metropolitan University, 31 Jewry Street, London, EC3N 2EY, UK
M.Dixon@Londonmet.ac.uk

Simon C. Lambert and Julian R. Gallop
e-Science, CCLRC Rutherford Appleton Laboratory,
Chilton, Didcot, Oxon, OX11 0QX, UK
S.C.Lambert@rl.ac.uk
J.R.Gallop@rl.ac.uk

Abstract Environmental pollution control relies heavily on human expert judgment supported by historical data and scientific models. Telemonitoring, by networks of heterogeneous sensor arrays, provides the opportunity for data mining models to be constructed from the historical data to supplement human expertise. This paper reports some progress made in the TELEMAC project by data mining. TELEMAC is concerned with enhancing the efficacy of anaerobic digestion in potentially unstable digesters. In the laboratory using full instrumentation it is possible to derive a good description of the digester state. With data mining it is possible to identify some constraints on sensor choice. This paper examines this data mining work from the perspective of a three layer Grid architecture to see what implications and requirements arise that could benefit the exercise of expert judgment. After placing the specific TELEMAC situation in a generic Grids context, we present a classification approach to attributes for metadata and indicate some examples of model resource discovery.

Keywords: anaerobic digestion, data mining, telemonitoring and control, wastewater treatment.

1. Introduction

Networks of sensor arrays, measuring properties of multiple instances of some physical process, raise some important issues in the context of Grids. An example is provided by the TELEMAC project [1], a European Union funded project on anaerobic wastewater treatment, in which individual treatment plants are equipped with a variety of sensors. The aim of TELEMAC is to improve the monitoring and control of digesters from a central telemonitoring and control centre, TCC [2]. The control of these plants could benefit from data mining and the leveraging of knowledge through the TCC.

Although the TELEMAC project was not conceived as a Grids project, nonetheless there is clear potential for applying Grid technologies. The focus is on three levels of grids: knowledge, information, and data rather than computation. Issues that arise include: 1) data heterogeneity, 2) the data mining methods themselves, 3) timebased issues, such as the updating of data mining models, 4) the role of human expertise.

In TELEMAC a user interacts with a heterogeneous environment of databases and data collection sensors. Grid technology could provide a standard framework for the interoperation of the distributed sites. In some views of Grids, metadata, agents, and brokers are key architectural components. Paraphrased here are observations from Jeffery [3] relevant to TELEMAC: "**Metadata:** Most examples of metadata in use today are neither structured formally nor specified formally so tend to be of limited use for automated interoperations and consequently require human interpretation. **Agents/Brokers:** Agents use metadata to take action; they can provide a monitoring function. Brokers act as go-betweens for agents."

This paper uses the experience of TELEMAC for illuminating some design issues for this class of application in a Grids environment. The paper is structured as follows. Section 2 considers the industrial context and associated biochemical processes. Data mining in TELEMAC is discussed in Section 3; the issues of sensor arrays, the role of sensor ranking, and diversity of sensors are addressed in a data mining context. Examples of data mining results are presented. In Section 4 we consider TELEMAC from the perspective of the three layer architecture Knowledge, Information, and Computation/Data Grids. It is here we address the issue of leveraging knowledge and grid resources. The role of human expertise in providing knowledge management in the plant monitoring and control cycle is presented and this shows the way the three Grids interact in this type of environment. In Section 5 we identify some specific attributes that are useful in the metadata for our data mining models and resources. A short summary of our conclusions finishes the section.

2. Industrial context

Anaerobic wastewater treatment is an important technology for the disposal of certain kinds of waste, in particular the by-products from alcohol production in wineries and distilleries [4]. It has great advantages such as efficiency, low production of sludge, and the possibility of energy recovery through co-generation. However it is an unstable process which is difficult to monitor and control with the consequence that plant is operated at low efficiency. Expert knowledge is required for efficient operation of the plant but that expertise is unlikely to be locally available at small, possibly remotely located, individual plants. Therefore the role of the TCC is crucial here in supporting expert human knowledge by a range of analysis and prediction techniques. The anaerobic digester plants operate on a range of engineering principles such as upflow sludge blankets, lagoons, upflow fixed-beds and continuous stirred tanks, CSTRs. Within TELEMAC there is a preponderance of CSTRs at the industrial level with typical volumes of 500 to $5000m^3$. The chemical oxygen demand, COD, of the wastewater is one measure of the outflow quality; organic loading rates within the digesters vary between 2kg and 20kg COD $m^{-3}d^{-1}$. Measurement of COD is generally not available on-line [2].

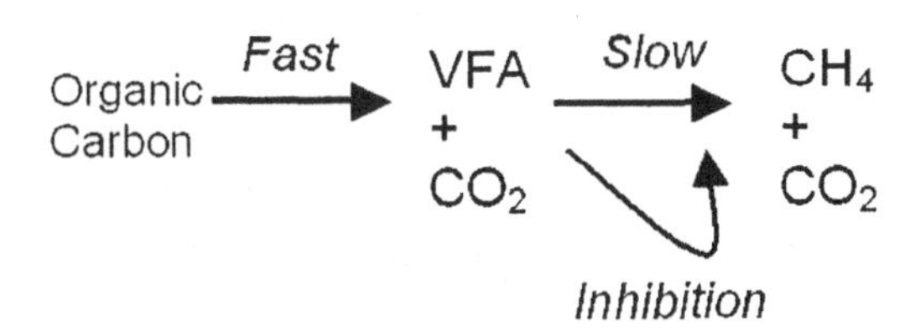

Figure 1. The biological process for anaerobic waste water treatment.

The biological process has two main steps; these are shown in Figure 1. In the first step a set of acidogenic bacteria generate volatile fatty acids and carbon dioxide. This conversion proceeds at a fast rate. Volatile fatty acids themselves are acetates and acetic acid or similar. The second step is a slow conversion of the volatile fatty acids to methane and more carbon dioxide by methanogenic bacteria. The problem is that a build up in the concentration of volatile fatty acids inhibits the methanogenic bacteria. This can lead to suppression of the second stage and ultimately to irreversible destabilisation of the digester; then it could take a period of several weeks or even several months to recover. A converse problem occurs if the digester is hydraulically overloaded and the biomass is washed out.

3. Data mining in TELEMAC

3.1 Introduction

The biological and chemical processes involved in anaerobic digestion are complex but there is good qualitative understanding of the main features. Although analytical models have been developed [5], there is still much scope for data mining of sensor data to complement them. Data mining helps to answer both static and dynamic questions, such as which sensors form the minimum set required for accurate estimation of key variables like concentration of volatile fatty acids, or what is the likely future value of such a variable given the current state of the digester plant [6].

3.2 Sensor ranking and diversity

A wide range of sensors are commercially available for use with anaerobic digesters. Characteristics of these and research sensors are summarized below.

3.2.1 Sensor types. 1) Classical plant instruments such as gas and liquid flow meters, pressure and temperature gauges, 2) Titrimeter to measure acid and base concentrations (up to 4 variables), 3) Infra-Red spectrometer (up to 5 variables), 4) TOCmeter to measure total organic content, 5) Thermal conductivity sensor for CO2.

3.2.2 Sensor modes. 1) Online sensors return a value at measurement time, 2) Offline chemical analysis returns a measurement significantly later and may be different in value than from an online measurement.

3.2.3 Sensor problems. 1) Sensor reliability - failure due to lack of precision, saturation, lag in recovery of measuring capacity, foaming in digester, and contamination, 2) Sensor accuracy - calibration, standard setting.

In Figure 2 *tempdig* is the temperature, *qin* is the influent liquid flow rate, *phdig* is the pH, *qgas* is the biogas flow rate, *co2gas* is the percentage of carbon dioxide in the biogas, *vfadig* is the concentration of volatile fatty acids, *tocdig* is the concentration of total organic content, and *coddig* is the concentration of chemical oxygen demand. With a full set of sensors it is possible to get a fairly complete chemical description of the current digester state. The figure shows expert judgement of the ranking of sensors by expected availability/reliability, with the simplest and most robust in the inner ring. These four levels of sensor are relevant when dealing with operational industrial systems which would lack such full instrumentation.

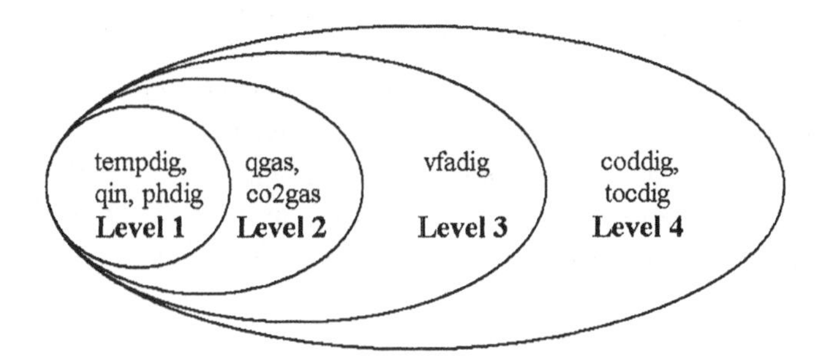

Figure 2. Venn diagram showing sensor ranking. The sensors are defined with their Level. Suffix dig indicates measurement of the digester content.

3.3 Data mining techniques used

3.3.1 Classification and Sequencing. A key aspect in assisting the digester expert to form a judgement is to characterise the data to form a set of digester states. This was done using cluster analysis. Although it is possible for a cluster analysis algorithm to select the number of clusters, the decision is in general hard to justify to the expert. Therefore some analysis using a range of cluster numbers was undertaken. It was found that with these datasets, a progression from small but numerous clusters to larger and fewer gave a relatively stable cluster assignment. This gave some confidence that the assignment to clusters is not arbitrary for these datasets. Having obtained some clusters, an analysis of time-based cluster sequences was also undertaken which gave a set of transition frequencies [7].

3.3.2 Regression models. Regression models have been used for several purposes: 1) Models for predicting data values for missing/faulting sensors were constructed with associated predictions of confidence intervals. This has allowed both current prediction and short term forecasting of the concentration of dissolved and suspended organics during sensor failure. 2) Highly accurate short term forecasting is feasible using multivariate autoregression; with reliable sensors this could be used for plant control. 3) Predictions from auto-regression are of little use over extended time on occasions of sensor(s) faulting, a frequent occurrence, because the models depend on known target values at previous times. Non linear multivariate regression performs satisfactorily for current and imminent states.

The models need to be evaluated against an independent test set of data to ensure that the model training does not result in over-fitting to errors in the training data. Statistical tests for quality of fit need applying. Such tests include residuals, mean squared and mean errors, squared Pearson correlation function (R^2), and paired sample t-tests for means. A range of models needs to be deployed. Linear models can provide good starting pointers. In some circumstances they can be sufficient in themselves E.g. for the most extensively instrumented digesters. In other cases artificial neural net models provide a markedly superior model judged by out-of-sample test set estimates. Unit root tests aid a decision on whether to model in differences or levels.

3.4 Examples of work done

Data mining has shown that 1) It is feasible to determine the ranking of sensors; E.g. in order to estimate a Level4 variable (Levels as in Figure 2) it is considerably better to have at least one Level3 sensor dataset (*coddig* requires either Level3 *vfadig* or Level4 *tocdig*). 2) Features between variables can mean that a second sensor adds little to the improvement of a model. E.g. strong colinearity means that if *tocdig* data is available then *vfadig* adds little additional modelling power.

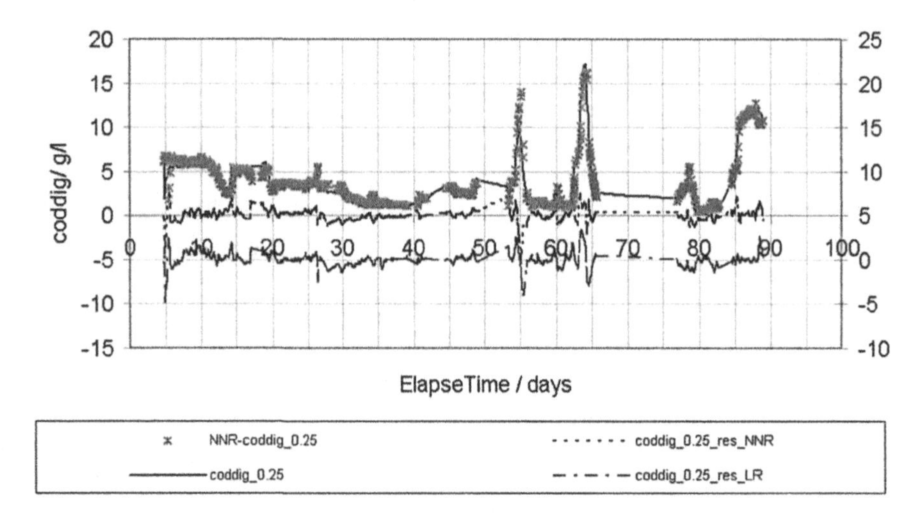

Figure 3. Forward prediction of coddig for 0.25days. Prefix or suffix of NNR or LR indicates neural net or linear regression respectively; res denotes residual.

Figure 3 shows a forward prediction of 0.25d for an INRA validated dataset using the sensor variables from Level1, Level2, and Level3 inputs to predict a Level4 variable, the concentration of *coddig* in g/litre. It compares the independent test set experimental data with the prediction of a neural net model and also shows the residuals on the left hand scale. The model had 8 logistic functions in two hidden layers (as 5+3) with *tempdig* eliminated; R^2=0.945, t-pair=1.3, mean residual error = 0.031, predicted mean square error=0.332. The residuals for a corresponding linear regression are shown on the right hand side scale. R^2=0.930 (in sample R^2=0.928), t-pair=0.21, mean residual error = 0.014. Figure 4 compares the independent test set experimental data with the prediction of a neural net model. 97% of the actual experimental data points fall within the 95% prediction confidence band.

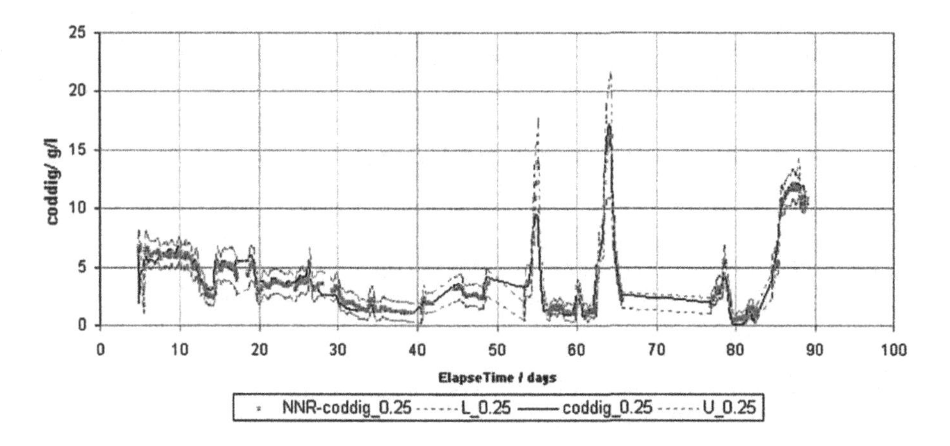

Figure 4. 95% prediction confidence bands [6] from forward prediction of 0.25days for a validated dataset for the concentration of coddig in g/litre.

3.5 Some issues of heterogeneity

In addition to the usual problems of heterogeneity associated with data and their schema such as consistency of names, scaling, units, and applicability range there are some heterogeneities which affect data mining models from arrays of sensors. Data heterogeneity arises at two levels, from the diversity of sensors installed on what are essentially different instances of the same process, and from intrinsic differences between processes. For the first of these, unavoidable heterogeneities arise from the following: 1) different types of sensors measuring a given physical quantity by a different process, 2) different initialisation calibrations of the same sensor types, 3) complete failure of a sensor, 4) partial failure of the sensor through contamination, saturation, or drift, 5) different sampling frequencies and process time-constants.

Also the anaerobic digesters themselves operate on different principles and are of different sizes. There are practical heterogeneities that arise from scaling variables; sometimes a key dimension is unknown or changing. However, these issues of heterogeneity have not been fully explored in TELEMAC.

4. The Grids context

4.1 Telemonitoring and control: the TELEMAC concept

Figure 5 shows how the TELEMAC project represents an important advance in remote monitoring and control of wastewater treatment plants. Profile 1 shows the traditional practice on an isolated plant. Profile 2 shows how TELEMAC laboratory prototypes evolved. Profile 3 shows the full TELEMAC solution to sharing expertise while maintaining local control. The Database, Telemonitoring system and Expert are based at or accessible to the Telemonitoring and Control Centre (TCC) and are remote from the local user. Other components in Profile 3 are local to individual plants. The icons for the local user show the transition from puzzled in Profile 1 to enlightened in Profile 3.

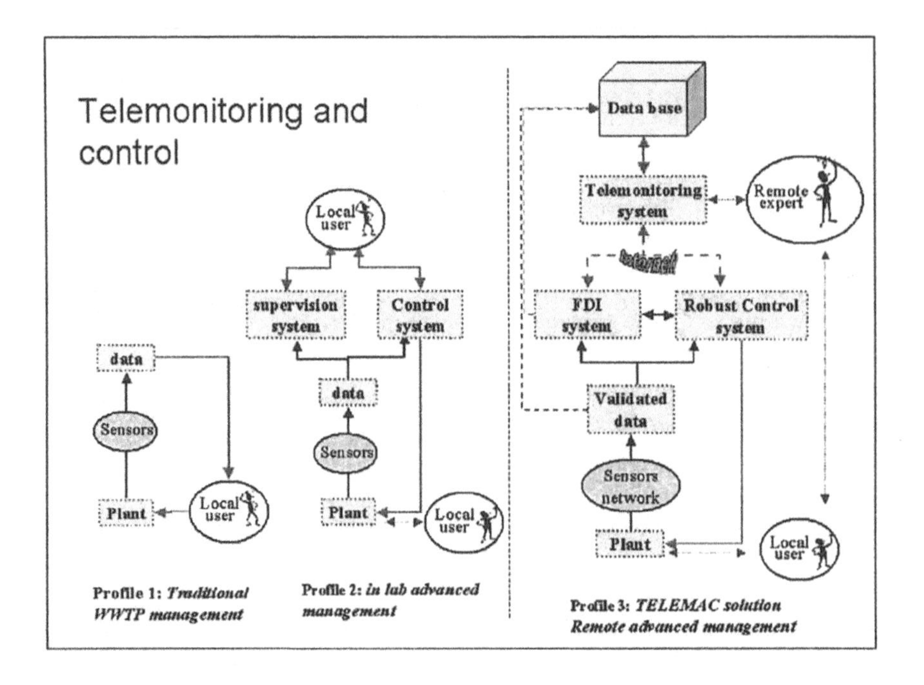

Figure 5. The evolution of monitoring and control of wastewater treatment plants.

Profile 3 introduces the monitoring and control of multiple plants from a single remote centre, the TCC. This is a step towards a full Grids-based system, though there is as yet no concept of identifying and combining resources according to specific needs: the system components and linkages are predefined and inflexible. It is possible to abstract the essential components of the above model so as to prepare for a Grids-based solution.

The **Local user** needs to be able to operate the plant in normal mode and receive warning of possible excursions. Users will seek and receive advice from a Remote Expert.

The **Remote expert** needs to monitor each individual plant, compare with reference models, issue advice and alerts to local operators/users. The remote experts service a TCC.

The **Local plants** can differ. Different plants have different arrays of sensors, have different volumes and operating principles. Each plant has its own data validation and consistency check for fault detection and isolation, **FDI**. Individual variables and combinations of variables are validated. In laboratory prototypes, multiple sensor consistency for the same variable can be used for calibration. Outputs of the FDI are used to provide robust control guidance. Each plant is serviced by a TCC; of course a single TCC may service multiple plants.

The **Telemonitoring and Control Centre** receives and stores validated data from local plants. It provides advice from monitored data in response to enquiries. It pools models to generalise expertise. It revises models as new situations are recognised. The TCC is responsible for holding the models and data for its plants. There are mathematical analytical and simulation models as well as data mining models.

4.2 Knowledge, information, computation/data Grids

A general architecture has been proposed for structuring knowledge, information, and data/computation in a Grids context [8]. This architecture, shown in Figure 6, represents the conversion of data to knowledge and then using the knowledge to exercise control. Explicitly the control is over the data and its processing but ultimately it is concerned with changing the data in the real world. Homogeneous access to heterogeneous distributed data occurs in the information layer. As well as including data mining technology the knowledge layer encompasses human experts and decision makers. This model is therefore compatible with the approach taken in TELEMAC.

4.3 The Grids perspective for leveraging knowledge

Figure 7 shows the mining of historical data to produce reference knowledge and models that can be applied to current behaviour of the digester plant. The cycle is closed by the observation of the resulting behaviours leading to a need for remining if there are deviations from what was expected. The ovals with broken lines indicate opportunities for leveraging knowledge obtained from elsewhere. For example, reference knowledge obtained about the behaviour of a digester in a state of hydraulic overload might be generalisable to other digesters of the same class, and usable in managing such states in future.

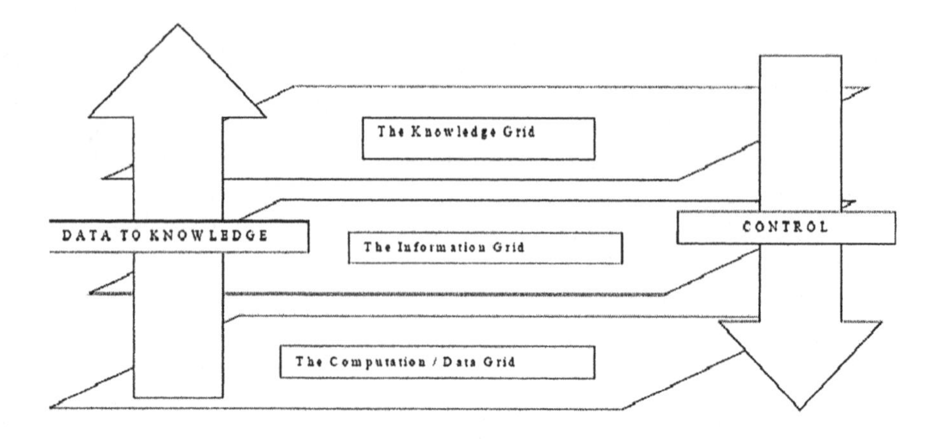

Figure 6. The Knowledge, Information, Computation/Data Grids [8]

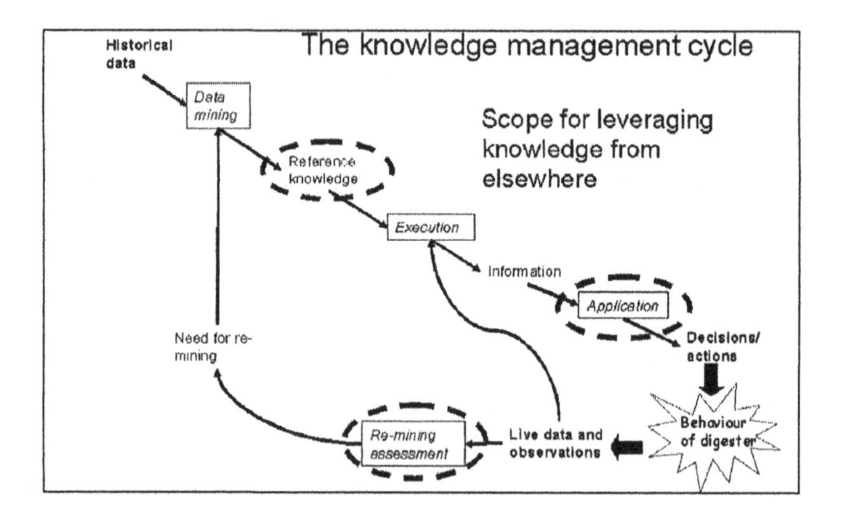

Figure 7. The knowledge management cycle.

Large companies are likely to opt for an intra-company TCC while the many small wineries might collaborate through geographically local TCCs. In either case there is scope for leveraging knowledge that has been derived about a particular situation by applying it in other circumstances, typically to a different plant. This leveraging should be done in a transparent way. It is therefore anticipated that a Grids infrastructure will provide the appropriate user transparency for this to proceed because it provides access to resources. Now it is not necessary for the Remote Experts to be located at every TCC.

4.4 Grid resources

With reference to Figure 7, it is possible to identify a number of classes of resource that can enable the leveraging of knowledge. These are:

Data mining tools. A selection of tools and methods such as those mentioned in Section 3.3 may be available at the TCC. Not every TCC will have the same set, so there is potential for offering the tools themselves for use as a resource.

Datasets. Datasets from sensor data are steadily accumulated at the TCC and constitute the raw material for data mining that is a valuable resource in its own right. An ontology for resolving heterogeneities needs to be included.

Mined data. The results of the data mining, in the form of neural nets, rules, and clustering parameters are obviously of potential value in dealing with situations on other plants. This is the classic example of transferring knowledge from one plant to another.

Human expertise. It is important not to forget that the expertise of the remote experts is itself a kind of resource that can benefit the operation of multiple plants in a Grid.

5. Grids based approach to TELEMAC

5.1 Generalising the problem

From a Grids perspective we can consider each network to consist of a set of nodes (in TELEMAC each of these is the local computer associated with a digester) and a set of decision support centre nodes (in TELEMAC a TCC). Figure 8 shows a network of sensor arrays. The sensors are labelled for reporting variables A,B,C,D,E etc. A1, A2 are two different sensors reporting on variable A. The plants local computer acts as the node, validating the data for that plant, and passing it to the TCC. In some circumstances control action may be passed from the TCC to a node for action on the plant controls. In Figure 9 the decision support centre node comprises the remote experts, the validated data and models, and the data mining and knowledge investigation tools (DMKI).

5.2 Metadata

Metadata is required in a Grids system to represent properties of the Grid resources and allow reasoning over them to locate and deploy resources. The terms applicability, transformability, and reliability emerged as important

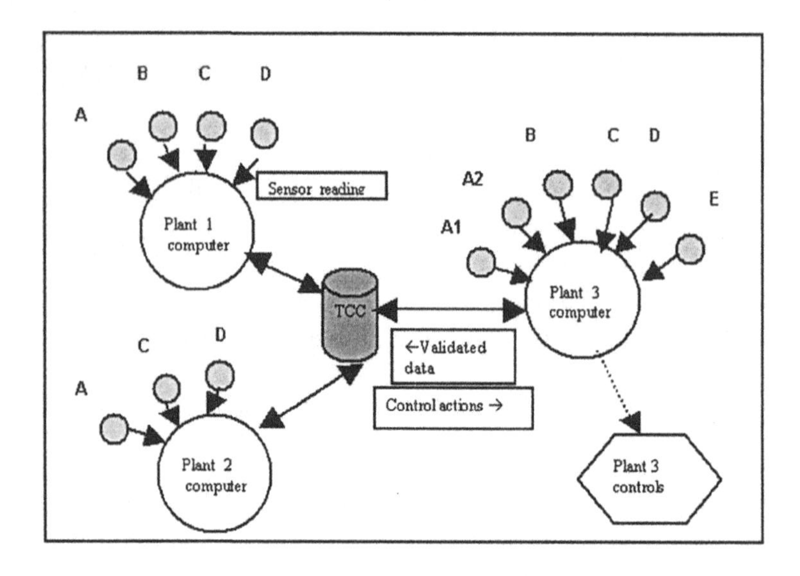

Figure 8. A network of sensor arrays.

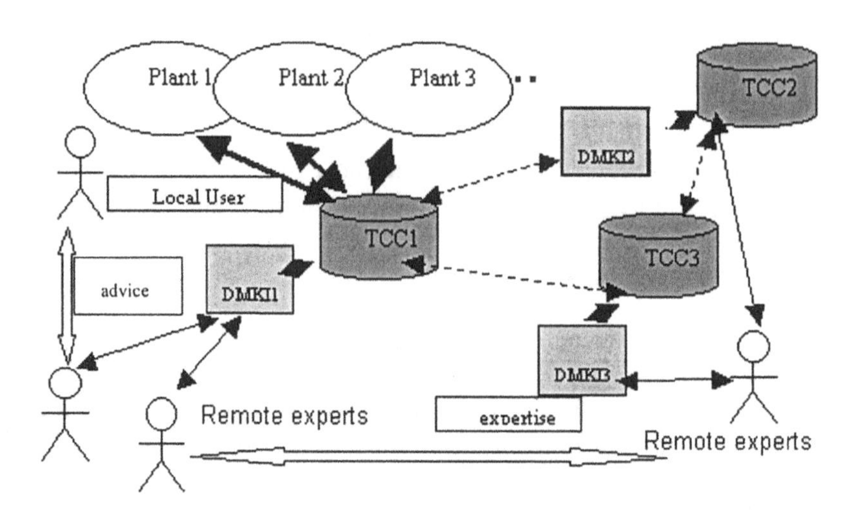

Figure 9. A network of data, information and knowledge sharing.

metadata attributes for reworking TELEMAC in a Grids architecture. These terms are discussed in relation to the data mining models and resources.

5.2.1 Data mining models. **Applicability:** this class of metadata identifies circumstances under which the model can be deployed with confidence on the basis of the model generation E.g. the type of process, and the range of sensors available. It would normally be based on expert knowledge.

Transformability: this metadata identifies expert judgement about whether the models estimates can be used in (gu)estimating different regimes.

Reliability: this metadata identifies the confidence in the derivation of the model viz: the goodness of the model assessed using training and testing data, and any constraints that need to be considered.

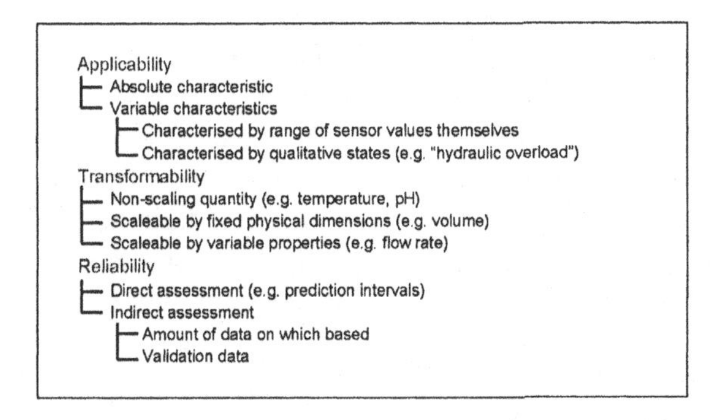

Figure 10. Metadata about datasets archived and available for data mining

5.2.2 Data mining datasets. Figure 10 shows the metadata relating to datasets available as a Grid resource.

Applicability:

Absolute characteristic: this is a fixed feature of the system that never changes e.g. digester process type but not a potentially varying characteristic such as internal volume.

Variable characteristics: Generally each variable series is characterised by statistical summary data such as stationarity or variance. The series from the sensors are considered individually to determine the span of the variable and missing values. Qualitatively different behaviours of the digesters are characterised as states bound by ranges on subsets of the variables. Using these states an expert would be able to assess a priori whether they were not suitable for modelling other states e.g. data relating to hydraulic overload would not give a good indication of the behaviour of organically overloaded states.

Transformability:

Direct instrument readings sometimes need transforming to a consistent scale.

Non-scaling: these are quantities that typically have a direct scientific role such as temperature and pH.

Scalable by fixed physical dimensions: typically converts extensive to intensive e.g. using volume to scale biogas flow rates to $m^{-3}d^{-1}$ or to convert between time and frequency. Within this category we include time scale synchronisation where a variable is mapped to a different interval.

Scalable by a variable: maps to a new variable of interest E.g. using differences to remove a trend in a variable or produce a derived variable E.g. HRT is Volume/¡inflow-rate¿ which is the length of time taken to feed into the digester the volume of liquid equal to the digesters volume.

Reliability:

Direct assessment: These are methods where the prediction on the target data generates an estimate of the error. E.g. Prediction intervals can be obtained directly from neural net models of the unseen targets. Bootstrapping is widely used as an alternative approach for non-heteroskedastic data; it produces multiple models each on a variant of the training data.

Indirect assessment: These are methods where an estimate of the error is based on the quality of the model fit to its training and validation data. e.g. information criteria and characteristics of residuals in linear regression.

5.3 Resource discovery

Having established a collection of resources with associated metadata, resource discovery proceeds by locating resources that satisfy the current needs of the user (at a TCC). Urgency and novelty of the digester state are factors that need to be taken into account when identifying potential resources such as data mining models that can be deployed. If a digester is in an alarming state which the Remote Experts have never seen before, then the experts would cast the net wider to look for resources that might help with the situation - accepting data mining models that are less reliable, for example, because at least they might offer some information of value. The broker would seek resources using such criteria [3]. Firstly it would need to match digester type and sensor set available in the archive; it would perform measurement unit conversion as appropriate. Then a suitable set of models would be selected with appropriate guidance. The system may even provide the Remote Expert with functionality that will advise on the urgency of the problem and whether it is novel.

5.4 Conclusions

TELEMAC is representative of a class of systems: networks of sensor arrays with significant heterogeneity and varying reliability. The sensors respond and report at different frequencies. Over time models need to be updated episodically as new data changes the characteristics being monitored. Expert knowledge can be deployed in different ways from advisory to automatic control. The knowledge base is used to infer behaviour of systems with different characteristics. The Grids architecture provides a knowledge, information and data architecture that enables a structured approach to developing this class of system.

Acknowledgments

This paper refers to work carried out under the IST project TELEMAC (Telemonitoring and Advanced Telecontrol of High-Yield Wastewater Treatment Plants). Especial thanks are due to J.P. Steyer (INRA), L. Lardon (INRA), O. Bernard (INRIA) and B. Le Dantec (ERCIM). The relation of TELEMAC to Grids has been studied in the scope of the CoreGRID Network of Excellence.

References

[1] TELEMAC: Telemonitoring and advanced telecontrol of high yield wastewater treatment plants, IST project no. IST-2000-28156 *http://www.ercim.org/telemac*. 2000.

[2] O. Bernard et al. An integrated system to remote monitor and control anaerobic wastewater treatment plants through the internet.. *Water Science and Technology* **52**(1-2): 457-464, 2005.

[3] K.G. Jeffery. Next generation GRIDs for Environmental Science. *Environmental Modelling and Software* . 2005, in press.

[4] H. Macarie. Overview of the application of anaerobic treatment to chemical and petrochemical wastewaters. *Water Science and Technology.* **42**(5-6):201-213, 2000.

[5] O. Bernard, Z. Hadj-Sadok, D. Dochain, A. Genovesi, and J.P. Steyer. Dynamical model development and parameter identification for anaerobic wastewater treatment process. *Biotech. Bioengin.* **75**(4):424-439, 2001.

[6] M. Dixon, J.R. Gallop, S.C. Lambert, and J.V.Healy. Experience with data mining for the anaerobic wastewater treatment process. *Environmental Modelling and Software.* 2005, accepted.

[7] M. Dixon, J.R. Gallop, S.C. Lambert, L. Lardon, J.V. Healy, and J.P. Steyer. Data Mining to Support Anaerobic WWTP Monitoring,*IFAC Workshop on Modelling and Control for Participatory Planning and Managing Water Systems, Proceedings CD. Venice http://epubs.cclrc.ac.uk/work-details?w=30122.* 2004.

[8] K.G. Jeffery. CRIS and Open Access. *Proc. World Library and Information Congress: IFLA 71, Oslo, Norway. http://epubs.cclrc.ac.uk/work-details?w=34228.* 2005.

Index